JOHN HOYLES

ARCHIVES INTERNATIONALES D'HISTOIRE DES IDEÉS

INTERNATIONAL ARCHIVES OF THE HISTORY OF IDEAS

39

JOHN HOYLES

THE WANING OF THE RENAISSANCE
1640–1740

JOHN HOYLES

THE WANING OF THE RENAISSANCE 1640–1740

STUDIES IN THE THOUGHT AND POETRY OF HENRY MORE, JOHN NORRIS AND ISAAC WATTS

MARTINUS NIJHOFF — THE HAGUE — 1971

ISBN 90 247 5077 6

PRINTED IN THE NETHERLANDS

To Andrée

ACKNOWLEDGMENTS

I am particularly grateful to the following for their help and advice: to Donald Davie for reading and commenting on the chapters concerned with the verse of Henry More and Isaac Watts; to T. E. Jessop with whom I discussed the chapters on Watts's thought; and to R. L. Brett for his painstaking consideration of my ideas as they evolved.

John Hoyles

Hull,
March 1970

TABLE OF CONTENTS

PART THREE

THE RESULT: ISAAC WATTS 141

GENERAL INTRODUCTION

It is not always easy to maintain a proper balance between the delineation of cultural development within a given literary field and the claims of practical criticism. And yet if the history of ideas is to be more than a pastime for the student of literature, it must be rooted in the precise art of discrimination. The following chapters attempt to describe and evaluate a particular cultural development by relating the background of ideas to the literary achievement of three writers. It will be sufficient here to outline the nature of the problem, and the method and approach employed.

The concept of cultural development implies a recognition of the connections between ideology and aesthetics. There are at least two ways of exploring such connections. The one, pioneered by Basil Willey, seeks to situate the critical moments of our cultural development in the background of ideas, without which the contribution of a particular author cannot be justly evaluated. The danger of such an approach is that the task of discrimination comes to depend over-heavily on extra-literary criteria. Writers stand or fall as they are better or worse moralists. The second approach, pioneered by F. R. Leavis, allows a constant appeal back from the extrapolated generalisation to the words on the page, regarded in the last resort as sole depository and guarantee for the work of discrimination. The danger here lies in the hallucination that words are only words, and that the power of the right word exists in a vacuum. It goes without saying that Willey and Leavis share many insights, and often avoid these dangers. Thus Leavis arrives at his "line of wit," and Willey at his conclusion that John Smith is both the best writer and most representative thinker among the Cambridge Platonists, through a combination of ideological and aesthetic discrimination. Unless these connections are made the business of criticism can become sadly impoverished.

It is also true that when these connections are made, the result can be irritatingly nebulous. Thus we still struggle to interpret and apply T. S.

Eliot's formula of "dissociated sensibility." But in a way this is as it should be, since no simple formula can adequately explain what one critic has called "the cultural revolution of the 17th century." [1] There is no scientific method to discover the connections between ideology and aesthetics, and if there were we would still be left with the related imponderables of tradition, the individual talent, the words on the page, and the discriminating reader. One of the reasons why Eliot's formula teases out of thought rather than clarifies, is that the bulk of exegesis on the 17th century cultural revolution isolates rather than connects the contributory elements. Thus on the one hand we have Miss Tuve's work on imagery, and on the other hand there are Fairchild's study of religious ideas, and W. P. Jones's study of scientific ideas. [2] As a result Eliot's "dissociation of sensibility" is either interpreted as a technical revolution at the level of the hermetically enclosed conceit, or as an ideological development based on a descriptive catalogue of extrapolated concepts. If it is agreed that neither conceit nor concept have literary meaning and value, as opposed to linguistic and philosophical meaning, except as they are related, then the critic may be equipped to describe and evaluate a particular area of cultural development.

The cultural development we are concerned with occurs between the age of Marvell and the age of Blake. Many descriptive titles may be applied to it, though none has any claim to be definitive or exclusive of the others. In terms of literary history, we are dealing with the metamorphosis from Metaphysical to Augustan, and the change in kind between the Elizabethan and Metaphysical on the one hand and the preromantic and modern on the other. [3] And in more general and nebulous terms we are dealing with the waning of the Renaissance and the transit to the modern mind. [4] Since the Renaissance was a cultural phenomenon in which the aesthetic and the ideological were inextricably combined, its waning may conveniently describe the dominant cultural process of the period under

---

[1] Samuel Leslie Bethell, *The Cultural Revolution of the 17th Century* (London: Dennis Dobson, 1951).

[2] Rosemond Tuve, *Elizabethan and Metaphysical Imagery* (Chicago: University Press, 1961). Hoxie Neale Fairchild, *Religious Trends in English Poetry* (5 vols.; New York: Columbia University Press, 1939–1962), vols. 1–2. William Powell Jones, *The Rhetoric of Science; A Study of Scientific Ideas and Imagery in 18th Century Poetry* (London: Routledge and Kegan Paul, 1966).

[3] The first of these changes is the subject of Geoffrey Walton's *Metaphysical to Augustan: Studies in Tone and Sensibility in the 17th Century* (London: Bowes and Bowes, 1955). The second is treated in Miss Tuve's *Elizabethan and Metaphysical Imagery*.

[4] The first of these phrases, unlike Huizinga's "Waning of the Middle Ages," is not current. The second is used by Walter J. Ong in "Ramus and the Transit to the Modern Mind," *The Modern Schoolman*, XXXII (May 1955), 307.

review. It is thereby implied that no one aspect of change in either concept or conceit can be described as responsible for this process. The temptation to find an overriding cause is present in the work of Walter J. Ong, who writes on the "widespread and mysterious shift from the audile to the visile in the whole way of thinking about cognition and the nature of man." According to Ong, the cause of this upheaval lies in Ramus's "simplification of logic." [5] To ascribe all to Ramus does not get us very far. On the other hand, one of the most striking characteristics of the waning of the Renaissance, or the transit to the modern mind, is in fact the shift within literary culture from the aural to the visual, and noone can doubt that with a problem of this kind, the connections between concept and conceit, idea and form, are of paramount importance. In order to investigate these connections, and test such general claims, three areas of cultural development can often be separated for special consideration and comparative study. These areas may be termed the aesthetic, the philosophical, and the religious. That they often overlap goes without saying. The critical period for each appears to be round about 1700.

Some of us were brought up to believe that the great dividing line in English literature occurs not at the Renaissance, nor with the Romantics, but in 1700. We were told that there was a difference in kind and quality between writers before 1700 and writers after 1700, and that the superior quality of the former was above all evident in the high standard of minor works nourished by the Renaissance. One only had to open the *Oxford Book of 17th Century Verse*, and then open the *Oxford Book of 18th Century Verse,* to be persuaded that the dividing line was there. Here then, in the shape of a received idea, is another "widespread and mysterious shift" to add to Ong's. Pursue Ong as he develops a book out of his ten-page article, and we are back in the world of Miss Tuve and T. S. Eliot. In Ong's words:

For the 16th and 17th century mind, the value in the object and the praise elicited by the object tend to be viewed as one whole. This mind does not feel the exterior objective world and the interior personal world as distinct from one another quite to the extent that we do. Objects retain a more personal or at least animistic glow.[6]

One of the ways of describing the process to which Ong, Eliot and Miss Tuve devote their attention, is to speak of a movement away from the art of discourse towards the art of description. Thus Ong, seeking to throw

[5] *Ibid.,* 308.
[6] Walter J. Ong, *Ramus: Method, and the Decay of Dialogue; From the Art of Discourse to the Art of Reason* (Cambridge, Mass.: Harvard University Press, 1958), p. 279.

light on the mysterious shift he has evoked, claims that towards the end of
the 17th century, the poetry of the Renaissance "shades gradually into
reflective poetry which does not talk to anyone in particular, but meditates
on objects, such as the moon." [7] The far-reaching implications of this
process are referred to by a leading 20th century French poet; Paul Valéry,
in an essay on Swedenborg, writes: "On voit donc la dissertation et la
dialectique remplacées par le récit et la description." [8] This shift from
discourse to description, from the aural to the visual, characterises the
waning of the Renaissance, and marks the transit to the modern mind.
More than a literary development, it is a total cultural phenomenon, and
Descartes is more responsible for it than Ramus. And yet of course, as
Michel Foucault points out, it transcends even the fortunes of the Cartesian
revolution. From Descartes onwards,

le texte cesse de faire partie des signes et des formes de la vérité; le langage
n'est plus une des figures du monde, ni la signature imposée aux choses depuis
le fond des temps. La vérité trouve sa manifestation et son signe dans la
perception évidente et distincte. Il appartient aux mots de la traduire s'ils
peuvent.[9]

According to Foucault, the Cartesian revolution sparks off a new and
essentially modern cultural movement, in which the word becomes
separated from the thing:

La profonde appartenance du langage et du monde se trouve défaite. Le
primat de l'écriture est suspendu. Disparaît alors cette couche uniforme où
s'entrecroisaient indéfiniment le *vu* et le *lu,* le visible et l'énonçable. Les
choses et les mots vont se séparer. L'oeil sera destiné à voir, et à voir seulement; l'oreille à seulement entendre. Le discours aura bien pour tâche de dire
ce qui est, mais il ne sera rien de plus que ce qu'il dit.[10]

Foucault and Ong may raise as many questions as they solve, but they at
least appear to be tackling the same problem. The American neoscholastic
and the French structuralist add some light to Eliot's "dissociation of
sensibility." The chapters which follow attempt to do the same, not so
much by philosophical or aesthetic generalisations, as by a detailed analysis
of the work of three writers who span the period in which this mysterious
shift took place.

If the existence of this general cultural phenomenon cannot be called in
question, we can move on to indicate the way in which it may be ap-

---

[7] *Ibid.,* pp. 287–288.
[8] Paul Valéry, *Oeuvres,* ed. Jean Hytier (2 vols.; Paris: Gallimard, 1957-1959),
I, 868.
[9] Michel Foucault, *Les Mots et les Choses* (Paris: Gallimard, 1966), p. 70.
[10] *Ibid.,* p. 58.

proached. In the aesthetic area of investigation it will be necessary to trace the way in which the Metaphysical tradition embodies relics of Renaissance culture, and the way in which this tradition wanes in the years following the Cartesian revolution, until by 1700 it has almost disappeared. It will also be necessary to describe the emergence of new elements, some of which lead on to Augustan neoclassicism, some to Romanticism. The religious lyric is a particularly convenient and circumscribed form in which to observe these developments. There will not only be decline and fall; there will also be attempts to arrest the movement, some salvaging of the tradition, and the occasional successful innovation. When we have accounted for the various elements which go into the making of religious lyricism – sublimity, theory of the imagination, poetic diction, classicism, expressionism – we shall be in a better position to assess the nature of the cultural gap between Marvell and Blake; for there is some continuity even in the widest gap.

The 1700 dividing line in the philosophical area of investigation has been broadly documented by Basil Willey. Willey sees a qualitative difference between the insights of Cambridge Platonism and those of the English Enlightenment. The Cambridge Platonists are valued as moralists, though they themselves give rise to the deists, who are not moralists but minute philosophers. In this scheme of things, the waning of the Renaissance, again largely through the impact of the Cartesian revolution, leads into the impoverished English Enlightenment. Enveloped in this process are the interrelated elements of mechanism, vitalism, occasionalism, eclecticism, utilitarianism and rationalism. By attempting to delineate these elements within the cultural envelope, we shall see to what extent all was decline and fall, and to what extent Platonic and non-Cartesian undercurrents lead on to Kant and Coleridge.

In the religious area of investigation we will trace the post-Reformation development of pietism up to the point where it is overtaken by Evangelicalism. Here the transit to the modern mind is marked by a move from the letter to the spirit. Contributory elements include latitudinarianism, moralism, modernism, socinianism, quietism and deism. Between the Caroline piety of Herbert and the Evangelical piety of Cowper, the cultural gap is large. The consensus has it that this was essentially a decline. We shall examine the process that fills the gap, and relate it to the general cultural picture.

The framework within which these three areas of cultural development are distinguished and related is formed by the work of three writers. Each of these writers represents a stage in the waning of the Renaissance. At each

stage the impact of the Enlightenment on ideology and aesthetics is measured. Each writer is chosen because he is open to such pressures at both
levels; all are poets and all are thinkers. The stages of development can be
schematically described as follows.

Attention is centred on the years immediately before and immediately
after 1700; we look back and we look forward from that vantage point.
The source of development is located in the rise of English Cartesianism in
the 1640s. Henry More stands out as the most important exponent of this
movement. At the same time he is the principal architect of an attempt to
revive Renaissance Platonism, and a prolific lyrical poet, whose verse
reflects his philosophical enterprise, and contains the seeds of modern
aesthetic development at a time when the Metaphysical stage of the Renaissance tradition was only just beginning its decline. No claim is made
that his verse is, in the main, anything but mediocre, but it is suggested
that Henry More's contribution to English cultural development is severely
underestimated if the connections between ideology and aesthetics which
his work as a whole reveals are not brought out.

Having looked back from 1700 and located a source of the waning of
the Renaissance, it will be useful to identify a second stage, where Henry
More's contribution is both consolidated and evaporated on the verge of
the English Enlightenment. Here in the years immediately preceding 1700,
the figure of John Norris stands out as exemplary. Norris represents the
heritage of the Cambridge Platonists at a time when most of their arguments and positions were an anachronism. As such he both salvages and
waters down their insights. Like Janus, he looks both ways; back to More,
and forward to Watts. At the same time he is an important minor poet in
the Metaphysical tradition. The connections here are crucial to an understanding of English cultural development.

The result of this development can be seen most clearly in the work of
Isaac Watts. Watts was a revolutionary poet, and the bulk of his verse was
composed in the first decade of the 18th century. He is also a representative
figure in the English Enlightenment, reflecting its most typical mood. His
contribution in both these areas has been underestimated, and the connections between them sadly neglected. His work is central to our description of the changes in English culture between 1640 and 1740, because it so clearly displays in prose and verse the stage at which the Renaissance, with its Metaphysical and Platonic traditions, has given way to
the new forms and ideas of Classicism and the Enlightenment.

Thus the cultural movement which has its source in Henry More produces results which can be seen in the work of Isaac Watts. What cannot

be left out of this picture is the fact that in this process the loss of the old outweighs the gain of the new. In the long run Classicism and the Enlightenment were gods that failed to replace a dying culture. Their function was essentially negative; when they had broken down the old habits in ideology and aesthetics, they were themselves in no fit state to resist the rising tide of Romanticism. It is thus no surprise to find in the work of More, Norris and Watts not only signs of the waning of the Renaissance but also intimations of the rise of Romanticism.

PART ONE

THE SOURCE: HENRY MORE

CHAPTER ONE

INTRODUCTION:
THE FOURTH GROUND OF CERTAINTY

Henry More went to Christ's College, Cambridge in 1631, the year before Milton left.[1] It is tempting to see in this fact a symbol of the watershed between Renaissance and modern. Neither man is transitional in the way Sir Thomas Browne is, for neither was content to accept the Metaphysical luxury of divided and distinguished worlds. Both forged their own worlds with an energy common to humanists in all ages. But where Milton stands at the end of a long line of Renaissance humanists, More's links are with those sources of the English Enlightenment which, as early as the 1640s, were converging into some sort of purposeful homogeneity. There are many intimations in More's work of the far-reaching changes which the Enlightenment would bring in literature, philosophy and religion. And while the English Enlightenment proved to be conservative, More's radical modernity reveals the associated origins of romanticism, idealism and pietism.

More's humanism is evident in the energy with which he aims at conquering several fields of knowledge. But where the previous generations of literary humanists were disciplined by the Ramist simplification of the Aristotelian categories, More's switches from one department of study to another seem to be determined by personal inclination rather than objective method. In his "Little Narrative of himself," he recalls that he began philosophizing because he could not stomach the Calvinist doctrine of predestination.[2] He successively went through a mathematical phase, "fell a theologizing," and then returned to geometry.[3] In later life he came

---

[1] See Marjorie Hope Nicolson, "The Spirit World of Milton and More," *Studies in Philology*, XXII (1925), 434.

[2] Richard Ward, *The Life of the Learned and Pious Dr Henry More* (London: J. Downing, 1710), p. 6.

[3] Letter to Lady Conway, 17 October 1664. Marjorie Hope Nicolson (ed.), *The Conway Letters: The Correspondence of Anne, Viscountess Conway, Henry More, and their friends, 1642-1684* (London: Oxford University Press; New Haven: Yale University Press, 1930), p. 231.

to regret his early "desire of philosophizing," [4] only to finish his career in the spirit of Newton, seeking to elucidate the Book of Revelation according to mathematical principles.[5] This kind of easy-going eclecticism was of course congenial to More's temperament, but it also bears witness to the disintegration of the earlier humanist synthesis, held together by Ramist dialectic. It was becoming increasingly difficult to establish common ground which would support investigation into more than one field of knowledge.

The new philosophy which called all in doubt, led youthful inquiring minds to question the methods of learning employed in the universities. Logic, metaphysics, even the new mathematics, were tried and found wanting as replacements for the deposed queen of the sciences, scholastic theology. No one has better expressed the sense of intellectual vacuum, at once stimulating and bewildering, which the discerning minds of the 1640s experienced, than the young John Hall (1627-1656). He wrote from Cambridge in 1649 with Miltonic cadence:

Therefore ... I could not devise any better means than to make the mind pliant and passible to any truth, to free her from all those inquinated prejudices of education, tradition, or childish observation, and then withal to plant such a doubtfulness in her, as should not easily assent to any one thing which was not fortified with strong reason and right experience. And to do this, there cannot but be extreme necessity of a person not meanly versed in the causes of error, and stratagems of reason, who should dig out such axioms as should rectify the mind, and lead her by the hand, in the most subtile contemplations, and so refine her, that she might be able to extract pure and large theories out of things most immersed and hid in matter.[6]

Hall's analysis of the university's predicament in the cultural milieu of the late Renaissance helps us to understand the significance of More's temperament, with its characteristic openness and with its eclectic doubtfulness so jealousy guarded.

The latitude of More's temperament is such that he will not "easily assent to any one thing which was not fortified with strong reason and right experience." But his categorical "doubtfulness" is qualified, and indeed guaranteed, by an even more categorical inner light, which he shares with the Cambridge Platonists. This inner light often finds ex-

---

[4] Henry More, *The Theological Works* (London: J. Downing, 1708), p. i.

[5] Letter to Dr J. Sharp, 16 August 1680. *Conway Letters*, p. 479. More and Newton were educated at the same school in Grantham. For a description of their affinities, see Edwin Arthur Burtt, *The Metaphysical Foundations of Modern Science* (London: Kegan Paul, Trench, 1925), pp. 256-263, 279.

[6] John Hall, *An Humble Motion to the Parliament of England Concerning the Advancement of Learning and Reformation of the Universities,* ed. A. K. Croston ("Liverpool Reprints," No. 7; Liverpool: University Press, 1953), p. 39.

pression in terms of a defence of the divine life in man. Thus, in his *Second Lash* at Thomas Vaughan, he writes:

For I say, that that Divine Spirit and Life ... is worth not only all the magic that thou pretendest to, but all that thou art ignorant of besides: yea, and Descartes' philosophy to boot.[7]

As Elisabeth Labrousse and Rosalie Colie have shown in their studies of Bayle and Dutch Arminianism, the European Enlightenment was in its origins inextricably bound up with the insights of pietism and the religions of inner light as developed in 17th century Holland.[8] It is therefore not surprising to discover that More's devotion to the cause of the Enlightenment is dominated by a passionately held inner light.

More was nevertheless prepared to apply the latitude of his temperament to his profession of Platonism. In the preface, "To the Reader," added to the 1647 edition of his poems, he explains that he would "be so understood, as a representer of the wisdom of the ancients, rather than a warranter of the same." [9] This may well be an afterthought, inserted into the second edition to excuse the welter of scientific system with which he had wrapped up his Platonism; and yet in the preface to "Psychathanasia" (1642), he had written in similar vein:

I desire no man to take anything I write, upon trust, without canvasing; and would be thought rather to propound than to assert what I have here or elsewhere written.[10]

The tone is similar to Milton's.[11] From the spirit of tolerance to the principle of religious toleration was but a small step, and More was not slow to take it.

Coleridge wondered whether Henry More was the first to advocate universal toleration.[12] Certainly More was among the first. A short passage in "Psychathanasia," and written therefore before 1643, sets the tone:

[7] *The Second Lash of Alazonamastix* (1651), as quoted in Ward, p. 64.

[8] Elisabeth Labrousse, *Pierre Bayle* (2 vols.; The Hague: Nijhoff, 1963-1964). Rosalie L. Colie, *Light and Enlightenment: A Study of the Cambridge Platonists and the Dutch Arminians* (Cambridge: University Press, 1957).

[9] Henry More, *Complete Poems*, ed. A. B. Grosart ("Chertsey Worthies Library"; Edinburgh: privately printed, 1878), p. 7. More's poems, "Psychozoia," "Psychathanasia," "Antepsychapannychia" and "Antimonopsychia," were first published as *Psychodia Platonica* in 1642. They appeared in a 2nd revised edition as *Philosophical Poems* in 1647.

[10] Grosart, p. 42.

[11] Cf. *Areopagitica:* "A man may be a heretic in the truth; and if he believe things only because his Pastor says so, or the Assembly so determines, without knowing other reason, though his belief be true, yet the very truth he holds, becomes his heresy". John Milton, *Works,* ed. Frank Allen Patterson (18 vols.; New York: Columbia University Press, 1931-1938), IV, 333.

[12] Samuel Taylor Coleridge, *On the 17th Century,* ed. Roberta Florence Brinkley (Durham, North Carolina: Duke University Press, 1955), p. 626.

>   Thus, thus vain man
> Entitles always God to his opinion;
> Thinks every thing is done as he conceives;
> Would bind all men to his religion;
> All the world else of freedom he bereaves,
> He and his God must have dominion,
> The truth must have her propagation:
> That is his thought which he hath made a God,
> That furious hot inust impression
> Doth so disturb his veins, that all abroad
> With rage he roves, and all gainsayers down hath trod.[13]

Between the two editions of More's poems, Milton's *Areopagitica* had appeared (1644), and by 1647 the hint of this solitary stanza has been taken up and expanded in the long episode added to the second canto of "Psychozoia." [14] In this episode More sets out to make an explicit and organised attack on ecclesiastical tyranny; but it is significant that the attack on Glaucis, who represents the enthusiasm of Rantists, Familists, Quakers and others, is not delivered by More himself, but by Glaucis's father, Psittaco. Psittaco is presented in a worse light than his daughter, for he symbolises Presbyterian scripture tyranny, and is old priest writ large. More, in the person of Mnemon, replies to Psittaco's tirade in the spirit of toleration:

>   Fie; Psittaco! hide such infirmities
> From stranger wight: Who would his own dear child
> Thus shamefully disgrace? With mine own eyes
> Have I thy Glaucis seen, and better things surmise.[15]

Milton had argued for toleration from the principle of the manysidedness of truth. Here More is content to speak of enthusiasts he has known, and leave us to draw our own conclusion. Elsewhere however he is more truculent, as when, at the end of the Interregnum, he declares:

There is nothing would make so much for the interest of Christianity, as if this right of liberty of conscience were known and acknowledged all over the world. . . . False religion and vain superstition would sink, . . . and that only would be found to swim whose innate truth was able to bear it up of itself.[16]

---

[13] "Psychathanasia," III, iii, 68-69. Grosart, p. 82.
[14] Stanzas 57-125.
[15] "Psychozoia," II, 119. Grosart, p. 30.
[16] *An Explanation of the Grand Mystery of Godliness* (London: J. Flesher, 1660), pp. xxviii-xxix.

On the principle of universal toleration the "Lady of Christ's" and the "Angel of Christ's" are agreed; both were pioneers.[17]

More arrived at his belief in toleration through his feeling of scepticism, but it is clear from the start that this feeling arises from, and is firmly wedged in, the context of the "Fourth Ground," or "Divine Life," so dear to the Cambridge Platonists. The key stanza in the added episode of "Psychozoia" runs as follows:

> Wherefore a fourth, sole ground of certainty
> Thou didst produce, to wit, the Spirit Divine.
> But now alas! here is the misery,
> That left to doubt we cannot well enjoin
> Nor this nor that, nor Faith-forms freely coin
> And make the trembling conscience swear thereto,
> For we ourselves do but guess and divine
> What we force other men to swear is true,
> Until the day-star rise our eyes with light t'imbue.[18]

Religious toleration and philosophical scepticism were congenial enough to the Enlightenment's way of thinking, but there is a difference in kind as well as degree between More's "Spirit Divine" and Shaftesbury's "Sensus Communis." There is a world of difference too between philosophical scepticism based on indifference, and More's own brand, based on a willingness to change horses in midstream in the interest of truth. On the one hand Samuel Parker writes:

I am lately grown such a despairing sceptic in all physiological theories that I cannot concern myself in the truth or falsehood of any hypotheses. For though I prefer the Mechanical Hypotheses before another, yet methinks their contexture is too slight and brittle to have any stress laid upon them.[19]

On the other hand Henry More, in embracing the new philosophy of Descartes, professes a scepticism that does not preclude enthusiasm, when he writes:

For mine own part I must confess these apprehensions do plainly oppose what heretofore I have conceived; but I have sworn more faithful friendship with truth than with myself.[20]

---

[17] For other similarities between Milton and More, see M. H. Nicolson, *Studies in Philology*, XXII (1925), 433-452.

[18] "Psychozoia," II, 103. Grosart, p. 28.

[19] Samuel Parker, *A Free and Impartial Censure of the Platonic Philosophy* (2nd ed: Oxford, 1667), p. 46.

[20] *Democritus Platonissans* (1646), "To the Reader." Grosart, p. 90.

More's basic mood is thus that of Milton and Donne – intellectual energy in the service of speculative inquiry:

> But now lets sift the verity
> Of this opinion, and with reason rude
> Rub, crush, touse, rifle this fine fantasy.[21]

Each and every hypothesis is grist to his mill. But as the age changed, and the doldrums of evidence took much of the wind out of the sails of speculation, More grew to regret the expense of his earlier energies. In the preface to his *Theological Works* he apologises

if in those things which are so evidently true and clearly demonstrated, a more than ordinary heat has sometimes accompanied so great a light, and may seem to have armed my style in some places with over-much sharpness and vehemence.[22]

And yet in other respects, his enthusiasms, though they may have changed, hardly abated. Indeed the light of which he was advocate could hardly subsist without heat. For all his devotion to the Royal Society, he had even less affinities with men like Sprat, Parker and Wilkins, than did his kindred spirit Glanvill. Although More took part with Glanvill in the empirical investigation of the world of spirits, he did not submit himself, as did Glanvill, to the corporate discipline and common ground of the Royal Society programme. He remained faithful to his original lights.

These lights were nourished in the heat of what can only be termed religious experience. His "Little Narrative of himself" consists mainly of an account of childhood moments to which he ascribes a decisive and permeating influence. It is significant that his reading of that source-book of Protestant mysticism, *Theologica Germanica,* resulted in what amounts to instant conversion. Characteristically he makes the whole process sound perfectly natural; there is no intrusion of divine grace. He speaks simply of a quickening of his spiritual sense which

that truly Golden Book did not then first implant in my soul, but struck and roused it, as it were, out of sleep in me: which it did verily as in a moment, or the twinkling of an eye.[23]

And yet the sense of urgent immediacy carries with it a moral asceticism no less stringent than that traditionally provided by the Calvinism against which More is reacting; for he goes on in the next sentence:

[21] "Antimonopsychia" (1642), stanza 6. Grosart, p. 130. Cf. Donne's third satire and Milton's *Areopagitica.*
[22] *Theological Works,* p. ii.
[23] Ward, p. 13.

But after that the sense and consciousness of this great and plainly Divine Duty, was thus awakened in me; Good God! what Strugglings and Conflicts followed presently between this Divine Principle and the Animal Nature! [24]

This sense of religious experience once and for all at a given moment, rather than a growth into various stages of illumination, is more characteristic of puritan and pietist religion than of mysticism proper; and not least among More's affinities with John Wesley is his deep-seated distrust of mysticism.

Richard Ward's hagiographical purposes lead him to ascribe a fair measure of mystical illumination to his illustrious forbear. Hence:

He was once for ten days together, *no where* (as he termed it) or in one continued fit of Contemplation: During which he eat, drank, slept, went into the Hall, and conversed, in a measure, as at other times; yet the thread of it for all that space was never once, as it were, broken or interrupted.[25]

and:

He hath told us . . . that not only his own urine had naturally the flavour of violets in it; but that his breast and body, especially when very young, would of themselves, in like manner, send forth flowery and aromatic odours from them; and such as he daily almost was sensible of, when he came to put off his clothes and go to bed. And even afterwards, when he was older, about the end of winter, or beginning of the spring, he did frequently perceive certain sweet and herbaceous smells about him; when yet there were no such external objects near, from whence they could proceed.[26]

But prolonged meditation and sensuous excitability in an "intellectual epicure" [27] and recluse are occupational hazards, and in themselves no indication of mystical illumination. And More himself never had any doubts on the subject; passages which seem to point to mystical illumination are usually manifestations of his inept handling of spiritual matters as in his view susceptible to empirical investigation. More knew that

Fancy becomes sometimes presentifical, as in madmen and those in high fevers, whose phantasms seem real external objects to them.[28]

He was never even potentially a mystic, and the childhood moments he speaks of would sit more easily in the pages of *Grace Abounding* than in the pages of *Centuries of Meditations*.

The central experience More recalls in his "Little Narrative" has the solidity and local colour which distinguish Bunyan's autobiography. He

---

[24] *Ibid.*
[25] *Ibid.*, p. 42.
[26] *Ibid.*, pp. 123-124.
[27] John Norris's phrase, from his "To Dr More, An Ode," *A Collection of Miscellanies* (3rd ed.; London: S. Manship, 1699), p. 73.
[28] *The Two Last Dialogues* (London: J. Flesher, 1668), p. 346. Quoted in Ward, p. 43.

describes two phases. First of all he is delivered from hell as he shakes off
the burden of condemnation:

On a certain day, in a ground belonging to Eton College, where the boys used
to play, and exercise themselves, musing concerning these things with myself,
and recalling to my mind this doctrine of Calvin, I did thus seriously and
deliberately conclude with myself . . .[29]

There follows his refutal of predestination, and he goes on:

Which Meditation of mine, is as firmly fixed in my memory, and the very
place where I stood, as if the thing had been transacted but a day or two ago.[30]

The deliverance is presented as a rationally argued meditation, but it is
none the less a deliverance which took place in the grounds of Eton College
at a given moment. In the second phase of his experience More is assured
of God's presence by an inward feeling, which comes to a head as he chews
over a passage from the last Latin pagan poet:

In that ground mentioned, walking, as my manner was, slowly, and with my
head on one side, and kicking now and then the stones with my feet, I was
wont sometimes with a sort of musical and melancholic murmur to repeat, or
rather hum to myself, those verses of Claudian; . . .[31]

There follows his refutal of atheism, and he goes on:

Yea even in my first childhood, an inward sense of the Divine Presence was
so strong upon my mind; that I did then believe, there could no deed, word
or thought be hidden from him.[32]

The assurance is presented as a natural sense, and this is not without consequence for the so-called trend from religion to moralism which the Cambridge Platonists are so often accused of perpetrating. But again, the assurance is incarnate in time and place, and, across the barriers of "Faith-
forms" which divided them, Bunyan would have approved.

These then are some of the salient features of More's mind and character. They are the only sure guide to a just appreciation of his works, for
his philosophy, theology and poetry make little sense outside the existential
ground on which they were erected. Unless his work is seen as a symptom
of the modern mind, emerging not only from the dark night of Aristotelian
scholasticism, but also from the high noon of Ramist humanism, it is re-
fracted into incongruous fragments, which at best illustrate the chaos of
divided but confused worlds. Thus, before we deal with the aesthetic
implications of what we see emerging in More's work, it is necessary to
relate his mind and character to its historical context of philosophical and

[29] Ward, p. 6.
[30] *Ibid.,* p. 7.
[31] *Ibid.*
[32] *Ibid.*

religious background. This context is particularly confused in its early stages, and it is here that More's ideas are developed. Within the existential ground we have looked at, his combination of light and latitude in both philosophy and religion strikes us as obscurantist. Why stick to Cartesian *and* Platonic notions? Why stick to spiritual *and* latitudinarian truth? If we can throw some light on these inconsistencies we shall be in a better position to appreciate that modernity which lies just below the surface of More's work, and which holds precious intimations of ground common to idealism, pietism and romanticism.

CHAPTER TWO

PHILOSOPHY: DESCARTES AND PLATO

Henry More contributed a great deal to the formation of the philosophy of the Enlightenment. He worked hard to sift the old verities; but he spoke so often in the name of Plato, and so often in the name of Descartes, that his voice was blurred in the years when it most needed to be heard. The Enlightenment, through the Royal Society, grew out of Descartes, and through the latitudinarian spirit, out of Plato. Once this had happened, More's attempts to submit his fourth ground of certainty to the criteria of experimental science led naturally to the absurdities of contradiction between Descartes and Plato, and to grotesque confusion between mind and matter.[1] Such a gothic conclusion to the career of a founder of the modern mind can only be explained by looking carefully at the origins of More's philosophy.[2]

More's formative years were spent in the Cambridge of the late 1630s and early 1640s, and his philosophical ideas reflect the various tendencies which at that time were converging to forge the Enlightenment. A generation passed before a sense of homogeneity and solidarity could be consciously proclaimed. Simon Patrick, in a pamphlet published in 1662, traces the origins of the new movement to that generation, "whose fortune it was to be born so late, as to have their education in the university since the beginning of the unhappy troubles of this kingdom." [3] This was the

---

[1] Cf. Burtt, pp. 129-130.

[2] Writing of "the true and genuine meaning of my interweaving of Platonism and Cartesianism so frequently," More declared that he made "use of these hypotheses as invincible bulwarks against the most cunning and most mischievous efforts of Atheism."
A Collection of Several Philosophical Writings (2nd ed. enlarged; London: W. Morden, 1662), p. vi. It is not his motives but his methods which lie open to the charge of obscurantism.

[3] Simon Patrick, *A Brief Account of the New Sect of Latitude Men, together with some reflections on the new philosophy, in answer to a letter from his friend at Oxford,* ed. T. A. Birrell ("Augustan Reprint Society," No. 100; Los Angeles: University of California Press, 1963), p. 5.

generation tutored by Whichcote and More, More himself having come under Whichcote's influence in the years 1637-1639. It was thus a generation nourished on Arminian and Platonic revival. It was also the generation which felt the first impact of Descartes.[4] Cartesian philosophy provided fresh material for those engaged in the struggle against Aristotle, and gave an impetus to the revival of Baconian empiricism. Unfortunately the university did not fully respond to either of these challenges; John Hall's proposals for the reform of university teaching were forgotten; and the Royal Society grew up very much outside the influence of the university, and was hence largely indifferent to philosophical first principles. More himself embraced the Cartesian philosophy before 1646 (the date of *Democritus Platonissans*), which suggests that it is hardly possible to distinguish between the respective influence Plato and Descartes may have had on the formation of the latitudinarian spirit. Some sixteen years later, Patrick, for his part, still couples Descartes and Plato as sources of true philosophy and guarantees of sound divinity.[5] Clearly More's generation needed both Plato and Descartes if it was to make any inroads into the dominant Aristotelian philosophy which the Presbyterian and Anglican hierarchies upheld. More used both to this end.

Enlightenment apologists from More to Bolingbroke reduce the pervasive scholastic ethos which died so hard, especially in the universities, to that traditional figure of diminution, "cobwebs"; a few brushes of the pen, and the protean Stagirite is out of sight, if not out of mind.[6] The English mind was in any case averse to demolishing what had lasted so long, unless it could be sure of having found something better to take its place. The Cartesian alternative never really caught on in the England of the Royal Society. Metaphysical certainty was avoided until generations nourished on Newton could fall back on the argument from design. More's contemporaries maintained a prudent scepticism, and we find John Wilkins, for example, assiduously refining the science of language, without having to choose between Descartes and Aristotle.[7] Such was the spirit of the Royal Society.

More, however, could not be indifferent towards a metaphysical system,

---

[4] Descartes was being read from 1640 onwards, though the first translation did not appear until 1649. See M. H. Nicolson, "The Early Stage of Cartesianism in England," *Studies in Philology,* XXVI (1929), 356-374.

[5] Patrick, p. 24.

[6] Cf. *ibid.*, p. 23: "The inquisitive genius of latter years like a mighty wind hath brushed down all the school-men's cobwebs."

[7] John Wilkins, *An Essay towards a Real Character and a Philosophical Language* (London: S. Gellibrand and J. Martin, 1668), p. 194.

which, in his opinion, sustained the Socinians. To Lady Conway, whose Quaker tendencies led him to smell Socinianism, he wrote:

The want of philosophy is most certainly the ground of the Socinians' gross mistakes in those grand points of our religion. . . . They are but Aristotelians in philosophy or nothing at all. I mean are for his system of the world, and understand not the laws of matter, nor the system of Descartes.[8]

For More, Aristotle was bad philosophy because he was bad religion. It is therefore not surprising to find him allegorising the Oxford school of rationalist theologians in the person of Graculo, on whose quilted cap

> were writ
> More trimly than the Iliads of yore
> The laws of Mood and Figure and many precepts more,

> All the nice questions of the School-men old
> And subtilties as thin as cobwebs bet,
> Which he wore thinner in his thoughts yrold.[9]

Graculo's companion is Corvino, who "argues by church authority"; [10] so that both Presbyterian and Anglican traditionalists, who believed in the divine right of their church government, are associated with rationalists and Socinians. The common factor, says More, is their Aristotelianism. Hence the enthusiasm with which More attacked Aristotle and embraced Descartes was no mere preference in metaphysics; it arose from his conviction that Aristotle was an affront to, and Descartes a support for, his fourth ground of certainty, and that "contemplations concerning the dry essence of the Deity are very consuming and unsatisfactory." [11]

More found in Cartesian psychology corroboration of his Platonic instincts. He was convinced that

every human soul is no abrasa tabula, or mere blank sheet; but hath innate sensations and notions in it, both of good and evil, just and unjust, true and false; and those very strong and vivid.[12]

As a Platonist, he knew

> that nothing's bare to sense,
> For sense cannot arrive at th'inwardness
> Of things, nor penetrate the crusty fence
> Of constipated matter.[13]

[8] Letter to Lady Conway, 5 July 1662. *Conway Letters,* p. 203.
[9] "Psychozoia," II, 75-76. Grosart, p. 26.
[10] See Henry More, *Philosophical Poems,* ed. Geoffrey Bullough (Manchester: University Press, 1931), p. 205, note.
[11] "To the Reader" (1647). Grosart, p. 7.
[12] "Little Narrative of Himself," Ward, p. 5.
[13] 'Psychozoia," I, 28. Grosart, p. 15.

It was natural that he should snatch at Descartes' theory of innate ideas as philosophical proof of his own "precious substratum within." [14] On the other hand there is no doubt that Descartes gave him impetus to work towards the Enlightenment. As M. H. Nicolson has pointed out, More

was in complete sympathy with the desire of his age to understand the natural world, and impatient of reactionary tendencies to oppose the cause of scientific investigation. . . . Descartes offered him when he most needed it, intellectual assurance of the validity of his own feelings in regard to the nature of man and the phenomena of the universe.[15]

More himself summed up his early position vis à vis Descartes in terms of unqualified enthusiasm:

But that which enravishes me the most is, that we both setting out from the same lists, though taking several ways, the one travailing in the lower road of Democritism, amidst the thick dust of atoms and flying particles of matter, the other tracing it over the high and airy hills of Platonism, in that more thin and subtile region of immateriality, meet together notwithstanding at last . . . at the same goal.[16]

The distinction nevertheless remains; More preferred the high road. And the goal, or substratum, which More valued, was more susceptible to Platonic than to Cartesian corroboration.

   The distinction between the light of inner sense and the common notions of the Enlightenment is at times an academic one. More speaks of "innate sensations and notions." But it is clear that he uses them, not as synonyms, but as distinct faculties of the soul; and there is no doubt which he regarded as more important. On the one hand there is John Wilkins, who writes:

As men do generally agree in the same principle of reason, so do they likewise agree in the same internal notion or apprehension of things.[17]

The emphasis is on the agreement, not on the quality of the apprehension. This is the lower road of Lord Herbert of Cherbury, leading to deism and the Enlightenment. On the other hand there is Henry More, who claims

that the real sensation of un-self-interested love (for as for the notion thereof it signifies no more than the picture of a rose or of a flame, as to the scent or warmth) is the most pleasing and delightful sensation that the soul of man can have experience of.[18]

This is the high Platonic road, traced by means of the distinction between sensation and notion.

[14] "To the Reader" (1647). Grosart, p. 7.
[15] M. H. Nicolson, *Studies in Philology*, XXVI (1929), 365.
[16] *Philosophical Writings*, p. xii.
[17] Wilkins, p. 20.
[18] Letter V, Ward, p. 285.

This distinction was part and parcel of the Enlightenment epistemology which More and the Cambridge Platonists had to live with. They could not resurrect a Renaissance mystique in an age whose most positive contribution to cultural development had been the separation of word and thing. If their light and divine life were real, they had to be things, whose essence escaped the strangle-hold of verbal description and notionhood. Hence John Smith's insistence on this very same distinction in his classic formulation of Cambridge Platonism:

Were I indeed to define divinity, I should rather call it a *divine life,* than a *divine science*: it being something rather to be understood by a spiritual sensation, than by any verbal description.[19]

In isolating the precious substratum within as a thing irreducible to a notion, the Cambridge Platonists laid the foundations of post-Renaissance religious epistemology. Only by claiming that the "true method of knowing . . . is not so much by notions as actions," and that "religion itself consists not so much in words as in things," [20] could they safeguard the autonomy of religious experience in a scientific world.

It is perhaps this Platonic obstinacy that Simon Patrick's Oxford correspondent has in mind when he accuses the "New Sect of Latitude Men" of having affinities with the Rosicrucians, and poisoning the fountain of philosophy.[21] Patrick makes no direct answer to this charge, unless it be in the passing reference to Platonism as the loving nurse of sound divinity. He concentrates instead on defending the mechanical philosophy, and welcomes the opportunity of extending to the cosmos the experimental investigation already applied to the human body:

Certainly it must be the office of philosophy to find out the process of this divine art in the great automaton of the world. This physicians have taken the boldness in part to do, in those little watches, the bodies of animals, and Descartes hath proceeded farthest in the like attempt in that vast machine, the universe.[22]

The question emerges forcibly; how, if at all, did More, as a "latitude man," assimilate mechanistic Cartesian cosmology into his vitalistic Platonic system?

More was an unrepentant syncretist. Commenting on the significance of his own *Conjectura Cabbalistica* (1653), he wrote:

---

[19] John Smith, *Select Discourses,* ed. Henry Griffin Williams (4th ed.; Cambridge: University Press, 1859), p. 1.
[20] *Ibid.,* p. 2.
[21] Patrick, p. 3.
[22] *Ibid.,* p. 19.

I think I have ... plainly proved that not only Platonism, but that which now deserves to be called Cartesianism, ... was part of the ancient Judaical Cabbala. ... The latter being as it were the Body, the other the Soul of that philosophy; the unhappy disjunction of which has been a great evil to both: the Metaphysicians growing vain in spinning out needless and useless subtilties and ridiculous falsities, concerning immaterial beings, ... and the Atomical Philosophers becoming over-credulous of the powers of matter, nay, I may say, too too impious and impudent in exploding the belief of immaterial beings.[23]

From this middle position, More enjoys the best of both worlds. He is able to steer a course midway between Paracelsus and Descartes. Far from regarding the infinity of worlds as a threat to the Paracelsian microcosm, he develops his theory of the infinity of worlds out of Platonic principles, and in "Psychozoia" creates the concept of "The Great Psychany." This particular instance of syncretism, for all its apparent remoteness from the Enlightenment, in fact represents a considerable step forward. More is modernising the concept of the microcosm. According to Paracelsus,

man is the lesser, and for his sake the Macrocosm, the greater world, was founded. ... This therefore is the condition of the Microcosmus, or smaller world. It contains in its body all the minerals of the world. Consequently the body acquires its own medicine from the world. There is a vast variety of things contained in the body of the microcosm which elude the observations of the senses. ... There are for example more than a thousand species of trees, stone, minerals and metals. ... Accordingly, know that the mysteries of the microcosm are to be mystically understood.[24]

To accept such views at their face value, even mystically interpreted, one had to be an alchemist or a Rosicrucian. Bacon had led the attack on Paracelsus; according to him,

the ancient opinion that man was *microcosmus,* an abstract or model of the world, hath been fantastically strained by Paracelsus and the alchemists, as if there were to be found in man's body certain correspondence and parallels, which should have respect to all varieties of things, as stars, planets, minerals, which are extant in the great world.[25]

More, as befits the man who crossed swords so bitterly with the alchemist and Rosicrucian, Thomas Vaughan, set out to discredit Paracelsus, by listing some of his more outlandish doctrines and concluded:

[23] *Philosophical Writings,* pp. xvi-xviii.
[24] Paracelsus, *The Hermetic and Alchemical Writings,* ed. and trans. Arthur Edward Waite (2 vols.; London: J. Elliott, 1894), I. 161. Quoted in M. H. Nicolson, *The Breaking of the Circle: Studies in the Effect of the New Science upon 17th Century Poetry* (rev. ed.; New York: Columbia University Press, 1960), p. 23.
[25] Francis Bacon, *The Advancement of Learning* (London: Oxford University Press, 1906), II, x, 2, p. 127.

These are the rampant and delirious fancies of that great boaster of Europe
Paracelsus, whose unbridled imagination and bold and confident obstrusion
of his uncouth and supine inventions upon the world has, I dare say, given
occasion to the wildest philosophical enthusiasms that ever were broached
by any either Christian or Heathen.[26]

But in spite of this onslaught, More was not prepared to abandon the
microcosm, which appealed strongly to all who were not out and out
Baconians. Metaphysical poetry thrived on the microcosm; Sir Thomas
Browne overcame his Baconian scruples and believed:

To call ourselves a microcosm, or little world, I thought it only a pleasant
trope of rhetoric, till my near judgement and second thoughts told me there
was a real truth therein.[27]

More, for his part, found the concept acceptable:

There is a participation on the virtue at least of all the life that is in the universal orb of life, at the creation of man's soul, . . . whence man may well be
termed a microcosm, or a compendium of the whole world.[28]

More's acceptance is conditional, and he goes on to relate the microcosm
to his "Great Psychany," in an attempt to rescue the Platonic heritage
from what he considers to be the absurd literalism of Paracelsus. As he
explains,

The abode of the body is this earth, but the habitation of the soul her own
energy, which is exceeding vast, at least in some. Every man hath a proper
world, or particular horizon to himself, enlarged or contracted according to
the capacity of his mind. But even sense can reach the stars; what then can
exalted Fancy do, or boundless Intellect? But if stars be all inhabited, which
writers no way contemptible do assert, how vast their habitation is, is obvious
to any fancy. Besides some inhabit God himself, who is unspeakably infinite.[29]

The shift in tone from Paracelsus to More is exemplary of the transit to
the modern mind. It is his Platonism which allows More to display such
euphoric modernism, and adumbrate the mood of Romantic aesthetics. He
spiritualises the literalist data of the Renaissance, without jettisoning the
old microcosmic reality. For More, the vitalism of the universe is the
natural corollary of the vitality of man's soul; and if man's soul be infinite, then an infinity of worlds preserves the correspondence. In this
footnote to his celebration of the "Great Psychany," there is confirmation

---

[26] *Enthusiasmus Triumphatus* (1656), p. 33, in *Philosophical Writings.*
[27] Sir Thomas Browne, *Religio Medici,* I, 34, in *Works,* ed. Geoffrey Keynes (4
vols.; London: Faber and Faber, 1928), I, 44. Quoted in M. H. Nicolson, *The
Breaking of the Circle,* p. 26.
[28] Note to "Psychozoia," II, 23. Grosart, p. 143.
[29] Note to "Psychozoia," II, 24. *Ibid.*

that More's syncretism is less gratuitous and more purposeful than often meets the eye.

Four years later we find More recruiting Descartes (whom he had read in between times) to support his own Platonic Cartesianism *avant la lettre*:

Nay and that sublime and subtile Mechanic too, Descartes, though he seem to mince it, must hold infinitude of worlds, or which is as harsh one infinite one. For what is his *mundus indefinité extensus,* but *extensus infinité*? Else it sounds only *infinitus quoadnos,* but *simpliciter finitus.* But if any space be left out unstuffed with atoms, it will hazard the dissipation of the whole frame of nature into disjointed dust; as may be proved by the principles of his own philosophy.[30]

There is unconscious irony in the last sentence; for, as More and Cudworth were later to discover, Descartes' dualism was to spawn that race of "professed theists of later times," who were to "make the whole world to be nothing else but a mere heap of dust, fortuitously agitated." [31]

More found no difficulty in assimilating Descartes' innate ideas and infinity of worlds into his Platonic system. For him there was no dualism; the two concepts corroborated and enlarged his fourth ground of certainty. But the Enlightenment, in its concentration on evidence and design, was to separate the concepts into an epistemological dualism. On the one hand God, on the other man, and, with a mechanistic universe in between, never the twain shall meet. This was to invite religion to become deistic or mystical, and philosophy to become Lockeian or Malebranchian. A generation later the rift had polarised into confrontations, such as those between Locke and Norris in England, and Bayle and Poiret in Holland. Bayle's description of Poiret is revealing in this respect:

C'est un homme d'une probité reconnue, et qui de grand Cartésien est devenu si dévot, que pour songer mieux aux choses du Ciel, il a presque rompu tout commerce avec la terre.[32]

More stood with neither Locke and Bayle nor Norris and Poiret. He stood for commerce between heaven and earth. Unlike Norris, thrust into the embrace of Malebranchian occasionalism, More was not, in his early period, forced to choose between two opposites.

Only in 1668 did More explicitly reject Cartesian dualism.[33] And yet

---

[30] *Democritus Platonissans* (1646), "To the Reader." *Ibid.,* p. 90.

[31] Ralph Cudworth, *The True Intellectual System of the Universe,* ed. and trans. John Harrison (3 vols.; London: T. Tegg, 1845), I, 217.

[32] Pierre Bayle, *Nouvelles de la République des Lettres,* April 1685, in *Oeuvres Diverses* (4 vols.; La Haye: P. Husson etc., 1727-1731), I, 269. Poiret was a voluminous editor of French quietists, including the notorious Antoinette Bourignon.

[33] In More's *Divine Dialogues* (London: J. Flesher, 1668), Cupophron and Hylobares represent the two extremes of Cartesianism, spiritual and materialist.

as early as 1647 More's enthusiasm for Descartes was far from uncon-
ditional. More was never a pure Cartesian. He used Descartes to support
his fourth ground of certainty; he did not derive this ground from Descartes. The 1647 preface is quite clear on this point:

Monsieur Descartes hath attempted bravely ["a demonstration of the soul's
immortality"] but yet methinks on this side of mathematical evidence. He and
that learned knight our own countryman [Francis Bacon] had done a great
deal more if they had promised less. So high confidence might become the
heat and scheme of poetry much better than sober philosophy. . . . Would it
not be an over-proportioned engine . . . too forcibly driving men to obedience
if they had their immortality as demonstrable as; that the three angles of a
triangle are equal to two right angles. Besides it would prevent that fitting
trial of the soul, how she would be affected if there were nothing to come;
whence she would not be able so sensibly to discover to herself her own
hypocrisy or sincerity.[34]

More had no use for a metaphysics which left no room for the free life of
the spirit. In 1651, defending a modernist Platonism against the Paracelsian excesses of Thomas Vaughan, he explicitly relates Descartes to his
principle of "divine spirit and life":

Descartes' philosophy is indeed a fine, neat, subtile thing; but for the true
ornament of the mind, bears no greater proportion to that principle I told
you of than the dry bones of a snake made up elegantly into a hat-band, to the
royal clothing of Solomon. But other natural philosophies, in respect of
Descartes his, are even less than a few chips of wood to a well erected fabric.[35]

Unfortunately the Enlightenment, in the form of the Royal Society, was
not interested in well-erected fabrics, and with the rejection of Descartes'
cosmology, More's existential idealism was left high and dry. When More,
in his modernist zeal, sought to verify his philosophical insights by the light
of experimental science, he merely revealed the absurdity of his confusion
between mind and matter.

For Coleridge, who saw More as a symptom of the decline of Renaissance Platonism, the confusion was not so much between mind and matter,
as body and matter:

Were there no nother operative causes, as there are many, for the partial
diffusion and sudden decay of Platonism in the 16th and 17th centuries, its
obscure and in part erroneous explanation of matter, and the frequency with
which Platonists confounded matter with body would have sufficed. In Henry
More who blended the doctrine of Descartes (viz. that matter is mere extension and that Body and Soul or Spirit are especially heterogeneous) with

---

[34] "To the Reader" (1647). Grosart, p. 7.
[35] *Second Lash* (1651), as quoted in Ward, p. 64.
[36] Coleridge, *On the 17th Century,* p. 621.

the notions of Plotinus, which are built, on the assumption of their being differences in degree, Body being the dying away of Spirit, and its last vibrations and echoes, this incongruity is especially prominent and revolting.[36]

No doubt Thomas Vaughan's views were as revolting to More, as were More's to Coleridge; for both More and Coleridge were modernisers in the tradition of Platonic idealism. We have seen how strongly More came out against Aristotle, but to Coleridge, More was tainted with barbarism, because entangled in the Aristotelian categories of abstract thought. It is precisely on More's notes to canto one of "Psychozoia," that Coleridge remarked with some irritation:

The three or four preceding pages convince me that H. More was a poetical philosophist who amused himself in calling Aristotelian abstractions by the names of Platonic ideas; but by no means a philosophic poet, framing in the life-light of a guiding Idea.[37]

It is not easy to dismiss Coleridge's view that More in particular, and Renaissance Platonism in general, are too often given to gratuitous mystification. The sort of speculation behind such a statement as "the low spirit of the universe, though it go quite through the world, is not totally in every part of the world," [38] was clearly not in the best interests of the Enlightenment.

More nevertheless soldiered on in defence of his fourth ground of certainty. He felt it necessary to defend its cosmological dimension as formulated in his concept of the "Spirit of Nature," the "Mundane Spirit," or the "Principium Hylarchium." He believed that "the Spirit of the Lord fills all the world," [39] not only the world of spirit, but the world of extension. He defined his "Spirit of Nature" as

a substance incorporeal, but without sense and animadversion, pervading the whole matter of the universe, and exercising a plastical power therein . . . raising such phenomena in the world, by directing the parts of the matter and their motion, as cannot be resolved into mere mechanical powers.[40]

Such remarks were taken by the Enlightenment as descriptive of a merely external cosmos, whereas it is clear that More intended them as a description of the cosmological dimension of his fourth ground of certainty, itself the basis of his existential idealism.

For More the "Spirit of Nature" was a philosophical first principle. In his own words, "that there is a Spirit of Nature . . . nothing can be more

---

[37] *Ibid.*, p. 623.
[38] "Psychozoia," canto I, Preface to the Reader. Grosart, p. 10.
[39] Note to "Psychozoia," I, 59. *Ibid.*, p. 140.
[40] Henry More, *The Immortality of the Soul* (London: W. Morden, 1659), p. 193.

evident in philosophy." [41] It was also the essential link between God and the universe, the highest mind and the lowest matter; for More "the Spirit of Nature . . . is the vicarious power of God upon the matter"; [42] "we may look upon this Spirit of Nature as the great Quartermaster General of Divine Providence." [43] The basis of this projected dimension lay fairly and squarely in More's Platonic interpretation of the microcosm. Thus:

The Mundane Spirit (of which everybody hath its part) inacted by Psyche, if any particular soul exert any imaginative act, needs must for a time at least be coloured as it were or stained with that impression, so that Psyche must needs perceive it, sith it affects her own spirit.[44]

Couched in this Platonic rigmarole is the spiritual truth More was concerned to defend at all costs.

Unfortunately More was himself in part responsible for creating the atmosphere in which the Enlightenment controversy between mechanists and vitalists took place; for he insisted upon testing his "Spirit of Nature" against the latest hypotheses on the nature of matter. Thus, in a consideration of Boyle's Hydrostatics, he writes:

It is a very pleasant discourse, though I be not altogether satisfied that his paradoxical inferences from the experiments are true. There will be a Spirit of Nature for all this, and I think for anything that ever will be alleged to the contrary, or excogitated to evade the unrelish of that principle.[45]

Eight years later he seeks the support of George Keith, the Quaker, and reports to Lady Conway that Keith "is very philosophically and platonically given, and is pleased with the notion of the Spirit of Nature." [46] It followed that the English Enlightenment, to the extent that it was theist and un-Cartesian, used More and Cudworth as tools in the mechanist-vitalist controversy. From Ray to Clarke and beyond, the orthodox theists watered down Cudworth and More to combat deism. A brief consideration of three phases in the development of this controversy, will indicate the fortunes of More's philosophical ideas in the period of the Enlightenment.

John Ray, in the 1690s, shows himself to be curiously divided between Renaissance and modern. He accepts a good deal of Cudworth's vitalism, quoting him at length, and including his onslaught against the mechanic theists; thus, "the pulse of the heart Dr. Cudworth would have to be no

---

[41] *Philosophical Writings*, p. xv.
[42] *The Immortality of the Soul*, p. 13.
[43] *Ibid.*, p. 203.
[44] Note to "Psychozoia", I, 59. Grosart, p. 140.
[45] Letter to Lady Conway, 17 March 1666. *Conway Letters*, p. 269.
[46] Letter to Lady Conway, 11 August 1674. *Ibid.*, p. 391.

mechanical but a vital motion, which seems to me probable." [47] And he sees no reason to reject the concept of Plastic Nature: "There seems to be necessary some Intelligent Plastic Nature, which may understand and regulate the whole economy of the plant: for this cannot be the Vegetative Soul, because that is material and divisible together with the body." [48] But he is adamant against More's theory of signatures: "As for the Signatures of Plants, or the notes impressed upon them as indices of their virtue, though some lay great stress upon them, ... because all that I find mentioned and collected by Authors, seem to me to be rather fancied by men, than designed by Nature to signify or point out any such virtues or qualities, as they would make us believe, I have ... rejected them." [49] Ray is discreet and conservative in his devotion to the scientific method. He does not discard the medieval categories, though he does not think them "agreeable to philosophic verity and accuracy" and prefers the "atomic hypothesis." [50] Nor is he above quoting Sir Thomas Browne on the quincunx.[51] He thus illustrates the mood of the English Enlightenment, and helps account for the persistence of the influence of More and Cudworth in the early 18th century.

In 1697, Leibniz, in a letter to Thomas Burnet, opted for a via media between the mechanical theories of Descartes and the vitalist position taken up by More and Cudworth:

Je crois que tout se fait mécaniquement, comme veulent Démocrite et Descartes, contre l'opinion de M. Morus et ses semblables; et que néanmoins tout se fait encore vitalement et suivant les causes finales, tout étant plein de vie et perception, contre l'opinion des Démocriticiens.[52]

In 1705 Leibniz engaged in a controversy with the Newtonians over the invention of the calculus. The dispute spread to other issues, and in 1710 Leibniz made his first attack on the Newtonian theory of gravity. In 1712 Leibniz referred to gravity as "an occult quality" which could not be reduced to principles of matter and motion; and in 1715 he crossed swords with Samuel Clarke on the question of vitalism.[53] The Leibniz-Clarke correspondence, originally published in 1717, reveals with extraordinary

[47] John Ray, *The Wisdom of God Manifested in the Works of Creation* (London, 1691), p. 30.
[48] *Ibid.*, p. 76.
[49] *Ibid.*, p. 85.
[50] *Ibid.*, p. 42.
[51] *Ibid.*, p. 80.
[52] Gottfried Wilhelm Leibniz, *Die Philosophischen Schriften*, ed. C. J. Gerhardt (7 vols.; Hildesheim: Olms Verlag, 1960), III, 217. This letter is dated 24 August 1697. It is quoted in *Conway Letters*, p. 456.
[53] See G. W. Leibniz and Samuel Clarke, *The Leibniz-Clarke Correspondence*, ed. H. G. Alexander (Manchester: University Press, 1956), Introduction.

clarity the difference between the English and European Enlightenments. Both men are concerned to castigate materialism, and both see each other's systems as excluding a justifiable measure of vitalism. Whereas Clarke rests his case on Newtonian mathematics, Leibniz relies on metaphysics. Leibniz's complaint against the Newtonian cosmology is that God is reduced to the level of a bad workman who has to maintain and repair his machine; in Leibniz's view miracles exist for grace not nature.[54] Clarke responds by accusing Leibniz of crass materialism, of eliminating God from the universe, and of ignoring the importance of mathematics.[55] Leibniz states his preference for metaphysics as the only way to combat the materialists, and claims that his monadology goes beyond Newton.[56] In a letter to Conti, a Venetian cleric who came out for Leibniz in Paris and for Newton in London, Leibniz attacked the general flabbiness of post-Newtonian English philosophy:

Je m'étonne que les sectateurs de M. Newton ne donnent rien qui marque que leur maître leur a communiqué une bonne méthode. J'ai été plus heureux en disciples. C'est dommage que M. le Chevalier Wren de qui M. Newton et beaucoup d'autres ont appris quand il était jeune, n'a pas continué de régaler le public. . . . Dans le temps qu'il était jeune, on se serait moqué en Angleterre de la nouvelle philosophie de certains Anglais. Lui et M. Flamstead avec M. Newton sont presque le seul reste du siècle d'or d'Angleterre par rapport aux sciences.[57]

For Leibniz, in the absolutist tradition of the European Enlightenment, England was a country which had turned its back on philosophy, and chosen to limit its speculation to the field of experimental science. The development of More's philosophy, from the relative autonomy of metaphysics to the strait-jacket of scientism, prefigures this decline.

Meanwhile the English went on using Cudworth to combat materialism. In 1706 Thomas Wise's *Confutation of Atheism* consisted of an abridgement of Cudworth's *System,* in which the enemies of religion, Descartes, Bayle, Hobbes and Spinoza, were set up against the friends of religion, More, Norris, Newton and Locke.[58] Cudworth's work was translated into English by the Bishop of Durham in 1731, and in the same year whole chunks of Cudworth were retailed to a wide reading public in *The*

[54] Ibid., pp. 11-12.
[55] *Ibid.,* pp. 12, 14.
[56] *Ibid.,* pp. 15 ff.
[57] G. W. Leibniz and S. Clarke, *Correspondance Leibniz-Clarke,* ed. André Robinet (Paris: Presses Universitaires de France, 1957), p. 43. This letter is dated 6 December 1715.
[58] See Colie, pp. 141-142.

Present State of the Republic of Letters.[59] A second complete English edition appeared in 1743, and in 1749 James Cawthorn's "The Vanity of Human Enjoyments" contained the following tribute to a writer who, in Rosalie Colie's words, "spoke to many religious souls in the 18th century troubled by the impieties of their age": [60]

> Ask at yon tomb, where Cudworth's mighty name
> Weeps o'er the ruins of his wit and fame,
> Cudworth, whose spirit flew, with sails unfurled,
> Through each vast empire of the ideal world,
> Pierced through the mystic shades o'er Nature thrown,
> And made the soul's immensity his own.[61]

But this was the indulgence of lip-service. Nobody had followed up the work of More and Cudworth. When they had served their turn as quotable precursors of a pious Enlightenment, they were cast aside as illuminati. So often had Cudworth been used by the orthodox theists, that Bolingbroke, in the interests of heterodox theism, felt it necessary to demolish with his posthumous blunderbuss any credit that More's Platonist friend might still enjoy in Augustan England.[62] Thereby was displayed the immobility of the English Enlightenment. For Bolingbroke was merely repeating in a general and diffuse way, the incisive diagnosis of More's Platonism made by Bayle as early as 1684. Bayle saw that More's mistake lay in trying to transpose his idealism into a shape that would fit in with current cosmological hypotheses:

Un théologien de Cambridge nommé More, dont on voit des lettres parmi celles de M. Descartes, a soutenu hautement que les âmes existent avant que d'être unies au corps, et qu'elles descendent du lieu de leur résidence, pour s'unir au corps, attirées par une odeur très-subtile qui s'exhale des petits embryons encore informes à peu près comme les oiseaux de proie sont attirés de bien loin par l'odeur de leur gibier. C'est bien ce que disait Cicéron, qu'il n'y a point de sentiment si absurde, que quelque philosophie ne l'ait soutenu. Il est néanmoins fâcheux qu'un philosophe, que a écrit si subtilement et si savamment contre le système de M. Descartes, soit tombé dans des pensées si grossières.[63]

---

[59] *The Present State of the Republic of Letters*, ed. A. Reid (18 vols.; London: William Innys, 1728-1736), VII (1731), pp. 66-69, 139-150, 196-203, 325-330.

[60] Colie, p. 143.

[61] Alexander Chalmers (ed.), *The Works of the English Poets from Chaucer to Cowper* (21 vols.; London: J. Johnson, 1810), XIV, 254.

[62] Henry St John, Viscount Bolingbroke, *Works*, ed. David Mallet (5 vols.; London, 1754).

[63] Bayle, *Nouvelles de la République des Lettres*, May 1684, in *Oeuvres Diverses*, I, 58.

The English Enlightenment did not pursue Bayle's judgement of More; it simply used the Platonists, until they were no longer in currency, and then cast them into oblivion.

Whatever may have been the fortunes of More's philosophy in the 18th century, there remains the problem of interpreting his support for Glanvill's view, that spirit is an empirical phenomenon susceptible to scientific investigation.[64] More's *Antidote against Atheism* contains thirteen chapters of case histories concerned with witches, ghosts, and miscellaneous spiritual phenomena.[65] In More's eyes these stories amounted to arguments against those arch-atheists, Hobbes and Spinoza. There was for example the Tedworth ghost; More reported that "some Hobbians have been at Tedworth and were convinced." [66] In a letter to Glanvill, he referred to "such coarse grained philosophers as those Hobbians and Spinozians, and the rest of that rabble," who "slight religion and the scriptures, because there is such express mention of spirits and angels in them, things that their dull souls are so inclinable to conceit to be impossible.[67]

More's opposition to Spinoza was singularly unfortunate, as more than one critic has pointed out. In the words of Rosalie Colie:

Had More and others like him been able to recognize and to use the extraordinary super-platonic unification Spinoza offered his readers, the materialist conquest More so feared might not so easily and so thoroughly have taken place. More's mistake was the mistake natural to his age: he failed to see in so extra-ecclesiastical a figure as Spinoza the intense sincerity that spoke so plainly to the neo-platonising 19th century, in the grip of a materialism more enveloping . . . than anything imagined by More or Cudworth.[68]

According to E. A. Burtt, More went a good way along with Spinoza in confronting the "seemingly impassible gulf of the Cartesian dualism," but not far enough:

Besides the penetrating analysis of Spinoza, More was the one thinker of importance in the age who dimly glimpsed a suggestive way out. But More confined the extension of the soul to the body plus a thin portion of the surrounding medium, which at best only solved part of the problem, . . . and in any case the notion was quite unacceptable to exact-minded people because deduced too largely from superstitious theosophical fancies[69]

[64] See Aharon Lichtenstein, *Henry More: The Rational Theology of a Cambridge Platonist* (Cambridge, Mass.: Harvard University Press, 1962), p. 183.

[65] *Antidote Against Atheism*, pp. 86-129.

[66] Letter to Lady Conway, 31 March 1663. *Conway Letters*, p. 216.

[67] "Dr More's Letter to Mr Glanvill", 25 May 1678, in Joseph Glanvill, *Sadducismus Triumphatus* (4th ed.; London: A. Bettesworth etc., 1726), pp. 9-10.

[68] Colie, p. 92.

[69] Burtt, p. 323.

Because of this, More was singularly ill-equipped to appreciate the work of Spinoza, and unable to distinguish between the "superplatonist" and the Hobbesian materialist.

More nevertheless had a sufficiently exact mind to subject spiritual phenomena to empirical, as well as theosophical, inquiry. The even more exact-minded Sprat had declared, with perhaps premature optimism:

Every man is unshaken at those tales at which his ancestors trembled: the course of things goes quietly along, in its own true channel of natural causes and effects. For this we are beholden to Experiments.[70]

More himself sifted the evidence, and frequently refused to credit tales that came to his notice. Thus:

I have heard of strange news since my last [letter] of one carried away and torn to pieces by the devil in Lincolnshire, which is seriously reported here and is believed by some, but I do not believe one syllable of it, but look upon it as a gullery.[71]

On another occasion he wrote: "I cannot believe any prodigy that serves a design, though some true ones may do so." [72] More cannot be accused of enjoying any confusion of mind and matter which he may have helped to perpetrate. In the conclusion to his analysis of the case histories he had assembled, he made the following apology:

It is not to be imputed to any vain credulity of mine, or that I take a pleasure in telling strange stories, but that I thought fit to fortify and strengthen the faith of others as much as I could; being well assured that a contemptuous misbelief of such like narrations concerning Spirits, and an endeavour of making them all ridiculous and incredible, is a dangerous prelude to Atheism itself, or else a more close and crafty possession and insinuation of it. For assuredly that saying is not more true in politics, *No Bishop, no King*; than this is in metaphysics, *No Spirit, no God*.[73]

The slogan "No Spirit, no God" provides the key to any intricacies and barbarities which mar More's philosophy; that the 18th century English Enlightenment shirked the issue is not to its credit.

With all its obvious limitations, More's gothic speculation serves his declared end of maintaining "our free sprite." [74] Coleridge was infuriated at More's inability, or refusal, to account for the unity of body and soul; he demanded a "middle term." [75] But it was hardly More's fault that the

[70] Thomas Sprat, *History of the Royal Society*, ed. J. I. Cope and H. W. Jones (St. Louis: Washington University Press, 1959), p. 340.
[71] Letter to Lady Conway, 5 April 1658. *Conway Letters*, p. 147.
[72] Letter to Lady Conway, 4 January 1662. *Ibid.*, p. 198.
[73] *Antidote Against Atheism*, p. 142.
[74] "The Preexistency of the Soul," stanza 89. Grosart, p. 127.
[75] Coleridge, *On the 17th Century*, p. 623.

Enlightenment separated man from God, body from soul, and left the carcass of a mechanistic universe between the two. Cudworth's "plastic nature" was a massive attempt to give Coleridge what he wanted, namely a world where, in Cudworth's own words. "God, as Plato (after Orpheus) speaks, will be not only the beginning and end, but also the middle of all things." [76] More's "middle life" serves the same purpose; there is

a Middle life or faculty of the soul of man betwixt the Divine and Animal; which ... we may call ... Reason; which is a power or faculty of the soul, whereby either from her innate ideas or common notions, or else from the assurance of her own senses, or upon the relation or tradition of another, she unravels a further clew of knowledge, enlarging her sphere of intellectual light, by laying open to herself the close connexion and cohesion of the conceptions she has of things, whereby inferring one thing from another she is able to deduce multifarious conclusions, as well for the pleasure of speculation as the necessity of practice.[77]

It is on the ground of this "middle life," alias "Reason," that More chooses to organise the defence of "our free sprite." Here is the source, rationale and purpose of his philosophical enterprise.

[76] Cudworth, I, 224.
[77] An Explanation of the Grand Mystery of Godliness, in Theological Works, p. 35.

CHAPTER THREE

RELIGION: LATITUDE AND PIETISM

The part More played in forming the latitudinarian spirit in religion can hardly be distinguished from his reconstruction of an existential idealism; but, to the extent that it can be identified as a separate strand in More's work, it speaks even more eloquently than does his philosophy for the emerging modern consciousness. More cannot however be held responsible for two end-products of latitudinarianism which seemed to later generations to constitute its essence. These were the political party which "won" the 1688 revolution on the one hand, and the rise of deism on the other. It must for example be remembered that in More's day there was no distinction between a latitudinarian and a Platonist.[1] Thus the sequel to More's theology lies in the growth of pietism, which, as Law and Wesley discovered in their own different ways, was the only radical alternative, in an age of Enlightenment, to the politically established and spiritually dead latitudinarianism of deist and orthodox alike.

In Simon Patrick's 1662 pamphlet we have the first recorded use of the term "latitude men." [2] It is significant that Patrick's Oxford correspondent refers to these original latitudinarians as a "new sect." It was inconceivable at the time that any group of men with new ideas about religion should be anything else. To the Anglican and Presbyterian traditionalists who believed in uniformity, anyone who cast doubts upon this principle was ipso facto a schismatic, a sectarian and a heretic; in their eyes the latitude men were no better than Socinians. Writing at a time when the Presbyterians were about to be excluded from Charles II's Anglican establishment, Patrick was on safe ground in riposting that, "as for rites and ceremonies of divine worship," the latitude men "do highly approve that virtuous mediocrity which our Church observes between the meretricious gaudiness

---

[1] See T. A. Birrell's introduction to Patrick's *Brief Account.*
[2] *Ibid.*

of the Church of Rome, and the squalid sluttery of fanatic conventicles." [3]
But this was pure form. There was a deeper charge to be met, based on the
belief that Aristotle and theology were interdependent, and that to change
one by embracing the "new philosophy" would inevitably lead to innovations in the other:

But methinks I hear some men say, all innovations are dangerous; philosophy
and divinity are so interwoven by the schoolmen, that it cannot be safe to
separate them; new philosophy will bring in new divinity; and freedom in the
one will make men desire a liberty in the other.[4]

Patrick answers this charge by pointing out that this is the "same argu-
mentation the Presbyterians used when they bore rule in the university,
and the new philosophy was interdicted in some colleges on that account."[5]
This is hardly an answer, for it was not only the Presbyterians who used
this argument, but Anglicans also, naturally apprehensive that the new
philosophy was the harbinger of atheism; thus Casaubon: "Men that are
much fixed upon matter and secondary causes and sensual objects may
forget that there be such things in the world as spirits, and at last that there
is a God and that their souls are immortal." [6] More himself was to become
as apprehensive when latitudinarians and Platonists went their several
ways; but, writing in 1662, he displays the optimism of the modernist.

Patrick, in this same year, made the claim that "true philosophy can
never hurt sound divinity." [7] More concurred. In a letter, he described
Descartes' philosophy as "the best engine I can find against erroneous
fabrics in religion." [8] In the preface to his *Immortality of the Soul* he ex-
patiated on this theme:

I think it is the most sober and faithful advice that can be offered to the
Christian world, that they would encourage the reading of Descartes in all
public schools or universities. That the students of philosophy may be
thoroughly exercised in the just extent of the mechanical powers of matter,
how far they will reach, and where they fall short. Which will be the best
assistance to religion that reason and the knowledge of nature can afford.
For by this means such as are intended to serve the Church will be armed
betimes with sufficient strength to grapple with their proudest deriders or op-
posers. Whenas for want of this, we see how liable they are to be contemned
and borne down by every bold, though weak, pretender to the mechanic
philosophy.[9]

[3] Patrick, p. 7.
[4] *Ibid.,* p. 22.
[5] *Ibid.,* p. 23.
[6] Meric Casaubon, *Letter to Peter du Moulin* (1669), as quoted in Meyrick
Carré, *Phases of Thought in England* (Oxford: Clarendon Press, 1949), p. 259.
[7] Patrick, p. 24.
[8] Letter to Lady Conway, 5 July 1662. *Conway Letters,* p. 203.
[9] *The Immortality of the Soul,* p. 13.

And in the 1662 preface to his collected philosophical works, he was even more explicitly confident in his modernist approach to the Bible, claiming that "if anyone presume that he has found such points of Cartesianism, or Platonism as I have applied to the Mosaic letter to be really true upon thorough examination, I dare confidently pronounce to him, that if they be so, those truths were ever lodged in the text of Moses." [10] Modernism is one aspect of More's latitude; another is pietism.

More's achievement was to establish a sound divinity which was above the sects, but not above the everyday realities of the moral life. Thus his reaction to his Calvinist childhood led to pietism rather than to moralism. The distinction is important, because the latitudinarian spirit evaporated with amazing rapidity into the moral self-sufficiency of Enlightenment deism. More's resistance to the temptations of moralism was strong for a Platonist. In areas of thought and doctrine in which Platonists tend to leave no room for the activity of "our free spirit," More is quite adamant; and his arguments, though some of them may have seeped through from his Calvinist heritage, have more in common with the arguments of 18th century enthusiasts. The context in which More's pietism arose needs to be restated if we are to correct the view that the latitudinarian spirit was by its very nature destined to disappear, once it had given birth to whiggery and deism.

One reason for the neglect of the pietistic strand in latitudinarianism is that Tuckney, in his initial attack on Whichcote's theology, is seen to have spoken prophetically of later developments in latitudinarianism. It is however clear that, vis à vis the Cambridge Platonists, he overstated his case. He had written of Whichcote's tendencies:

Mind and understanding is all; heart and will little spoken of.... A kind of moral divinity minted; only with a little tincture of Christ added: this is not Paul's manner of preaching.[11]

The moral divinity of the Cambridge Platonists would indeed lead to deism; but it was also a divinity which had much to say about the heart and will, and was even more opposed to the elevation of "right reason" as a theological criterion than Tuckney shows himself to be.[12] It is true that later Whichcote was viewed as an apostle of the Enlightenment; but in Whichcote's day to defend spiritual light against Calvinist orthodoxy was to contribute to the Enlightenment. Whichcote had written:

---

[10] *Philosophical Writings,* p. xix.
[11] "Eight Letters of Dr Antony Tuckney and Dr Benjamin Whichcote," in Whichcote's *Moral and Religious Aphorisms,* ed. S. Salter (1753), Letter II. Quoted in Henry More, *Philosophical Poems,* ed. Bullough, p. xix.
[12] For More's attack on "right reason," see "Psychozoia," II, 99. Grosart, p. 28.

The more mysterious the more imperfect: that which is mystically spoken, is but half spoken: As darkness is, in compare with light; so is mystery, in comparison with knowledge.[13]

He had also declared: "The religious represent God to themselves as amiable; the superstitious represent God to themselves as formidable." [14] It is not therefore surprising to find editions of Whichcote appearing in 1697 for consumption in an age of Enlightenment, and in 1753 in an age of pietism. Shaftesbury felt it necessary to apologise for "the unpolished style and phrase of our author, who drew more from a college than a court, and was more used to School-learning and the language of an university than to the conversation of the fashionable world." [15] Samuel Salter on the other hand congratulated himself on living in "an age . . . in which such a generous freedom of thinking, chastened and tempered by the genuine spirit of true piety and most exalted devotion," such as Whichcote's, "meets with the esteem and applause it so well deserves." [16] In other words Whichcote's latitude, his "generous freedom of thinking," is inseparable from his spirit of piety. While remembering that Tuckney was critical and Shaftesbury appreciative of the former, it must not be forgotten that Law and Wesley cherished Whichcote's kindred spirit, Henry More, chiefly for the latter.[17]

The moralism of the Enlightenment left no room for pietism to function; if left no incentive to religious effort. Platonism inevitably tended to minimise the importance of evil; thus we find More saying:

> Who misconceives, conceives but his own ill,
> Brings forth a falsehood, shows his want of skill.[18]

Tuckney was right; this is not Paul's manner of preaching; but then neither is it Shaftesbury's. There may not be much sense of sin in More's moral divinity, but there are two ways in which he avoids the moralism of the Enlightenment.

In the first place he has a sense of two natures, without which pietism would have no basis. He distinguishes as follows:

---

[13] Benjamin Whichcote, *Moral and Religious Aphorisms,* ed. W. R. Inge (London: E. Matthews and Marrat, 1930), No. 1014.

[14] *Ibid.,* No. 947.

[15] Shaftesbury, *Sermons of Whichcote* (1697), preface, as quoted in Inge's Whichcote, p. xviii.

[16] Salter's 1753 preface to the *Aphorisms,* as quoted in Inge's Whichcote, p. xxiii.

[17] See J. H. Overton, "Henry More," *DNB.*

[18] "Insomnium Philosophicum," Grosart, p. 179.

I mean not Nature's harsh obdurate light,
The shameless eye-brows of the Serpent old,
That armed with custom will not stick to fight
With God and him affront with courage bold:
But that sweet temper we may oft behold
In virgin youth as yet immaculate,
And unto drudging policy unfold,
Who do without design, now love, now hate,
And freely give and take withouten price or rate.[19]

These two natures, rooted in the moral being, correspond closely to the "old man / new man" categories of pietistic theology. Whether the divine principle of grace is planted in the soul at conversion, or merely awakened, is a matter of dry speculation in the light of the existential reality of the "fight." In another place More refers to Grace and Nature as both of divine origin:

It is God alone
That gives both strengths whenever we do swink.[20]

But, as Bullough points out, this does not annihilate the freedom of the soul's responsibility; [21] for all our dependence on God, "we do swink."

In the second place More comes out very strongly against that principle of Enlightenment moralism, to which Norris was drawn a generation later, namely, "self-love." In two long letters on the subject, he sets his "divine principle" against the new concept. For the Enlightenment, the circle of felicity and benevolence was based on the concept of self-love. To More it seemed "as unnatural and forced a conceit, to found all that love we owe to God and the whole creation upon self-love, or to resolve it thereinto, as to attempt to cram the whole bulk of the universe into the eye of a needle." [22] He believed that "self-love cannot raise the soul towards the Divine Nature. Nothing can ascend up into heaven but what comes down from it." [23] But More is not against self-love out of Platonic principle alone; later on in this letter it becomes clear that his opposition is based on the positive alternative of the mystery of regeneration:

The wind bloweth where it listeth, but thou knowest not from whence it comes. So deep a mystery is real regeneration. But if there be no new principle of Love ingenerated in regeneration, ordinary people might easily discern in

---

[19] "Psychozoia," II, 123. *Ibid.,* p. 30.
[20] "Psychozoia," III, 48. *Ibid.,* p. 37.
[21] *Philosophical Poems,* ed. Bullough, p. 223.
[22] Letter IV, Ward, p. 258.
[23] Letter V, ibid., p. 274.

what corner the wind stands: all then is from self-love, and circles into self-love again.[24]

Pietism thrived on such theology, and those men of the Enlightenment who attempted to corner the wind, could not radically mark this emergent religious consciousness.

In the 18th century the religious awakening emerged in the form of what the established philosophical, social and political Enlightenment could only call "enthusiasm." More's theology can be seen as ensuring that deism was not the only kind of enlightened religion. The generation that sat at the feet of Tillotson would make no sense of More's pietistic emphasis on regeneration. It would rejoice in those "other performances, whether of morality or religion, arising from mere self-love," which, according to More, "are at best but as preparations, or the more refined exercises, of a sort of theological Hobbianism." [25] More would have nothing to do with those cardboard weapons which the orthodox in Tillotson's day wielded against the deistic scarecrows of the pseudo-Enlightenment. That he left Trinitarian controversy to be settled by scripture, may be a relic of his Calvinist past; [26] but that he attacked the emphasis placed on future rewards, is a sure sign of his pietism, and a foreshadowing of the Evangelical reaction to the dry speculation of the 18th century religious establishment.

Of future rewards More writes: "I never yet understood that the hope of an inheritance should make a man a son. Regeneration makes us sons: not the belief of an inheritance." [27] To read More on regeneration is to read More on himself; for it is not with the doctrine as such that he is concerned, but rather the experience which gives rise to the doctrine. He speaks of "immediately entering the lists, and of using all possible endeavours, that our own will, by which we relish ourselves, and what belongs to us, in things as well of the soul as of the body, might be opposed, destroyed, annihilated; that so the Divine Will alone, with the New Birth, may revive and grow up in us." [28] And drawing the doctrinal conclusion, he speaks as Law and Wesley spoke in their generation:

The old man; while it doth but exercise, all this time, its own nature divers ways, and adjusts itself to outward multifarious opinions and practices in religion, and bends and winds itself about this way and that way; is still a mere serpent, the mere old man; as a dunghill, turn it into what shapes and postures you will, still remains a dunghill. The Divine Seed alone is that

[24] *Ibid.*, p. 282.
[25] "Little Narrative of Himself," *Ibid.*, p. 14.
[26] See "Psychozoia," canto I, Preface to the Reader. Grosart, p. 10.
[27] Letter V, Ward, p. 288.
[28] "Little Narrative of Himself," *Ibid.*, p. 14.

which is acceptable unto God; and the sole invincible basis of all true
religion.[29]

It is hardly surprising that Law and Wesley found much to their liking
in More's work.

There is for instance More's argument from the two natures, in which
a parallel is made between the needs of the "old man" and the needs of the
"new man." On the one hand:

> When we are clothed with this outward world,
> Feel the soft air, behold the glorious sun,
> All this we have from meat that's daily hurled
> Into these mouths.

On the other hand:

> He gives his own dear body and his blood
> To drink and eat. Thus daily we are fed
> Unto eternal life. Thus do we bud,
> True heavenly plants, such in our lasting food.[30]

Law devoted pages of discourse to this kind of sacramental pietism. There
is also in More a sense of deliverance from "the dark chains, and this so
sordid captivity of my own will," which he ascribes to the moment of his
initial spiritual awakening: "there shone in upon me daily a greater assurance than ever I could have expected, even of those things which before
I had the greatest desire to know." [31] Wesley gave a similar account of his
conversion.

More's latitudinarian spirit is thus qualified and conditioned by an
ethical impetus, which, though in its intensity of moral asceticism may
seem to be derived from a Calvinist emphasis on grace from without, is in
fact an awakening of the precious substratum within. It is thus not incompatible with the newly tapped sources of Cartesian introspective
egoism. Indeed, to give More his historical due, it marks, in a decisive way,
the metamorphosis from Renaissance Protestantism to modern Protestantism, from Calvinism to pietism; a metamorphosis which Troeltsch detected in the age of Jurieu and Bayle, and which More thus succinctly
foreshadowed.[32]

In More's work this metamorphosis is recorded in a blurred fashion,
because of the awkwardness and enthusiasm with which he gives philoso-

---

[29] *Ibid.*
[30] "Psychathanasia," III, i, 31-32. Grosart, p. 69.
[31] "Little Narrative of Himself," Ward, p. 15.
[32] See Elisabeth Labrousse, *Pierre Bayle,* II, 443.

phical expression to his theology. Bayle's comments on Cudworth's "plastic nature" apply equally well to More's "mundane spirit"; neither is relevant to a valid defence of the religious life:

La dispute sur les Natures Plastiques de M. Cudworth n'intéresse point la religion. C'est une hypothèse inventée depuis peu, et suivie de peu de gens. Qu'elle fournisse un prétexte de chicane ou non aux Athées, peu importe. Cela ne nuit point à tant d'autres arguments victorieux que ce savant anglais emploie et développe merveilleusement contre l'Athéisme.[33]

Bayle's point becomes clear if we consider that More's "mundane spirit" is but the Holy Spirit writ large in the cosmos, and is conceived as a support, rather than a proof, for the validity of practical piety. Thus More declares that,

> God's spirit is no private empty shade
> But that great ghost that fills both earth and sky
> And through the boundless universe doth lie,
> Shining through purged hearts and simple minds
> When doubling clouds of thick hypocrisy
> Be blown away with strongly brushing winds.[34]

It is in spite of its philosophical clumsiness that More's work reveals the metamorphosis from Renaissance to modern Protestantism. Take for example his crusade against literalism:

For as many as are born of the Spirit, and are not mere sons of the Letter, know very well how much the more inward and mysterious meaning of the text makes for the reverence of the Holy Scripture and advantage of godliness. . . . It is the atheist's highest interest, to have it taken for granted, that there is no spiritual meaning, either in Scripture or Sacrament, that extends further than the mere grammatical sense in the one, or the sensible, gross, external performance in the other.[35]

Here is evidence of the switch from letter to light; from Calvinism, with its emphasis on literary humanism, learning and The Book, to a Cartesian pietism, with its emphasis on the self-sufficiency of the inner light with direct access to the divine life.

With the break-up of scholastic and rationalist systems of theology, concentration on the inner life of the spirit became the only way in which to maintain the reality of religious life. Time and time again, More returns

---

[33] Bayle, *Réponse aux Questions d'un Provincial,* in *Oeuvres Diverses,* III, 891.
[34] "Psychozoia," II, 91. Grosart, p. 27.
[35] Henry More, *Conjectura Cabbalistica* (1653), "Epistle Dedicatory ... To Dr Cudworth," in *Philosophical Writings.*

to this theme, with such insistence that he appears to be rehearsing a catechism:

> If then said he, the spirit may not be
> Right Reason, surely we must deem it sense.
> Yes sense it is, this was my short reply.
> Sense upon which Holy Intelligence
> And Heavenly Reason and Comely Prudence
> (O beauteous branches of that root divine!)
> Do springen up, through inly experience
> Of God's hid ways, as he doth ope the eyn
> Of our dark souls and in our hearts his light enshrine.[36]

This concept of two reasons is similar to that developed by Law and Coleridge. It also constitutes a reference to what have been loosely termed 17th century reason and 18th century reason, differentiated by Cassirer as follows:

In the great metaphysical systems of . . . Descartes and Malebranche, of Spinoza and Leibniz, reason is the realm of the "eternal verities," of those truths held in common by the human and the divine mind. What we know through reason, we therefore behold "in God." Every act of reason means participation in the divine nature; it gives access to the intelligible world. The 18th century takes reason in a different and more modest sense. It is no longer the sum total of "innate ideas" given prior to all experience, which reveals the absolute essence of things. Reason is now looked upon rather as an acquisition than as a heritage.[37]

There can be little doubt that a good deal of the confusion inherent in More's work is due to his devotion to both concepts of reason. Cassirer might well have defined 18th century reason in the words of More himself:

By Reason I understand so settled and cautious a composure of mind as will suspect every high-flown and forward fancy that endeavours to carry away the assent before deliberate examination; she not enduring to be gulled by the vigour or garishness of the representation, nor at all to be borne down by the weight or strength of it; but patiently to try it by the known faculties of the soul, which are either the common notions that all men in their wits agree upon, or the evidence of outward sense, or else a clear and distinct deduction from these.[38]

This is Baconian reason, an acquisition rather than a heritage, with no mention of participation in the divine nature.

[36] "Psychozoia," II, 99. Grosart, p. 28.
[37] Ernst Cassirer, *The Philosophy of the Enlightenment* (Boston: Beacon Press, 1951), p. 13.
[38] Henry More, *Enthusiasmus Triumphatus* (1656), p. 38, in *Philosophical Writings*.

More however, unlike his Baconian contemporaries, did not abandon the concept of "heavenly reason." He would not shirk the dilemma of constructing a theological epistemology in an age of Enlightenment. Stillingfleet was one of the few latitudinarian divines who raised the problem, although he proffered no more than a hypothetical solution. "Supposing reason to be pure and not corrupted and steeped in sense as now it is," he suggested "it would discover spiritual evidence to be the most real and convincing evidence." [39] The insights of the Cambridge Platonists allowed them to be more than hypothetical. Thus John Smith, whose *Discourses* were published only two years before Stillingfleet's work, asserts the validity of this very same hypothesis: "When reason once is raised, by the mighty force of the Divine Spirit, into a converse with God, it is turned into sense: that which before was only faith . . . now becomes vision." [40] More was equally convinced. He distinguished between the relative weakness of "natural reason" and "a more palpable evidence," namely revelation, which, he claimed, was "more intelligible and convictive to the generality of the world, who have neither leisure nor inclination to deal with the spinosities and anxieties of human reason and philosophy." [41] Elsewhere he agreed with Stillingfleet and Smith that reason, raised to the state of illumination, could provide this "more palpable evidence". Thus the 23rd conclusion in his *Brief Discourse of the True Grounds of the Certainty of Faith in Points of Religion* (1668) is "that there is a divine certainty of faith, which, besides the grounds that the moral or human certainty hath, is supported and corroborated by the spirit of life in the new birth, and by illuminated reason." That there may be no doubt as to the nature of such reason, he adds that "this is not to be argued, but by an internal sense to be felt." [42] In another place he wrote that "the beginning of reason is not reason, but something which is better: but what can be better than Science but God?" [43] And he tried to define the beginning of reason in the following terms:

I should commend to them that would successfully philosophise, the belief and endeavour after a certain principle more noble and inward than reason itself, and without which reason will falter, or at least reach but to mean and frivolous things. I have a sense of something in me while I thus speak, which I must confess is of so retruse a nature that I want a name for it, unless I should adventure to term it Divine Sagacity.[44]

[39] Edward Stillingfleet, *Origines Sacrae: or A Rational Account of the Grounds of Christian Faith* (3rd ed.; London: Henry Mortlock, 1666), p. 251.
[40] Smith, p. 17.
[41] *The Immortality of the Soul*, p. 2.
[42] *The Two Last Dialogues*, p. 484, and *Theological Works*, p. 768.
[43] *Philosophical Writings*, p. ix.
[44] *Ibid.*, p. vii.

More seems to be basing his theological epistemology on the principle of the operation of the Holy Spirit. How else can one interpret the pre-occupation common to the following declarations?

There is a kind of sanctity of soul and body that is of more efficacy for the receiving and retaining of Divine Truths, than the greatest pretences to Discursive Demonstration.[45]
All the subtile cords of reason, without the timely recovery of that divine touch within the hidden spirit of man, will never be able to pull him back, out of that abhorred pit of atheism and infidelity. So much better is in-nocency and piety than subtile argument, and earnest and severe devotion than curious dispute.[46]
Believe it, Christianity is another kind of thing, than some bold wits would make it; and is but a dead husk, where the assistance of the spirit is not both acknowledged and experienced.[47]

Such is the pietism which provides the guiding line of More's theology.

Although More stressed the authority of the indwelling spirit, it should not be forgotten that he never renounced a measure of Anglican ortho-doxy. This he felt was essential in an age when so many light-infested sects were basing their doctrines and practices on the primordial of spiritual experience. This he makes quite clear in the preface to his *Theological Works,* where he takes up a considered orthodox via media between for-malism and enthusiasm:

For whereas some in an hypocritical flattery of the external person of Christ, shuffle out all obligation to the divine life (which is that mystical Christ within us) and pervert the Grace of God in the Gospel to looseness and liber-tinism; and others on the contrary (whether out of the power of melancholy that calls the thoughts inward, or the scandal they take from abuse of the personal offices of our blessed Saviour (they feeling the generality of Chris-tians make the external frame of religion but a palliation for sin) or whether for the obscurity of some articles of the Christian faith) have become plainly infidels and misbelievers of the whole history of Christ, and will have nothing to do with his person, but look upon the mystery of Christianity as a thing wholly within us, and that has no other object than what is either acting or acted in ourselves: I have with all earnestness of endeavour, and with un-deniable clearness of testimony from Reason and Scripture demonstrated the truth and necessity of both Christ within and Christ without, and have plainly set out the wonderful wisdom and goodness of God in contriving so powerful a means as the very exterior economy of Christianity is for the renewing of our natures into the glorious image of his Son, who is the life of God, and the soul's sure pledge of an happy immortality.[48]

[45] *Ibid.*
[46] More's "Interpretation General," Grosart, p. 166.
[47] Letter IV, Ward, p. 266.
[48] *Theological Works,* p. ii.

And yet, Anglican or not, More is too honest to brush his pietism under the carpet. This balanced synthesis contains too many parenthetic qualifications, which betray a depth of feeling and sympathy for the pietism of the sectarian enthusiasts, for it to be a genuine Anglican compromise in anything but form. The last sentence of the passage reveals the sacramental nature of More's pietism. Clearly this allowed him to feel at home in the pre-1688 Church of England, and was the source of his basic dislike of Quakerism. In this he closely resembles William Law, whose pietism derived from his understanding of sacramental Christianity. Both men had a nagging love-hate relationship with Quakerism, though More's was the more violent because he was in touch with the excessively enthusiastic first generation of Quakers. Nevertheless, in the parenthesis "they feeling . . .", More almost identifies himself with the position of the dissenting enthusiasts. His via media, fine and orthodox though it is, betrays a clear preference for the inner Christ.

The sectarian enthusiasts towards whom More devoted most attention were the Quakers, the Familists, and the Behmenists. His own preference for the inner Christ allowed him to develop a fairly honest and just critique of the groups. Like the Quakers, the Familists and Behmenists were taken by More to be performing a positive rôle within the structure of Restoration Christianity. He considered that "at present, by a kind of oblique stroke, God does notable execution upon the dead formality and carnality of Christendom by these zealous evangelists of an internal Saviour." [49] At the same time he realised that there were severe limitations in those sects already constituted which militated against any extension of the gospel of the inner Christ. His criticism of Boehme is particularly judicious in this respect:

But admit that J. Behmen drives all inward in his writings, as if he had forgot that Christ without him who suffered at Jerusalem, . . . and withal that he has healed Familism of that unsoundness and rottenness of corrupt Sadducism; yet for all that the invincible obscurity of his writings will prevent his being over-popular, and his mistakes in his pretended inspirations in matters of philosophy ruin his authority amongst the more knowing and sagacious sort of persons.[50]

The core of More's argument against Boehme and the Familists did not however lie here. It lay rather in his refusal to accept that Boehme and the Familists were divinely inspired. In what amounts to a psychological analysis of their religion he pinpoints the symptoms of enthusiasm. What is interesting is that he does this, not in the spirit of abuse, but with a very

[49] *The Two Last Dialogues*, p. 354.
[50] *Ibid.*, p. 336.

real appreciation for the value of a religion based on the faculty of love and the operation of the spirit. This analysis exactly reflects his own ambivalent position vis à vis the light-infested sects; antipathy is tempered with sympathy.

Pursuing his consideration of Boehme, More writes as follows:

I will . . . allow him to be a very serious and well-minded man, but of a nature extremely melancholic. And . . . I conjecture that he had been a reader of H. N. [i.e. Henry Nicholas [51]] and Paracelsus his writings. Both which being enthusiastical authors fired his melancholy into the like enthusiastic elevations of spirit, and produced a philosophy in which we all-over discover the footsteps of Paracelsianism and Familism, love and wrath, sulphur and sal-nitre, chemistry and astrology being scattered through all. I do not deny . . . but that both H. N. and J. Behmen were inspired; but I aver withal that their inspiration was not purely spiritual, intellectual and divine, but mainly complexional, natural and demonial. . . . Complexional love, the noblest motion impressed upon us by the spirit of nature, first oppressed in the constriction, compunction and anguish of a down-bearing melancholy, and after burning and flaming out into a joyful liberty, and carrying captive with it those severer particles, that would have smothered it, into a glorious triumph of light and cheerful splendour of the spirits, which makes the soul overflow with all kindness and sweetness, this, I conceive, is all the peculiar inspiration or illumination these Theosophists had at the bottom. Which yet is not so contemptible, but that they justly magnify it above the grim ferocities of the superstitious factions in the embittered Churches of the world, who have not so good an inspiration as this.[52]

The language in which More couches his analysis, adumbrating some of the insights of English Romanticism, together with the wholly sympathetic afterthought, betray his real position. While those who practised the religion of the spirit fell short of More's high ideal, they nevertheless represented the best that the religious activity of the Restoration could rise to. More's distinction between divine love and sublimated "complexional love" is highly theoretical, and his glowing description of the latter suggests that in practice the two are indistinguishable. His preference for the inner Christ leads him to analyse the springs of religious activity in terms of psychological states of mind, without for all that discrediting such states of mind as either valueless or spurious.

More's emphasis in all his work on the inner Christ led several persons to believe that he was himself a Quaker.[53] And in a sense his whole attitude contains the main brunt of Quaker grievance and aspiration; so that he

[51] Henry Nicholas (or Niclaes), who flourished 1502-1580, was the founder of the Familist sect.
[52] *Ibid.*, pp. 349-351.
[53] See Letter to Lady Conway, 14 July 1671. *Conway Letters*, p. 341. See also Letter to Lady Conway, 26 February 1675-6. *Ibid.*, p. 425.

was able to be instrumental in the conversion of George Keith to Quakerism, and perhaps partly responsible for this leading Quaker's return to the
Anglican fold a generation later.[54] But More's pietism in itself is enough
to account for his dislike of Quakers as a body. The Quakers had come out
of Cromwell's England, and had more in common with Ranters and
Familists than with the sect of wealthy and enlightened dissenters they
were to become.

More's aversion to the practices of religious enthusiasts was such that he
remonstrated with one of them:

Nor am I at all, Philalethes, enthusiastical. For God doth not ride me as a
horse, and guide me I know not whither myself; but converseth with me as a
friend.[55]

He made the same distinction between reasonable and unreasonable
enthusiasm in the preface to his collected philosophical works:

I must ingenuously confess that I have a natural touch of Enthusiasm in my
complexion, but such as, I thank God, was ever governable enough, and I have
found at length perfectly subduable. In virtue of which victory I know better
what is in Enthusiasts than they themselves.[56]

It was a distinction between on the one hand, "the seasonable suggestions
of that Divine Life and Sense that vigorously resides in the Rational Spirit
of free and well-meaning Christians," and on the other hand, "that religious frenzy men run into, by lying passive for the reception of such im-
presses as have no proportion with their faculties." [57] This distinction allows his to spend a brief moment, after a long catalogue of the abuses of
religious enthusiasm, in an encomium of the "true and warrantable
Enthusiasm":

To such Enthusiasm as this, which is but the triumph of the soul of man
inebriated, as it were, with the delicious sense of the divine life, that blessed
root and original of all holy wisdom and virtue, I must declare myself as
much a friend, as I am to the vulgar fanatical Enthusiasm a professed
enemy.[58]

This distinction also allows him to make his via media a synthesis rather
than a compromise:

For assuredly that Spirit of Illumination which resides in the souls of the
faithful, is a principle of the purest Reason that is communicable to the
human nature. And what this Spirit has, he has from Christ.[59]

---

[54] See Letter to Lady Conway, 11 August 1674. *Ibid.*, p. 391. Keith's "The Deism
of William Penn and his Brethren" (1699) marked his return to Anglicanism.
[55] *Second Lash*, as quoted in Ward, p. 49.
[56] *Philosophical Writings*, p. x.
[57] *Conjectura Cabbalistica*, p. 2. *Philosophical Writings*.
[58] *Enthusiasmus Triumphatus*, p. 45. *Philosophical Writings*.
[59] *Ibid.*, p. 39.

More's position throws light on the relationship between pietism and enthusiasm.

Pietism had nothing to gain from separation, from sectarianism. It sought to reconstitute the religious life on a basis which was available to any branch of the Christian religion, and in time had its adepts in every sect. More speaks with the voice of pietism when he claims:

I am above all sects whatsoever as sects; for I am a true and free Christian; and what I write and speak is for the interest of Christ, and in behalf of the life of the Lamb, which is despised.[60]

He attacks the Socinians, not because they are too free, but because they are too straight: "The Socinians are free enough in all conscience; and a little too bold in some respects, but their genius is too straight and short for some things." [61] This shows remarkable willingness to see the other side in an age when Socinians were, with Hobbes and Spinoza, thought to be revolutionary atheists. In his attitude to Quakers, we find all the symptoms of a common zeal for truth and holiness, symptoms which reveal the pietistic ground of More's own theological writing and religious experience. Wrapped up in his love-hate relationship, he feels compelled to speak out:

These things ... I have been forced to utter to the world; for it was as fire within me, and this discharging of my conscience, as it is mine own ease and satisfaction, so I do not despair but if there be that sincere zeal to truth and holiness that is pretended, that it will redound to the safety of these melancholy wanderers that look up and down for Truth with that Candle of the Lord, the Spirit that he has lighted in them.[62]

More's wryly sympathetic description of the Quakers sounds almost like a self-portrait. And indeed both Quakers and Cambridge Platonists contributed to the emergence of a new religious consciousness, the roots of which lay in the latitudinarian spirit, and the future of which lay in the development of pietism and Evangelicalism. In opting for the inner Christ, More showed that he welcomed developments along these lines.

Pietism and Evangelicalism redefined the religious consciousness of the Protestant Reformation. They coincided with the Cartesian revolution in philosophy, and with the rise of sentiment in culture generally. Giving priority to the spirit over the letter, they reflected and contributed to the decline of the Renaissance and the emergence of Romanticism. More's contribution to the development of this new consciousness can best be seen

[60] *Second Lash*, as quoted in Ward, pp. 188-189.
[61] Letter to Lady Conway, 29 August 1662. *Conway Letters*, p. 208.
[62] *An Explanation of the Grand Mystery of Godliness*, in *Theological Works*, p. 372.

and summed up in his encomium on "the work of the heart" as opposed to "those umbratile skirmishes of the brain in Fancy and exterior Reason." [63] More spoke up in defence of the "mysteries of the heart," and described those "of the head" as nothing more than "an outward shop of fancies and fine pictures." [64] He believed that "the heart is the proper pavilion of either the spirit of the world, or the spirit of God," and in one of his rare rhapsodies claimed that through the heart occurred the operation of

a certain Divine Magic, that draws all the heavenly powers into the centre of our souls, imbibing the comfortable dews of Paradise, to the ineffable refreshing of the Garden of God. Through this sluice is let in all the nourishment to the new birth. . . . Whence the centre of our soul in the heart requires more diligent observation than that more peculiar one in the head. For though this seems more peculiarly ours, yet the other joins us with that which is more to us than we are to ourselves, whether it be the spirit of the world or of God, and makes us feelingly communicate with life and substance; whenas the other without this would only lead us into a field of shadows and dreams. Wherefore . . . he that is a candidate for the Kingdom of God, let him above all things cultivate the heart; for through this only is the inlet into the Kingdom of Light.[65]

This celebration of the religion of feeling must be taken into account in any analysis of More's thought. It seriously modifies the prevailing view that More was first and foremost a latitudinarian, with a touch of the Rosicrucian about him. More is as much a precursor of 18th century evangelicalism as he is of 18th century deism.

[63] *The Two Last Dialogues*, p. 35.
[64] *Ibid.*, p. 36.
[65] *Ibid.*, pp. 36-37.

CHAPTER FOUR

AESTHETICS: FROM METAPHYSICAL
TO ROMANTIC

It may seem perverse to find characteristics of Romanticism in the work of a pre-Augustan poet; but only in the context of an emerging modernity, figuring the break-up of Renaissance literature and the foretaste of Romantic literature, can we make sense of More's poetry, and relate it to a principle common to his philosophical and theological work. More was the only Cambridge Platonist to write poetry, and though few would judge his reputation enhanced by this work, it would be misleading not to take it into serious consideration. Such a consideration would correct the traditional view, implied in Coleridge's attitude towards the Cambridge Platonists, that while More and Cudworth's ideas could be regarded by the Romantic poets as important for aesthetic theory, their literary performance was without value. This divorce between More's poetic achievement, for what it is worth, and his relevance to aesthetic theory, obscures the homogeneity of More's modernity. More has a position in literature corresponding to his position in philosophy and theology. This can be established firstly by examining his relevance to aesthetic theory, not only in an absolute Coleridgean sense, but also relative to his own literary context at the watershed between Renaissance and modern; and secondly by putting into evidence his literary achievement.

It is easy enough to deduce in the abstract a central aesthetic principle from the structure of More's idealism and pietism. The ideological content of Coleridgean aesthetics is to be found ready made in many a page of More's work. There is the distinction between "right reason" and "Heavenly Reason," [1] the "principle more noble and inward than Reason itself," [2] the reality of "the precious substratum within," [3] and the concept of "the habitation of the soul her own energy." [4] The same is true of

---

[1] "Psychozoia," II, 99. Grosart, p. 28.
[2] *Philosophical Writings*, p. vii.
[3] "To the Reader" (1647). Grosart, p. 7.
[4] Note to "Psychozoia," II, 24. Ibid., p. 143.

Cudworth, though to a lesser extent. Cudworth was not a poet and hence totally unconcerned to apply to aesthetics and literature any of the highly Coleridgean arguments he had developed to combat atheistic materialism. Consider for example the unrealised potential of the following:

Whereas human art cannot act upon the matter otherwise than from without and at a distance, nor communicate itself to it, but with a great deal of tumult and hurly-burly, noise and clatter, it using hands and axes, saws and hammers, and after this manner with much ado, by knockings and thrustings, slowly introducing its form or idea (as for example of a ship or house) into the materials; nature in the mean time is another kind of art, which insinuating itself immediately into things themselves, and there acting more commandingly upon the matter as an inward principle, does its work easily, cleverly and silently. Nature is art as it were incorporated and embodied in matter, which doth not act upon it from without mechanically, but from within vitally and magically.[5]

One can immediately appreciate the relevance of this to Romantic aesthetics, to the rejection of 18th century poetic diction for example. It is so near to, and yet so far from, the preoccupations of Wordsworth and Coleridge. Hence the added significance of More's pronouncements in this area; for More, being a poet, does not always leave it to the Romantics to spell out the appropriate aesthetic conclusions.

This is nowhere so apparent as when he describes the Neoplatonic theory of primary and secondary imaginations. His source is Plotinus; [6] but he explicitly applies his psychological theory to the activity of the poet, and in doing so foreshadows not only the critical theory of Wordsworth and Coleridge, but also G. M. Hopkins' concept of the "Parnassian poet." [7] The primary imagination "grasps all"; "she sees and sways" the secondary imagination

> As she thinks good; and if that she think good
> She lets it play by itself, yet looketh on,
> While she keeps in that large strong-beating flood
> That makes the Poet write, and rave as he were wood.[8]

This application of Neoplatonic categories to the work of the poet is re-

[5] Cudworth, I, 235-236.
[6] See *The Enneads*, ed. and trans. Stephen MacKenna (2nd ed.; London: Faber, 1956), pp. 282-287 (IV, iii, 26-32). See also Bullough's gloss in More's *Philosophical Poems*, p. 187.
[7] Gerard Manley Hopkins, Letter to A. W. M. Baillie, 10 September 1864, in *A Selection of his Poems and Prose*, ed. W. H. Gardner (London: Penguin Books, 1953), p. 156.

inforced in the next verse, so that it becomes impossible to ignore the aesthetic theory:

> Prophets and Poets have their life from hence,
> Like fire into their marrow it searcheth deep,
> This flaming fiery flake doth choke all sense,
> And binds the lower man with brazen sleep:
> Corruption through all his bones doth creep,
> And raging raptures do his soul outsnatch:
> Round turning whirlwinds on Olympus steep
> Do cast the soul that erst they out did catch:
> Then stiller whispering winds dark visions unlatch.[9]

It is not enough to say that More's poetic theory "is that of Sidney, Spenser, Sylvester and Milton." [10] With the proviso that in practice two thirds and more of this theory was spent in the service of pietism (binding the lower man) and idealism (Platonic and not poetic vision), it is not incongruous to claim that it is the theory of the Romantics.

The Platonic and pietist reservations do not totally disqualify an appraisal of More's aesthetic theory, though they do severely limit its application. More could not be a Romantic, or even preromantic poet, because it was not his poems which mattered, but "the divine spirit and life that lies under them." [11] Hence Coleridge's disappointment when he found More lacking that absolute aesthetic theory he was looking for:

Whenever an attempt is made, as in H. More's, n.b. not Hannah, "Song of the Soul" to popularise philosophy, Ideas must perforce be represented by words, but words in their primary import always referring to things and images, and here in order to be rendered attractive and interesting to be supported by images of things, as similitudes or allegories. What wonder that Platonism at least should appear to sober minded men, who have become acquainted to it by such books, the veriest romance or fairy tale.[12]

Hence also, one suspects, Coleridge's savage demolition of Cambridge Platonism:

They commence with an abstraction, that is an object. Hence whatever is in its nature incapable of being contemplated objectively, as the I, We, with all the affections and passions, are not explained at all, . . . though in every object these subjects are supposed, in order to its being an object.[13]

---

8 "Psychozoia," I, 59. Grosart, p. 18.
9 "Psychozoia," I, 60. Ibid.
10 *Philosophical Poems,* ed. Bullough, p. lxxi.
11 *Second Lash,* as quoted in Ward, p. 64.
12 Coleridge, *On the 17th Century,* pp. 617-618.
13 *Ibid.,* p. 621.

And hence, in a general sense, the compatibility of Cambridge Platonism with religion as opposed to its incompatibility with poetry. Basil Willey follows Coleridge in stressing this incompatibility:

At best the imagination could be made to serve the understanding by deliberately using it, after the manner of the prophets, to produce what Coleridge, defining "allegory" called the "translation of abstract notions into a picture-language." The philosophical poems of Henry More were the outcome of a conscious attempt to produce poetry on these principles, and may be taken as a comment on the usefulness, for poetry, of such a theory. The fact is, that Cudworth and More, although they were probably better equipped theoretically to vindicate the imagination than any of the moderns before the Italian critics of the 18th century, were simply not poets or critics, but moralists and religious philosophers.[14]

Willey quotes John Smith's description of the "imaginative powers" which breathe "a gross dew upon the pure glass of our understandings." [15] Moore Smith, on the other hand, in the introduction to his edition of Herbert of Cherbury's poems, describes that poet's philosophy as "of that Platonic type which is itself akin to poetry." [16] Clearly it depends on the individual case. Lord Herbert happened to be a poet and a Platonist; More was a Platonist who wrote verses. To generalise from either the incompatibility or otherwise of Platonism and poetry, would appear to be a hazardous undertaking. If a generalisation is called for from these two particular cases, it must surely be along the lines of a distinction between a clear Renaissance tradition which nourished Lord Herbert, and a dubious modern experiment to which More was committed.

More's modern consciousness was such that, for all the gothic elements still encrusted in his work, he could not play on, or bewail, the disintegration of the old cultural synthesis, in the way the Metaphysical poets did. The mood was a tempting one, and the Metaphysicals went on exploiting it long after it had ceased to be a real proposition. As we have seen, More was too sure of his new philosophical and religious insights to enjoy the prospect of divided and distinguished worlds. Metaphysical minds, on the other hand, were resisting change even when they played with it. Thus the minor poet William Strode (d. 1645) reflects the impact of Descartes' attack on the music of the spheres and its microcosmic correspondence, when he claims:

[14] Basil Willey, *The 17th Century Background* (London: Penguin Books, 1962), p. 145.
[15] Smith, p. 22.
[16] Lord Herbert of Cherbury, *Poems,* ed. G. C. Moore Smith (Oxford: Clarendon Press, 1923), p. xx.

> Philosophy can scarce deny
> The Soul consists of harmony.[17]

Another minor poet, James Howell (1593-1666), repeats Donne's witty exploitation of cultural disintegration in rather more plaintive tone:

> What? is mild heaven turned to brass
> That neither sigh nor sob can pass?
> Is all commerce twixt earth and sky
> Cut off from Adam's progeny? [18]

Clearly by the 1660s it was impossible any longer even to play with the idea; it had become an echo through repetition, and one went on repeating it at the risk of banality. Perhaps the final Metaphysical tone was struck by Simon Patrick, as he entertained the prospect of a new age, with a quizzical epitaph on the disappearance of the old, in language strongly reminiscent of Donne's "First Anniversary" written fifty years previously:

Aristotle's Intelligences that moved the solid Orbs, have leave to play; and since that arched roof is gone, I know not how the elementary fire will be kept in. But if it should chance to prove true (and who knows what posterity will believe, since we have been so hardy as to admit Antipodes) that the earth is a planet and the sun a fixed star ... it would make foul work in the vulgar philosophy.[19]

The speculation and doubtfulness which the Metaphysical poets exploited to such effect would soon be dispelled by the new certainties established under the aegis of the Royal Society.

The aesthetic implications of the new philosophy had been spelt out from the beginning. One of the main purposes of Lord Herbert of Cher-

---

[17] Quoted in John Hollander, *The Untuning of the Sky: Ideas of Music in English Poetry 1500-1700* (Princeton: University Press, 1961), p. 295. Descartes' *Compendium Musices* appeared in 1618.

[18] James Howell, "Upon a Fit of Disconsolation, or Despondency of Spirit", from *Poems on Several Choice and Various Subjects* (1663), printed in Leslie Birkett Marshall (ed.), *Rare Poems of the 17th Century* (Cambridge: University Press, 1936), p. 121.
Cf. Donne's "First Anniversary" (1611):
"If this commerce 'twixt heaven and earth were not
Embarred, and all this traffic quite forgot,
She, for whose loss we have lamented thus,
Would work more fully, and powerfully on us."
John Donne, *Complete Poetry and Selected Prose*, ed. John Hayward (London: Nonesuch Press, 1955), p. 207.
Poetry and Selected Prose, ed. John Hayward (London: Nonesuch Press, 1955), p. 207.

[19] Patrick, p. 20. Cf. Donne's "First Anniversary":
"And New Philosophy calls all in doubt,
The element of fire is quite put out. (...)
'Tis all in pieces, all coherence gone."
Nonesuch Donne, p. 202.

bury's *De Veritate* (1624) was to "disengage the common notions which
it is not lawful to dispute from the wrapping of words that enclose them." [20]
Two of the leading lights of the early Royal Society, Samuel Parker and
John Wilkins, pursued the same ideal in their research on language. Wilkins set out to expose the "many wild errors, that shelter themselves under
the disguise of affected phrases; which being philosophically unfolded,
and rendered according to the genuine and natural importance of words,
will appear to be inconsistencies and contradictions." [21] Parker investigated
the function of metaphor in his manifesto of neoclassical aesthetics:

When therefore any thing is expressed by a metaphor or allegory, the thing
itself is not expressed, but only some similitude observed and made by Fancy.
So that metaphors being only the sportings of Fancy compare things with
things, and not marks or signs of things.[22]

Parker points his moral with a beautiful parody of one of the purple passages of the Cambridge Platonists. In the first of his *Discourses,* John
Smith had summed up the spirit of Cambridge Platonism in the superb
rhetoric of the following paragraph:

While we lodge any filthy vice in us, this will be perpetually twisting up itself
into the thread of our finest-spun speculations; it will be continually climbing
up into the τὸ Ἡγεμονικόν – the hegemonical powers of the soul, into the
bed of reason, and defile it: like the wanton ivy twisting itself about the oak,
it will twine about our judgments and understandings, till it hath sucked out
the life and spirit of them.[23]

Nothing could be further from the linguistic ideals of the Royal Society,
and Parker judiciously uses the passage in an attack on the style and spirit
for which it speaks so eloquently:

Thus their wanton and luxuriant fancies climbing up into the bed of reason,
do not only defile it by unchaste and illegitimate embraces, but instead of
real conceptions and notices of things, impregnate the mind with nothing but
airy and subventaneous phantasms.[24]

It is an ironic commentary on the principles Parker stood for, that his
argument is most effective when it uses, albeit by way of parody, the
techniques of imagery and rhetoric which he is so concerned to eliminate.

There is no doubt that More was on the side of the moderns; and nowhere is this more apparent than in his first Cartesian prose work, *An Antidote Against Atheism* (1652). He shows that, not only in prose style but
also in literary tone, he is aiming at something new. He could have been

[20] Quoted in Carré, p. 222.
[21] Wilkins, Epistle Dedicatory.
[22] Samuel Parker, p. 78.
[23] Smith, p. 5.
[24] Samuel Parker, p. 78.

writing under the influence of Hobbes, whose Gondibert essay came out the year before; and he is certainly foreshadowing the ideas of Parker and Wilkins:

I did on purpose abstain from reading any treatises concerning this subject, that I might the more undisturbedly write the easy Emanations of mine own mind, and not be carried off from what should naturally fall from my self, by prepossessing my thoughts by the inventions of others. I have writ therefore after no copy but the eternal characters of the mind of man, and the known phenomena of nature.... Though I cannot promise my reader that I shall entertain him with so much winning rhetoric and pleasant philology as he may find elsewhere; yet I hope he will acknowledge, if his mind be un-prejudiced ... that he meets with sound and plain reason, and an easy and clear method.[25]

More thus embraced with enthusiasm what some poets of his time were wailing over. Ralph Knevet (1600-1671) for example articulates the malaise of a Metaphysical poet, writing in a new age with which he is out of tune, when he writes in his "Infirmity":

> I want a volubility of tongue
> To traffic for applause,
> Although I know the laws
> And rights of rhetoric. I am not strung
> For sound and music shrill.
> My tongue's a silent quill.
> My wit is dumb and doth rehearse
> Things by mere signs and characters.[26]

Lord Herbert's common notions were now free from their verbal and metaphysical wrappings; the Metaphysical poet was tongue-tied, and the way was open for neoclassicism.

More may give the appearance of being a minor transitional poet caught between two worlds, but his contribution to aesthetics lies in his having traced out a third way which is neither Metaphysical nor Augustan. This third way lay between the "laws and rights of rhetoric," and the rehearsal of things "by mere signs and characters"; it lay in the "easy emanations of my own mind." This was a radically new formula. Un-fortunately it was not fully exploited until the phases of neoclassicism and preromanticism had exhausted the aesthetic implications of the new phi-losophy. For Cartesians and Newtonians, expressionism was no substitute for an objective correlative in the cosmos. On the whole the Enlighten-

---

[25] *Antidote Against Atheism*, pp. 1-2. *Philosophical Writings.*
[26] Printed in *Rare Poems*, ed. Marshall, p. 134.

ment replaced the Renaissance's appeal to the logically trained mind by an appeal to reason's ear; [27] and the Newtonian preromantics merely embellished this appeal by filling in the sense and sunshine of the universe, thus adding a visual dimension which, in certain writers like Thomson, by its very detail, becomes detachable from the underlying physico-theological purpose.

If it is clear that neoclassicism's chief innovation was to substitute for the Renaissance's "laws and rights of rhetoric," the Enlightenment's rehearsal of things "by mere signs and characters," it is less often realised that preromanticism made no radical departure from neoclassicism in this respect.[28] Take for example David Mallet's *Excursion* (1729), where one finds the following passage:

> But see, the flushed horizon flames intense
> With vivid red, in rich profusion streamed
> O'er Heaven's pure arch. At once the clouds assume
> Their gayest liveries; these with silvery beams
> Fringed lovely, splendid those in liquid gold:
> And speak their Sovereign's State.[29]

What is seen, is principally merely seen; it speaks only by a forced Miltonic syntactical link. The preromantics of this period write best when they forget their physico-theological framework and concentrate on visual detail. Thus for example Henry Brooke's *Universal Beauty* (1734-1736) is most striking when the poet forgets the universal and creates the particular:

> Here buoys the bird high on the crystal wave,
> Whose level plumes the azure concave shave.[30]

But there is a strict limit to what can be done along these lines, and this limit seems to be reached with Brooke's "tinge the topaz with a saffron dye," [31] and the numerous purple passages in Savage's *The Wanderer* (1729). Savage uses words to "paint amusing landscapes on the eye"; his trout have "crimson stains," his dawn vapours look "like veins blue-wind-

---

[27] See especially Joseph Addison, "The Spacious Firmament on High," *The Spectator,* No. 465, in *Works,* ed. Henry G. Bohn (6 vols.; London: Bohn's British Classics, 1856), III, 485-486.

[28] For a stimulating and extensive investigation of the distinctions between preromanticism and Romanticism, see Allan Rodway, *The Romantic Conflict* (London: Chatto and Windus, 1963).

[29] Chalmers, XIV, 17.

[30] I, 374-375. *Ibid.,* XVII, 341.

[31] III, 52. *Ibid.,* XVII, 346.

ing on a Fair-one's arm," and his "white clouds" are "streaked" with "mild vermilion." [32] All this is very fine, and justifies the claim that "Newton demands the Muse." [33] But *The Wanderer* is far from being a vision in the sense this word had for say Blake or Coleridge. For these preromantics – Thomson, Mallet, Savage and Brooke – "all is phenomenon," and "only wondrous facts" are "revealed to view." [34]

The preromantics were thus incapable of realising and practising the implications of More's gnomic formula:

> Who Divine Sense by Reason would descry,
> Unto the sunshine listens with his ear.[35]

Addison and the rest of the Enlightenment listened hard with reason's ear; Thomson and the preromantics offered Lockeian sense and Newtonian sunshine to the same ear; the sunshine of divine sense did not arise before the advent of Blake and the Romantics.

More's own poetry rarely reflects the expressionist aesthetics that can be deduced from his philosophy. It is frequently vitiated by relics of Renaissance poetics and intimations of neoclassicism. One of the factors which prevents More from translating his theory into practice is the overriding influence of Spenser. In poetic diction, Platonic allegory and stanzaic form, More was "a poet in the loll and trot of Spenser." [36] He would not have denied the charge; for him Spenser was the only poet. Hence we find that the only explicit aesthetic principle More held was essentially a Spenserian one: "Every poem is an Idyllium. And a poet no more sings himself, than a painter draws his own picture." [37] There can be few declarations which so categorically reject the expressionist element in poetry. Unfortunately the vast body of More's poetry is written with this principle in mind. It is derivative, obscure and unreadable. Above all, it is wide open to Coleridge's charge that one of the main faults of "our elder poets not of the first class, and of none more than of H. More" is "that generally they are regardless of the influence of associations, not merely such as are the accidental growth of a particular age and fashion, but of those that are grounded on the nature of man and his circumstances." [38]

---

[32] Richard Savage, *Poetical Works,* ed. C. Tracy (Cambridge: University Press, 1962), 129, 133, 144.

[33] Richard Glover, "Poem on Sir Isaac Newton" (1728), line 11. Chalmers, XVII, 13.

[34] Henry Brooke, *Universal Beauty,* V, 162, 199. Chalmers, XVII, 359.

[35] "Psychozoia," II, 97. Grosart, p. 28.

[36] Thomas Vaughan, *The Man Mouse Taken in a Trap* (1650), Epistle Dedicatory, as quoted in More, *Philosophical Poems,* ed. Bullough, p. lxix.

[37] "To the Reader" (1647). Grosart, p. 7.

[38] Coleridge, *On the 17th Century,* p. 625.

In other words, More's verse does not spring, as does his best prose, from the easy emanations of his mind. When it is not archaically Spenserian, it suffers from the faults common to those who attempted allegory in a scientific age.

Anachronism and modernism jostle uneasily in More's consciousness. Thus, in an explanatory note to the line "Duessa first invented magic lore," [39] he writes:

Duessa is the natural life of the body, or the natural spirit, that, whereby we are liable to magic assaults, which are but the sympathies and antipathies of nature, such as are in the spirit of the world.[40]

This obscure attempt to give a scientific basis to Spenserian allegory makes the explanatory note more important and readable than the obscurer text it glosses. More's feeling that it is necessary to regulate the strangeness of allegorical fiction, by explaining that it is only a natural process after all, is typical of those who wrote allegorical epics after Spenser and Milton. In this respect More foreshadows the miserable efforts of Cowley, Ken, S. Wesley and Mrs Rowe. And yet, even as a Spenserian allegorist, writing on the verge of the neoclassical Enlightenment, More reveals the possibility of expressionist aesthetics. More is clearly saying: "we are liable to magic assaults," we have access to the "spirit of the world." He almost implies that the marvellous in poetry derives its form from "the sympathies and antipathies of nature," as opposed to some prescribed technique of allegory. Of course More is in fact saying that these magic assaults must be resisted; but it only needed someone to accept the imagination in this sense as truth, for a fully fledged movement of Romantic expressionism to be launched, with full scope given to Coleridgean associationism.

There are passages in many Metaphysical and pre-Augustan poets which, taken out of their context, read like preromantic natural descriptions with all the painstaking detail that Thomson was capable of. The distinction usually made is that the earlier poets conceived their detail as rhetorical amplification from logical categories, so that the detail is in no way perceived by the senses in contact with the physical world, but conceived with a view to argument, praise, dispraise, persuasion, dissuasion etc.[41] Take for example Lord Herbert's "Elegy over a Tomb" (1617), where an apparently maximum amount of sensuous detail is incorporated into the logico-rhetorical structure of the poem.[42] There is the sun, the light, waves, hair, sky, air, red, white, blue, flowers and breath

[39] "Psychozoia," II, 29. Grosart, p. 22.
[40] *Ibid.*, p. 143.
[41] See Rosemond Tuve, *Elizabethan and Metaphysical Imagery*, Chapter 10.
[42] Herbert of Cherbury, pp. 32-34.

in the first verse alone. But in fact such detail can hardly be termed sensuous; it is not perceived; it is conceived. The words do not indicate the things, they do not point to an external reality which is more real than the words themselves; the words as words contain their own reality and create their own world. Nothing could be more different from the preromantic way of writing a poem. Similarly in "To Her Eyes," Lord Herbert is not interested in the relations between the eyes and the external world.[43] In the first place these eyes are described as affecting "more the mind than sense," and "are not so much / The works of light, as influence." And in the second place there is no external world, because all worlds and the woman's inner soul are contained in her eyes. This is a Metaphysical conceit of course; but the point is that any apparent sensuous detail exists and is defined in the context of a conceit, an argument, a praise, which creates its own world, and does not refer to something outside.

The preromantics on the other hand, were describing the visible phenomena of physical nature, and were able to do so because Newton had shown that visible phenomena were what mattered, and because the metaphysical reality which underpinned the Augustan status quo was argued from design. More's passages of detailed natural description may be classed as transitional between these two groups of poets. Take for example his description of the Arctic Pole:

> Where the numbed heavens do slowly roll:
> . . . where cold raw heavy mist
> Sol's kindly warmth and light resists.
> Where louring clouds full fraught with snow
> Do sternly scowl, where winds do blow
> With bitter blasts, and pierce the skin,
> Forcing the vital spirits in.[44]

This detail is in fact part of a rhetorical figure, of which it is an amplification. The argument runs:

> Confine me to the Arctic Pole,
>
> . . . .
> Yet by an Antiperistasis
> My inward heat more kindled is.[45]

And the passage is removed further from the directness of preromantic

[43] *Ibid.*, pp. 35-36.
[44] "Resolution," Grosart, p. 175.
[45] *Ibid.*

observation, since it is a paraphrase of a Horatian ode.[46] There is never-theless, in spite of these qualifications, an implied contact between the forces of nature and personal feeling; it is neither the rhetorical figure, nor the detailed description, as such, which are the be-all and end-all of the passage. More is concerned with his inward heat and vital spirits. He uses these in the service of Platonic vision; but they could so easily become the "genial spirits" of the Romantic imagination in the service of poetic vision.

These implications are borne out if tested against an even more remark-able passage of apparently preromantic description. The objects described are:

> Fresh varnished groves, tall hills, and gilded clouds
> Arching an eyelid for the glowing Morn;
> Fair clustered buildings which our sight so crowds
> At distance, with high spires to heaven yborn;
> Vast plains with lowly cottages forlorn,
> Rounded about with the low wavering sky,
> Cragg'd vapours, like to ragged rocks ytorn.[47]

This passage can be seen as transitional between the landscape of Spen-serian allegory and the 18th century prospect poem. It was published in the same year as Denham's *Cooper's Hill*, which suggests that Denham was not the only originator of the loco-descriptive poem. Indeed, taken out of its context, it represents a considerable step forward from the emblematic moralising of 17th century loco-descriptive poets towards the more precise pictorial geography practised by Dyer, Mallet and Savage.[48]

Dyer's case is particularly acute. For him poetry has ceased to be an independent art; its rôle is reduced to an imitation of painting and land-scape gardening. Dyer is not really writing poetry at all; he is merely describing landscape. In *Grongar Hill* he seeks to arrange a certain amount of natural objects in a prospect that will be aesthetically pleasing according to the canons of taste prevailing in the arts of painting and landscape gardening. In a verse epistle, "To Aaron Hill Esq.," he writes of

[46] Horace, *Odes*, I, 22. See Maren-Sofie Rostvig, *The Happy Man: Studies in the Metamorphoses of a Classical Ideal* (2 vols.; "Oslo Studies in English," Nos. 2 and 7; Oslo: Akademisk Forlag; Oxford: Blackwell, 1954-1958), I, 201.
[47] "Psychathanasia," III, i, 25. Grosart, p. 68.
[48] See especially Dyer's *Grongar Hill* (1726), Mallet's *The Excursion* (1729) and Savage's *The Wanderer* (1729).

> Surprising pictures rising to my sight,
> With all the life of colours and of line,
> And all the force of rounding shade and light,
> And all the grace of something more divine! [49]

The poem exists so to speak in the external world; all the "poet" can do is point to it; there is no question of his creating a world. In "An Epistle to a Famous Painter," he explicitly acknowledges the superiority of the painter over the poet:

> As yet I but in verse can paint,
> And to the idea colour faint
> What to the open eye you show.[50]

Words have no power in themselves to create anything; they can only stand for something more real outside.

More's prospect however has very little to do with the Newtonian world of nature. His groves are "varnished," because they are seen, not through the eye of the landscape gardener or in the Newtonian prism, but in "heaven's great eye." [51] In intention at least, More's prospect is as remote from ordinary landscape as those 17th century descriptions of "Jerusalem the Golden" enamelled and varnished in Biblical symbolism. But More is using the material of ordinary landscape, and identifying the total reality of his prospect with Platonic vision. Man's perception of landscape is a partial view; "but all things lie ope-right unto the sight / Of heaven's great eye; their thin-shot shadowings / And lightened sides." [52] 18th century prospect poems claim for their landscape the totality and completeness of view, which More allows only to Platonic vision. It may well be that the distant view, by which later prospect poetry was enabled to embrace a totality of landscape, has its origin in the Platonic vision from above. In the minor poem, "Insomnium Philosophicum," More writes of those who enjoy the Platonic vision:

> And while the creatures' goodness they descry
> From their fair glimpse they move themselves up higher,
> Not through contempt or hate they from them fly
> Nor leave by flying, but while they aspire
> To reach their fountain, them with sight more clear
> They see. As newly varnished all appear.[53]

[49] Chalmers, XIII, 252.
[50] *Ibid.*, XIII, 251.
[51] "Psychathanasia," III, i, 23. Grosart, p. 68.
[52] *Ibid.*
[53] "Insomnium Philosophicum," *ibid.*, p. 180.

The Platonic vision does not exclude objects of mundane nature. And yet the distinction between More and the preromantics remains. The 18th century prospect was a portion of mundane nature elevated into a self-sufficient picture external to the mind of man, analogous to the creations of painter and gardener. More's prospect, in the context of his interpretation of the Platonic vision, has in theory no meaning without the soul's active participation. It is true that the reality of mundane nature is seen only by the world's great soul; but "she views those prospects in our distant eye"; [54] and it is possible for the soul to be united to the "mundane sprite" and "corporate with God." [55] It is thus possible for the soul to grasp the reality of nature, beyond the partial prospect perceived by the senses. Such intimations would be fully exploited by Wordsworth and Coleridge over the heads of those preromantics who assiduously recorded their sense-data.

One of the reasons why More was not attracted to Metaphysical poetry, as other 17th century "singing Platonists" tended to be, was because his philosophical lights led him to pioneer the aesthetics of infinity.[56] Instead of playing with the barriers of matter, his Platonic instincts simply aspired to infinity. In his lyrics he seldom strikes a Metaphysical note. "Devotion" contains an element of Herbertian concreteness:

> Good God! . . .
> How can I then all difficulties devour!
> Thy might,
> Thy spright
> With ease my cumbrous enemy control.[57]

But such devotional expressionism is rare; it can have little place in infinity, where the "cumbrous enemy" has no meaning. The opening lines of "Charity and Humility" are equally isolated:

> Far have I clambered in any mind,
> But nought so great as love I find.[58]

More rarely "clambers"; in his infinity he soars. In "The Philosopher's Devotion," the dominant Addisonian strain (cf. "The spacious firma-

---

[54] "Psychathanasia," III, i, 25. *Ibid.*, p. 68.
[55] "Psychathanasia," III, i, 26. *Ibid.*
[56] M. H. Nicolson, in *The Breaking of the Circle*, p. 165, says that More "transferred to Space some twenty adjectives and epithets that had formerly been applied only to Deity." Cf. Burtt, p. 140.
[57] Grosart, p. 176.
[58] *Ibid.*, p. 181.

ment on high") shows up the very slight Metaphysical relic (he is celebrating the dance of the spheres):

> In due order as they move
> Echoes sweet be gently drove
> Through heaven's vast hollowness
> Which unto all corners press.[59]

More did not go on believing that infinity had "corners." And yet, if his declaration of intent – "the infinity I'll sing of time and space" [60] – inspires little confidence in the reader who knows that a century later Young's *Night Thoughts* still sing of infinity, it must be remembered that More retains at least an element of control over his muse; his verse does not merely celebrate in a void the abstract attributes of the deity, but contains expressionist potential:

> Strange sights do straggle in my restless thoughts
> And lively forms with orient colours clad
> Walk in my boundless mind.[61]

And after all, More was the first to sing infinity; what is so annoying about reading "In endless spaces up and down I fly . . . / More than the journey of ten thousand year / An hundred times told over," [62] is that so many people repeated the flight in subsequent generations.

The new age was nurtured on the sublime, and waxed Pindarical with the greatest of ease. Locke's philosophy provided some of the impetus needed; as MacLean has put it, "the strange notion that the larger the object contemplated by the mind, the greater would be the thought provoked, was a popular 18th century conception, denoting the mind's reliance on sensation." [63] Pietism was also largely responsible; Fénelon had caught the mood when he wrote: "J'embrasse tout, et je ne suis rien, je suis un rien qui connaît l'infini: les paroles me manquent pour m'admirer et me mépriser tout ensemble." [64] Young rang the changes on this theme ad nauseam – "Distinguished link in being's endless chain! / Midway from nothing to the Deity! . . . / Helpless immortal! insect infinite!

[59] *Ibid.*
[60] *Democritus Platonissans*, stanza 4. *Ibid.*, p. 91.
[61] *Ibid.*, stanza 2.
[62] "Insomnium Philosophicum," Grosart, pp. 178-179.
[63] Kenneth MacLean, *John Locke and English Literature of the 18th Century* (New Haven: Yale University Press, 1936), p. 57.
[64] Fénelon, *De l'existence et des attributs de Dieu* (Paris: Didot, 1853), p. 127.

/ A worm! a God! I tremble at myself" – ; [65] and Henry Brooke, in his old age, fell into the same rut:

> What shall we call this son of grace and sin,
> This demon, this divinity within,
> This flame eternal, this foul mouldering clod –
> A fiend or seraph – a poor worm, or God? [66]

The sublime was always on the verge of bathos, but never more so than in the work of those indefatigable Newtonian pietists, James Hervey and Edward Young. The former was capable of writing, with a straight face, and for the edification of a large public: "I gaze, I ponder; I ponder, I gaze: and think ineffable things. I roll an eye of awe and admiration." [67] The latter was definitively lampooned by George Eliot, who remarked of him:

No writer whose rhetoric was checked by the slightest truthful intentions, could have said,
> "An eye of awe and wonder let me roll,
> And roll for ever."
Abstracting the more poetical associations with the eye, this is hardly less absurd than if he had wished to stand for ever with his mouth open. [68]

These developments form the sequel to More's original attack on "the groveling mind and moping purblind eye," [69] an attack which many of the abuses of the late Metaphysicals justified. In committing himself to the aesthetics of infinity, More was combating the groveling wit and purblind conceits of baroque decadence.

More's commitment to the aesthetics of infinity coincided with the shift from Platonic vision to prospect poetry, both of which required sublimity:

> What ever's great, its shape these eyes of ours
> And due proportions from high distance see
> The best. [70]

Only once in his lyrics does More rise above this mere indication of transitional elements:

[65] Edward Young, *Night Thoughts,* I. Chalmers, XIII, 420. This 23-line paragraph contains no less than 21 exclamation marks!

[66] Henry Brooke, *Redemption* (1772). Chalmers, XVII, 442.

[67] James Hervey, *Meditations and Contemplations* (London: T. Hamilton, 1808), p. 325.

[68] George Eliot, *Essays,* ed. Thomas Pinney (London: Routledge and Kegan Paul, 1963), p. 368. This essay, entitled "Worldliness and Other Worldliness: the Poet Young," was originally published in the *Westminster Review,* LXVII (January 1857), 1-42.

[69] "Ad Paronem," Grosart, p. 177.

[70] *Ibid.*

When I my self from mine own self do quit
And each thing else; then an all spreaden love
To the vast universe my soul doth fit,
Makes me half equal to all seeing Jove.
My mighty wings high stretched then clapping light
I brush the stars and make them shine more bright.
Then all the works of God with close embrace
I dearly hug in my enlarged arms.[71]

This is one of the few passages which allow us to call More a poet. It is remarkable because More succeeds in avoiding the merely ornamental excesses of Metaphysical poetry – "I brush the stars" is no Clevelandism – and at the same time avoids letting the aesthetics of infinity eliminate the pre-Augustan vocabulary of lyrical devotion. What is more, the passage expresses emotion; the joy is highly personalised, and is able to link the "self" to the vast universe. Not again until Wordsworth will the aesthetics of infinity encourage such a measure of lyrical expressionism.

More's frequent references to the fire and energy of the poet do not in themselves support a Romantic aesthetic. Usually they merely reveal a combination of the chemistry of Platonic rhapsody and received classical notions on the sublime. In terms of historical development, More's description of the rhapsody –

Thus waxen hot with holy notion,
At once I'll break forth in a flame;
Above this world . . . I'll take my flight.[72]

– announces the Pindarics and physico-theological flights of Enlightenment lyricists. Norris, Watts and others would describe the ascent "to the everlasting coasts." [73] But for More, the Platonic rhapsody was meaningless unless grounded in its corollary, a reappraisal of the inner self, a cultivation of the consciousness, cut off from contact with the natural world:

So I all heedless how the waters roll
And mindless of the mirth the birds express,
Into myself 'gin softly to retire
After hid heavenly pleasures to enquire.[74]

---

[71] "Cupid's Conflict," ibid., p. 171.
[72] "Resolution," ibid., p. 175.
[73] "A Hymn upon Christ's Ascension," ibid., p. 187.
[74] "Cupid's Conflict," ibid., p. 170.

The introspective exercise allows the energy and fire of the poet to be grounded on more than aspiration, and makes possible a deeper contact between soul and nature than the physico-theological framework will permit. Already in this extract, the poet feels nature, in spite of his apparent negation of its reality, with an interior intensity more characteristic of Wordsworth than of the preromantics.

More's claim for the poet's energy is frequently associated with this reality of the interior consciousness. He declares that he is consumed

> With eager rage, my heart for joy doth spring,
> And all my spirits move with pleasant trembeling.[75]

Such potential for lyrical renewal goes hand in hand with an attack on the "cobweb niceties" of the Metaphysical poets and the indifference of the intellectual reader

> that doth want the fire
> And inward vigour heavenly furious
> That made my enraged spirit in strong desire
> Break through such tender cobweb niceties
> That oft entangle these blind buzzing flies.
>
> Possessed with living sense I inly rave
> Careless how outward forms do from me flow.[76]

It is difficult to make sense of such a passage without relating it to the decline of the Metaphysical lyric and the creation of conditions which would lead to the lyrics of Blake and Wordsworth.

This is not the only passage in More's verse which relates to the development of aesthetic theory. "Cupid's Conflict" contains a defence of his poetic style; it is couched in similar language, and must have the same aesthetic implications:

> The meaner mind works with more nicety
> As spiders wont to weave their idle web,
> But braver spirits do all things gallantly
> Of lesser failings not at all afraid:
> So Nature's careless pencil dipt in light
> With sprinkled stars hath spattered the night.[77]

Enlightenment neoclassicism, as summed up by Pope, would methodise "Nature's careless pencil," and weave webs as nice as those of the Metaphysicals, albeit with clear notions. More's techniques and purposes are

---

[75] *Democritus Platonissans*, stanza 4. *Ibid.*, p. 91.
[76] "Ad Paronem," *ibid.*, p. 177.
[77] "Cupid's Conflict," *ibid.*, p. 172.

as removed from those of neoclassicism as they are from those of the
Metaphysicals. He may "have taken pains to peruse these Poems of the
Soul, and to lick them into some more tolerable form and smoothness"; [78]
but he did not believe that "rhymes should run as smooth and glib as
oil." [79] To Metaphysical and Augustan alike, he declared:

> My thought's the fittest measure of my tongue,
> Wherefore I'll use what's most significant,
> And rather than my inward meaning wrong
> Or my full shining notion trimly scant,
> I'll conjure up old words out of their grave,
> Or call fresh foreign force in if need crave.[80]

Expressionism is the only criterion:

> And if my notions clear though rudely thrown
> And loosely scattered in my poesy,
> May lend men light till the dead night be gone,
> And morning fresh with roses strew the sky:
> It is enough, I meant no trimmer frame
> Nor by nice needlework to seek a name.[81]

The symbolism which More rouses himself to in this passage is foreign
to the logical conceits of Renaissance poetry, and inimical to the contained antitheses of neoclassicism; it conjures up vast horizons, because
it derives from an expressionism, based on the freedom and self-sufficiency of the individual consciousness.

Unfortunately More shared the Enlightenment's awareness of the split
between prose and poetry, and felt it necessary to justify his poetry by
making it as prosy as possible. He found it difficult to reconcile his lyrical
instincts with the demands of philosophical argument. He would have
liked to have written his philosophical poems in a lyrical vein, "with a
great deal of vigour and life"; this "would have agreed well enough with
the free heat of poesy, and might have passed for a pleasant flourish, but
the severity of my own judgment and sad genius hath cast in many correctives and coolers into the canto itself, so that it cannot amount to more
than a discussion." [82] This is true of all More's poetry to a greater or lesser
degree; it is interesting that he recognises it himself. When his poetry

---

[78] "To the Reader" (1647). *Ibid.*, p. 6.
[79] "Cupid's Conflict," *ibid.*, p. 172.
[80] *Ibid.*
[81] *Ibid.*
[82] *Democritus Platonissans*, "To the Reader." *Ibid.*, p. 90.

amounts to no more than a discussion, the "correctives and coolers" have compromised the "free heat of poesy." But at those rare moments when he allows himself to write in the middle of this free heat, his success is undoubtedly due to his lyrical expressionism. His technique on these occasions is introspective, even autobiographical. Thus he claims to have written "Psychozoia," "with no other design than that it should remain by me a private record of the sensations and experiences of my own soul." [83] In fact the record is largely of speculation and notions rather than experience and sense; but there is an element of Wordsworthian retrospective meditation, which would not be out of place in *The Prelude*:

> For I ev'n at those years was well aware
> Of man's false friendship, and grown subtility,
> Which made me snuff the wind, drink the free air
> Like a young colt upon the mountains high,
> And turning tail my hunters all defy.
> Ne took I any guide but th' innate light
> Of my true Conscience, whose voice to deny,
> Was the sole sting of my offended spright:
> Thus God and Nature taught their rude Cosmopolite.[84]

The resemblance is more than an accident of style. Wordsworth perfected and practised an aesthetic of the modern consciousness which had broken with the techniques of the Renaissance. More gave precious intimations, not only of the religious and philosophical dimensions of this revolution, but also of its aesthetic implications.

---

[83] Ward, p. 16.
[84] "Psychozoia," II, 122. Grosart, p. 30. Cf. the corresponding passage in his "Little Narrative": "Even in my first childhood . . .". Ward, p. 7.

CHAPTER FIVE

MORE'S WORK AS LITERATURE

Southey wrote of "Psychozoia": "There is perhaps no other poem in existence which has so little that is good in it, if it has anything good." [1] Coleridge commented: "Southey must have wearied himself out with the poem, till the mists from its swamps and stagnants had spread over its flowery plots and bowers." [2] Southey on reflection agreed: "I have not done full justice to him as a poet. Strange and sometimes uncouth as he is, there are lines and passages of the highest poetry and most exquisite beauty." [3] And so began Henry More's literary reputation.

The Victorians added little to Coleridge's judgment, though some seemed to enjoy wallowing in the swamps and stagnants. Thus Campbell likened More's poetry to "a curious grotto, whose gloomy labyrinths we might be curious to explore for the strange and mystic associations they create." [4] Gilfillan referred to "that poetic-philosophic mist, which like the autumnal gossamer, hangs in light and beautiful festoons over his thoughts, and which suggests pleasing memories of Plato and the Alexandrian school." [5] And Grosart took up the refrain, valuing More's poetry "for its imaginative qualities and wildness of fancy and exquisite niceness of expression of the most gossamery thinking and feeling, and its pre-Raphaelite-like studies of nature, and now and again – alas! at long intervals, and mainly in the minor poems – wonderfulness of rapture and aspiration." [6] No doubt they found what they were looking for – mystic associations and pre-Raphaelite gossamer; but even if such Romantic empathy can be justified on the grounds that otherwise More would have no literary reputation, it is hardly fair to isolate elements of his poetry which are sus-

[1] Southey, *Omniana*, II, 157, as quoted in Coleridge, *On the 17th Century*, p. 625.
[2] Coleridge, *Table Talk*, A, p. 393, as quoted in *ibid*.
[3] Southey, *MSS Chetham Library*, as quoted in Grosart, p. xxxi.
[4] Campbell, *Specimens* (1844), p. 297, as quoted in *ibid*.
[5] George Gilfillan, *Memoirs of the Less Known British Poets* (1862), vol. 12, pp. 221-222, as quoted in *ibid*.
[6] Grosart, p. xxix.

ceptible to such empathy, and construct a critical evaluation thereon.
More's contribution to literature cannot be evaluated outside the context
of his life and work, and without understanding it as an outcome of his
philosophical, religious and aesthetic insights.

Grosart, in spite of his taste for gossamer, made a serious attempt to see
More as a whole. In his introductory sonnet, "To Edward Dowden Esq.,"
he relates More the sage to More the poet:

> In supreme bygone ages,
> He stood in the forefront of England's sages,
> Revered of all. As arrow from the bow
> His great thoughts sped straight to men's hearts; and shook
> Gray superstitions, as with stroke of levin.
>
> . . . .
>
> As poet dark – but as a starry night,
> Or leaf-screened book, gleaming with flecks of light.[7]

And at the end of his introduction, Grosart repeats his previous reference
to More's "Wordsworthian consciousness of his largeness of soul and intellectual strength," [8] in a summary of his threefold achievement. There is
his "strenuous assertion of the ethical as well as intellectual side of all
truth"; his "rejection of religion that rested on mere dogma or creed"; and
his "self-introspection as an exemplar of a human soul," which led him to
write verse as "lovingly and lingeringly as anything in *The Prelude*
itself." [9]

In More's prose and poetry there are passages which are detachable
from the backcloth of polemical speculation, and indicate an emerging
modern consciousness. Usually the patches of literary value are moments
when More uses the anachronistic or disintegrating material of Renaissance imagination, notably Spenserian diction and Metaphysical wit, but
manages to appropriate such material to his introspective expressionism.
A key passage which will help to show how he does this is the following:

He hath made me full lord of the four elements; and hath constituted me em-
peror of the world. I am in the fire of choler and am not burned; in the airy
sanguine, and yet not blown away with every blast of transient pleasure, or
vain doctrines of men; I descend also into the sad earthly melancholy, and
yet am not buried from the sight of God. I am, Philalethes (though I dare say
thou takest me for no bird of paradise) Incola Coeli in Terra, and inhabitant
of paradise and heaven upon earth – I sport with the beasts of the earth; the

---

[7] *Ibid.*, immediately after the title page.
[8] *Ibid.*, p. xxi.
[9] *Ibid.*, p. xlvi.

lion licks my hand like a spaniel; and the serpent sleeps upon my lap and stings me not. I play with the fowls of heaven; and the birds of the air sit singing on my fist.[10]

At first sight it is difficult to see in what sense this Biblical rhapsody points to an emergence of the modern consciousness; it represents the style and content of pre-Augustan prose. Just so; this is what it is meant to be, almost a pastiche of the style and content of Thomas Vaughan, to whom More is writing.[11] More is arguing with Vaughan in Vaughan's own idiom; and, as the passage goes on to show, he is appropriating, to consolidate the reality of his divine life and free imagination, all the manifestations of magic and the old cosmology, which Vaughan has hurled at him. More pursues his rhapsody at the same high pitch:

All these things are true in a sober sense. And the dispensation I live in, is more happiness above all measure, than if thou could'st call down the moon so near thee by thy magic charms that thou may'st kiss her, as she is said to have kissed Endymion; or could'st stop the course of the sun; or, which is all one, with one stamp of thy foot stay the motion of the earth.[12]

As Ward pointed out, "it is hard to represent the wit, reason, zeal, fancy, sportfulness and seriousness, divine boast, and rapture of mind there is contained in this writing." [13]

It is instructive to compare those qualities in More's prose, which Ward pinpoints with such enthusiasm, with Vaughan's particularly spicy brand of personal abuse. One senses that Vaughan's most telling blows come, when he descends from the realm of speculative polemic, into the arena of libellous vituperation. In the preface to his *The Man Mouse Taken in a Trap and Tortured to Death for Gnawing the Margins of Eugenius Philalethes*, he draws More's character in that combination of Baconian and Rabelaisian style, so beloved of English satirists from Hall and Marston to Oldham and Cleveland:

It is supposed he is in love with his Faerie Queen, and this hath made him a very elf in philosophy. He is indeed a scurvy, flabby, snotty-snouted thing. He is troubled with a certain splenetic looseness, and hath such squirts of the mouth, his readers cannot distinguish his breath from his breech. . . . But I have studied a cure answerable to his disease, I have been somewhat corrosive, and in defiance to the old phrase, I have washed a Moore clean. I have put his hog-noddle in pickle, and here I present him to the world, a dish of soused nonsense.[14]

---

[10] *Second Lash*, as quoted in Ward, pp. 90-91.
[11] For a brief summary of the More-Vaughan controversy, see Thomas Vaughan, *Works*, ed. Arthur Edward Waite (London: Theosophical Society, 1919), pp. 468-473.
[12] *Second Lash*, as quoted in Ward, p. 91.
[13] Ward, p. 48.
[14] Quoted in More, *Philosophical Poems*, ed. Bullough, p. lxix.

A purple passage in identical vein occurs in Vaughan's preface to *Magia Adamica* (1650), with which *The Man Mouse* was published. More is once again subjected to a flourish of excremental wit:

His observations are one continued ass's skin and the oysterwhores read the same philosophy every day. 'Tis a scurril, senseless piece, and – as he well styles himself – a chip of a block-head. His qualities indead are trancendent abroad but they are peers at home. His malice is equal to his ignorance. I laughed to see the fool's disease – a flux of gale which made him still at the chops whiles another held the press for him, like Porphyry's basin to Aristotle's well. There is something in him prodigious. His excrements run the wrong way, for his mouth stools, and he is so far from man that he is the aggravation to a beast. These are his parts, and for his person I turn him over to the dog-whippers, that he may be well-lashed and bear the errata of his front imprinted in his rear.[15]

Vaughan has his place in English prose, half way between the gusto of Nashe and the conciseness of Swift; and on this ground More could hardly hope to compete with his opponent. But for More, polemic as well as abuse was distasteful; in an even battle Vaughan had slightly the better of the argument. The distinction between the two lies elsewhere. While Vaughan excels in his forte of Rabelaisian vituperation, More excels in giving rein to a rhapsodic expressionism. In Ward's words, More "was not for a mere notional apprehension of these high matters." [16] More's refusal to be limited to notional controversy results in a negative capability which creates its own gusto out of his imaginative vision.

More's gusto embraces relics of Renaissance wit as well as intimations of Romantic imagination. Vaughan's own language was clearly infectious; and More enjoys a fair share of pun and paradox in his polemic with Eugenius Philalethes. We have seen his Bird of Paradise witticism; and very similar is this retort:

If I be a Precisian, . . . it must be from hence, that I precisely keep myself to the naked truth of Christianity. If this be to be a Puritan, Eugenius, I am a Puritan: But I must tell thee that by how much more a man precisely takes this way, the more Independent he will prove.[17]

More's double pun, first on "Precisian" and "precisely," then on "Independent," was part of the game of Renaissance polemic, and fair ripost to a man who had written, "in defiance to the old phrase, I have washed a Moore clean." The gothic elements in More's prose are very often part and parcel of a Metaphysical wit that has not completely lost its old habits

---

[15] Thomas Vaughan, pp. 130-131.
[16] Ward, p. 47.
[17] *Second Lash*, as quoted in Ward, p. 188.

of gratuitous speculation. This is evident when More writes of marriage in the following terms:

It is a debt that all owe to nature, upon a bond or obligation almost as strong as that of death. But if men were not permitted to leave this life, before they got one to leave in their stead, virginity would be a compulsory immortality upon earth, and some men would be hugely divided betwixt the love of themselves and of women.[18]

But it is gratuitous speculation that remains within the bounds of possibility, when he bursts out:

O that Dr Banes that whitleather wit had but had the hap to have been at Tedworth in those transactions. What tough tugging would there have been betwixt the evidence of sense and the prejudicate fancies that his taurine blood had hatched against the existence of demons.[19]

And usually More makes use of Metaphysical wit in the service of truth, as when, stooping from the maze of speculation to a homely utilitarian simile, he writes:

I conceive those souls that are good here, are more settledly and resolvedly good hereafter from their being here; and with more ease; as he that can dance with shackles, will dance with more ease without them: and he that can run in his boots, will more nimbly and more easily run in his stockings.[20]

At other times, what seems to us gratuitous speculation, is in fact a seriously held piece of scientific theory, which the Metaphysical wit serves to demonstrate; as when More writes:

The low spirit of the universe, though it go quite through the world, yet it is not totally in every part of the world; also we should hear our antipodes if they did but whisper: Because our lower man is a part of the inferior spirit of the universe.[21]

Grosart's facetious comment – "Is this an anticipation of the telephone?" [22] – illustrates the dangerous path More was following in using wit to support truth.

More may use Metaphysical wit to sharpen the edge of notional controversy; it nevertheless remains true that, as literature, such passages interest us for the impression they give of More's imaginative consciousness, whether it be grappling with speculative truths on the basis of the fourth ground of certainty, or whether it be flexing its muscles and rejoicing in its

---

[18] Letter to Lady Conway, 29 August 1662. *Conway Letters*, p. 208.
[19] Letter to Lady Conway, 31 March 1663. *Ibid.*, p. 216.
[20] Letter VII, Ward, p. 294.
[21] "Psychozoia," canto I, Preface to the Reader. Grosart, p. 10.
[22] Grosart, p. xliv.

scope and energy. It is at this level of literary appreciation, that isolated passages, purple or otherwise, take on a meaning above that of style or content, and form an image of More's real literary achievement. This image does not distinguish between the motions of ordinary life, the search for speculative truth, and the sense of creative imagination. As such it approximates to Keats's "poetical character." More's poetical character is by no means a purely literary one; but with the reservation that its aesthetic implications are secondary to its philosophical and religious dimensions, it does relate the various facets of More's work to their organising and unitive source, and provide the only satisfactory criterion by which to measure his contribution to literature.

More's poetical character is best seen, as is Keats's, in his letters. This autobiographical articulation is in itself a no mean contribution to literature. The tone of the following passage is that of frank and casual introspection, with no hint of exhibitionism or self-pity. The gusto is Keatsian because it betrays a confidence in the solidity and validity of its intuitions, without claiming to be more than a means of self-expression:

I scarce find myself here at all, saving in the trouble of my body, which has been as sad as lead, which I conceive is from the flaccidity of the mouth of my stomach, which Helmont makes the seat of the soul, and is a further argument that she's absent from her usual residence. Which if she be I dare swear she is at my Lord Conways in Shandos street.... Either this or my incessant tumbling down too much small beer and fruit to mitigate that troublesome and wasting heat in my body caused by those fierce elements and materials of green choler, is the reason of this flaccidness of the mouth of my stomach, as that of my extreme proneness to heaviness and sorrow.... But I never deal with any passion that troublesomely invades me with sleights and diversions but bid them battle on the open field, and by a serious ramble for a whole afternoon... I got some considerable ground against my enemy, after which I was better in both body and mind.... Madame, what you speak in compliment I acknowledge if rightly understood, to be a real truth, viz. that in what place so ever I enjoy most of myself that I am sure to have the best company there. For I profess, if I know myself aright, I am nothing else but an aggregate of my friends.[23]

The Metaphysical arguments in this passage are identical to those out of which Lord Herbert of Cherbury wove his subtle lyrics and elegies. More appropriates the machinery of the Metaphysical conceit to the expression of personality. His method of dealing with troublesome passions reminds one of Keats putting on his best clothes to gain ground against melancholy. In this way the motions of ordinary life reveal More's poetical character.

[23] Letter to Lady Conway, 3 September 1660. *Conway Letters*, pp. 164-165.

Keats expressed his sense of the creative imagination in his theory of the "chamber of maiden thought," and the various passages which issued from it. More had a similar sense of the imagination's autonomy. Describing the strange sights and lively forms which people his mind, he compares them to

> men ybrought
> Into some spacious room, who when they've had
> A turn or two, go out, although unbad.
> All these I see and know, but entertain
> None to my friend but who's most sober sad;
> Although, the time my roof doth them contain
> Their presence doth possess me till they out again.[24]

More's sense of creative imagination, although he is not wholly happy with it, constitutes a second aspect of his poetical character.

The third ingredient of More's poetical character, his commitment to the search for truth, was of course geared to his fourth ground of certainty. Speculative truth might often be misleading, but it had to square with imaginative insight if it was to have any meaning. Keats, with equal foresight, saw that one had to be a philosopher, even if all the philosophical minds one knew were never content with a half-truth. False philosophy had to be castigated, and the life of the imagination upheld. With such a poetical character, More could hardly not write just a little bit like Blake and Keats. The following passages are eloquently exemplary:

> Such is thy putid muse, Lucretius,
> That fain would teach that souls all mortal be:
> The dusty atoms of Democritus
> Certes have fall'n into thy feeble eye,
> And thee bereft of perspicacity.
> Others through the strong steam of their dull blood
> Without the help of that philosophy,
> Have with more ease the truth not understood,
> And the same thing conclude in some sad drooping mood.[25]

> What doth move
> The nightingale to sing so sweet and clear,
> The thrush, or lark that mounting high above

---

[24] *Democritus Platonissans*, stanza 2. Grosart, p. 91.

[25] "Psychathanasia," I, i, 6. *Ibid.*, p. 43. Cf. Blake's "Mock on, Mock on Voltaire, Rousseau."

> Chants her shrill notes to heedless ears of corn
> Heavily hanging in the dewy morn?[26]

The striking affinities to poems by Blake and Keats are no mere accidents of style or content; they are the visible tip of the iceberg of More's total enterprise, as it emerges out of Renaissance culture into the modern mind.

---

[26] "Cupid's Conflict," *ibid.*, p. 173. Cf. Keats, "Ode to a Nightingale."

PART TWO

THE VERGE: JOHN NORRIS

CHAPTER SIX

INTRODUCTION: A TRANSITIONAL FIGURE

The work of Norris has suffered from the scant justice of footnotes and passing references. To a greater extent than More, his significance has been obscured by compartmentalisation, no attempt having been made to relate his poetry, philosophy and theology to a common pursuit. As a poet, he is remembered perfunctorily as the last of the Metaphysicals, not so much because his work shows affinities with Herbert's, as because Herbert was his predecessor at Bemerton vicarage. Herbert is the poet who transcends his ecclesiastical function; Norris is Norris of Bemerton, and his poetry is forgotten. From the meagre critical attention he has received we may glean the following hints.

In one view his poetry is valued as a throw-back to Elizabethan lyricism; "not a little of it reflects the grace of an earlier time, when Spenser sang amid fields, and certainly voices a spirit of things which can only express itself in song." [1] Remarking on the absence of "religious poetry" in the early 18th century, Dobrée refers to "that fierce pressure to be found earlier in the Metaphysicals, even as far towards this period as John Norris of Bemerton, and later in Smart and Blake." [2] This generally accepted view of Norris as the last of the Metaphysicals was not the 18th century view. A verse tribute to Norris, published in 1732, refers to him as the initiator, with Cowley, of the neoclassical tradition in sacred poetry; Norris is "our second psalmist" who writes with "philosophic energy," and his readers "in that soft pleasing dress / Instructive ethics see." [3] Maren-Sofie Röstvig's treatment of Norris as an exponent of the classical tradition of

---

[1] John Norris, *Selected Poems*, ed. J. R. Tutin ("Pembroke Booklets," No. 2; Hull: privately printed, 1905), Introduction.
[2] Bonamy Dobrée, *English Literature in the Early 18th Century 1700-1740* (Oxford: Clarendon Press, 1959), p. 151.
[3] Richard Gwinnett, *Pylades and Corinna. Vol. 2.* (London, 1732), p. 217.

retirement poetry between Cowley and the Newtonians tends to substantiate this view.[4]

Perhaps the most solid hints towards an interpretation of Norris's poetry
are made by Geoffrey Walton, who devotes a whole chapter to "The Poetry
of John Norris of Bemerton: A Plea for Recognition." [5] Walton accepts
the general view that "in Norris one finds a Metaphysical wit, which,
though the emotional and intellectual tension is relaxed, is still recognizably
Metaphysical," but claims that far from "exemplifying a final senility of
the Metaphysical manner, Norris injects new life into it." [6] And where
Miss Rostvig sees continuity in a neoclassical idiom, Walton claims that
"Norris's slightly bantering tone saves him from the complacency of the
18th century." [7] Here at least the door is opened to an interpretation of
Norris as an important transitional poet, neither redundant nor a precursor, but closely involved on the one hand with the line of Donne, Herbert, Marvell and Vaughan, and on the other with the emerging forces
and forms of the Enlightenment.

Norris has a greater reputation as a philosopher than as a poet. Perhaps
for this reason his philosophy has been pulled out of its context to a greater
extent than has his poetry. As the English Malebranche, lying in the
shadow of a greater thinker, he has been extracted from his local habitation, to serve as a link between the Cambridge Platonists and the 19th
century renaissance of idealism. Thus J. H. Muirhead ascribes to Norris
the achievement of adding one more footnote to Plato.[8] A preoccupation
with the continuity of transcendental categories of thought appears to
characterise those passing references which critics have felt able to make
in tribute to Norris. In 1910 Flora Mackinnon drew attention to the value
of Norris's philosophy "as an expression of the transition from Dualism
to Idealism." [9] In 1939 Fairchild claimed Norris as "a link between the
neoplatonism of the Cambridge school and that of Shaftesbury." [10] Here
at least there is a hint that Norris played some part in the development of
English thought between More's early Cartesianism and Berkeleyan
idealism. But elsewhere Norris is described as an unoriginal thinker to be
broken down to a series of sources which include Plato, Descartes, Male-

[4] Rostvig, I, 367-373.
[5] G. Walton, pp. 141-157.
[6] *Ibid.*, pp. 143-144.
[7] *Ibid.*, p. 146.
[8] John H. Muirhead, *The Platonic Tradition in Anglo-Saxon Philosophy: Studies in the History of Idealism in England and America* (London: Allen and Unwin, 1931), p. 106.
[9] Flora Isabel Mackinnon, *The Philosophy of John Norris* ("Philosophical Mono-graphs," Vol. 1, No. 2; New York: The Psychological Review, 1910), p. 92.
[10] Fairchild, I, 108.

branche, Philo and Augustine.[11] And in 1940, J. K. Ryan, while admitting that Norris "is at the same time a genuine mystic and an advocate of scholastic rationalism," concluded that in the last resort he was "a neo-scholastic born two centuries too early." [12]

Perhaps the most valuable hints towards an interpretation of Norris's philosophy are proffered by Meyrick Carré, who sees a certain originality in Norris's eclecticism, in spite of its resultant "loose confusion of Platonic idealism and recent empiricism." [13] Carré at least appears to recognize Norris's work as a valuable testimony to a cross-roads in European thought, where the insights of the medieval and Renaissance mind were grappling with those of the Enlightenment. This aspect of Norris's philosophy has been underestimated because of the way in which his magnum opus appears to spring up as a fully armed system out of the blue. But, as he points out in the preface, his *Theory* is a synthesis of "several passages disseminated up and down" his previous writings, which themselves "glance at the notion here undertaken to be displayed." [14] In other words Norris evolved his philosophy bit by bit in response to the pressures of the age. When viewed in this light, Norris can be seen to have been closely involved at one and the same time with the persistence of the medieval and the emergence of modern structures of thought.

Norris's contribution to the religious controversy of his age has passed unnoticed. He has been treated as a useful footnote to a study of the rational theology of Cambridge Platonism,[15] but his attack on Toland's brand of deism has not received the attention it deserves.[16] There has consequently been no attempt to account for the apparent discrepancy between that side of Norris which saw fit to pursue in theology those paths towards moralism laid down by the Cambridge Platonists, and the other side which sought to eradicate the seeds of deism. Only by relating Norris's religious thought to the common ground upon which his poetry and philosophy were erected, can critical justice be done.

The few references to Norris which do not confine themselves to one

---

[11] Muirhead, p. 105.
[12] J. K. Ryan, "John Norris: A 17th Century English Thomist," *The New Scholasticism*, XIV, No. 2 (April 1940), 113, 145.
[13] Carré, p. 272.
[14] John Norris, *An Essay Towards the Theory of the Ideal or Intelligible World* (2 vols.; London: S. Manship, 1701-1704), p. ii. For an exposition of Norris's systematic philosophy, see Muirhead, pp. 72-107, and Frederick J. Powicke, *A Dissertation on John Norris of Bemerton* (London: George Philip, 1894), pp. 36-76.
[15] Lichtenstein, p. 176, footnote No. 48.
[16] John Norris, *An Account of Reason and Faith, in Relation to the Mysteries of Christianity, in Reply to J. Toland's Christianity Not Mysterious* (London: S. Manship, 1697).

aspect of his work do not take us very far. Draper for example pays lip-service to "the follower of the Cambridge Platonists, who is remembered as writing a reply to the deist Toland," but is only interested in Norris as author of "several lugubrious lyrics," and "early exponent of the common graveyard theme of the worthlessness of life." [17] And Bullough contents himself with the remark that "the mystical poetry of John Norris of Bemerton and the treatise in which that enthusiastic man attempted to answer John Locke were the last offshoot in the 17th century of the great Platonic tradition." [18] All the critical evidence points to the unconvincing conclusion that "Norris was historically speaking a kind of sport." [19] And yet, from the evidence of Norris's own work, one is forced to an opposite conclusion. There is perhaps more truth in Dunton's eulogy of Norris than one would normally expect from a panegyric. Dunton wrote of his friend and associate:

> Directed by his leading light, we pass
> Through Nature's rooms, and tread in every maze.
>
> . . . .
>
> Norris is Nature's darling, free to taste
> Of all her store.[20]

If we must choose between Norris as "a kind of sport," and Norris as "Nature's darling," there can be no doubt that the eulogy comes nearer than the disparagement to a just appreciation of his importance. The surface obscurantism can only be dispelled if his poetry, philosophy and religion are interpreted as all of a piece, giving expression to a unique if heterogeneous consciousness.

[17] John William Draper, *The Funeral Elegy and the Rise of English Romanticism* (New York: University Press, 1929), p. 17.

[18] Geoffrey Bullough, *Mirror of Minds: Changing Psychological Beliefs in English Poetry* (London: Athlone Press, 1962), p. 92.

[19] Hollander, p. 299.

[20] John Dunton, *Characters of Eminent Conformists* (1710), in *Life and Errors*, ed. J. B. Nichols (London, 1818), pp. 671, 672.

CHAPTER SEVEN

NORRIS AND THE ENLIGHTENMENT

Since Norris's reputation rests primarily on his Platonic idealism and Metaphysical poetry, it is necessary to establish to what extent he occupies a position on the threshold of the Enlightenment. If we take Browne's "America and untravelled parts of truth," and Glanvill's "unknown Peru of Nature," as an expressive indication of the spirit of the previous generation; [1] and if we take the age of Watts and Addison, with its self-conscious Enlightenment, as having passed the threshold; then it must appear that Norris is nearer to Watts than to Glanvill. The age of Browne and Glanvill was an age of exploratory enthusiasm and insatiable curiosity. These qualities faded as men realised they were rid of the cobwebs of the Schools and no longer haunted by the ghost of the Stagirite. When Watts rescued one last science – logic – from the disrepute it had lain in since Bacon had begun the great assault on Aristotle, his self-congratulatory dedication to "so polite and knowing an age" was already a cliché. [2] Norris is also conscious of living in an enlightened age, but he appears to be less comfortable and less complacent about it. This sense of being in the Enlightenment, but not quite of it, can be pin-pointed at the beginning and at the end of his literary career.

In the 1687 preface to his *Miscellanies,* he refers to "such a refining age as this wherein all things seem ready to receive their last turn and finishing stroke." [3] There is here a note of incredulity, verging on the whimsical, if not the ironic. In similar vein, Norris addresses his readers in 1704; he has doubts about the success of the second part of his *Theory,*

---

[1] Sir Thomas Browne, *Pseudodoxia Epidemica* (1646), and Joseph Glanvill, *The Vanity of Dogmatizing* (1661), as quoted in Willey, *17th Century Background,* p. 48.
[2] Isaac Watts, *Logic, Or the Right Use of Reason in the Inquiry after Truth,* Dedication, in *Works,* ed. D. Jennings and P. Doddridge (6 vols.; London, 1753), V, iii.
[3] *Miscellanies,* "To the Reader" (1687; in the third edition of 1699 the date of this preface is misprinted as 1678).

by reason of its encountering so many prejudices, and its appearing in an age of so much fineness and exactness. So that I have at once both old prejudices, and new light to contend with. 'Tis a great disadvantage to come abroad in a discerning age.[4]

Here is a clear indication of Norris's feeling that he is living on the threshold of a new age, and must therefore be fighting on two fronts, as a Baconian against the residue of Aristotelian hegemony, and as a Platonist against the excesses of the Enlightenment. In other words, Norris welcomes progress, but is somewhat sceptical of the goal. Unlike Watts and Addison, who were indefatigable modernisers and vulgarisers, Norris has no wish to bring either philosophy or poetry down from the mountain top. On the contrary, he wishes to restore them to their "primitive and genuine greatness." [5] Hence his quizzical use of the word "refinement." For the Enlightenment, refinement meant above all polish, the rubbing off of the rough edges left over from a gothic and scholastic past; for Norris it no doubt still kept some of the Platonic sense of purification and the purging of moral and intellectual dross. Hence the ambivalence in Norris's interpretation of his own age.

In 1689 he referred in a sermon to "this cold frozen age." [6] Of course all Platonists feel cold in this world from time to time; [7] but this is no passing complaint from a world-weary idealist. In its context it is a plea for more warmth and spirit in pulpit oratory. Norris felt that in this respect the age had over-refined. Sprat, Wilkins and Tillotson had conditioned the sermon-hearing and sermon-reading public not to feel the cold, and to cherish the light of knowledge above the heat of zeal.[8] So it is that Norris contended with the new light. But he was too much at grips with the old prejudices not to be at the same time an apostle of the new light. In an early essay, he notes that the Moderns' sense of "living in a more refined and mature age of the world" is their only advantage over the Ancients, but he implies that it is a weighty and decisive one.[9] And in his "General Apology for the Christian Religion," he attributes the insufficiencies in the Law of Moses to the fact that the full Law of Nature was "too refined for the grossness of that age." [10] For Norris, the full Law of Nature meant

---

[4] *Theory*, II, Preface.
[5] *Miscellanies*, "To the Reader".
[6] John Norris, "Sermon preached in Bath, 30 July," in *Reflections upon the Conduct of Human Life, with reference to the Study of Learning and Knowledge. In a Letter to the Lady Masham* (2nd ed.; London: S. Manship, 1691), p. 213.
[7] Cf. Norris's poem "The Aspiration": "How cold this clime!" *Miscellanies*, p. 95.
[8] Some 250 of Tillotson's sermons were published in 14 volumes between 1695 and 1704.
[9] "Of the Advantages of Thinking," *Miscellanies*, p. 119.
[10] "General Apology for the Christian Religion," *ibid.*, p. 183.

what it had meant to earlier apostles of the Enlightenment. He acknowledged the common notions of Lord Herbert of Cherbury: "Men are made so generally alike, and take the rise of their motions from the same springs, that to know human nature, the best and most direct way is to know one's self.[11] And he equated such notions or motions with the innate ideas of Descartes and the universal reason of the Cambridge Platonists:

Thou carriest thy divine master and teacher, Truth, within thy own bosom. ... While she teaches thee in the school of the breast, even that eternal and universal Reason that shines upon all minds with a pure, steady and uniform light, gives to all men the same common answers.[12]

Norris may have had reservations about the Enlightenment, but these reservations are barely visible, when he himself stands so squarely in the high road that leads from Lord Herbert to Bolingbroke, from Descartes to Voltaire.

It would be natural to expect Norris to have made a useful, if late, contribution to the eradication of scholasticism. On the contrary, all the evidence suggests that, far from continuing the work of the Cambridge Platonists, Norris preferred to live with Sir Thomas Browne in divided and distinguished worlds. This is perhaps not without relevance to the persistence in Norris's poetry of the Metaphysical tradition. His attacks on Aristotle are certainly less virulent than those of his predecessors. Possibly, as an Oxford man, he had less prejudice against scholasticism than did his Cambridge colleagues. At times he appears strangely indifferent to the campaign of the anti-Aristotelians, as when, in a gloss on one of his poems, he half-heartedly apologises for using an illustration based on Aristotle:

This according to the Aristotelian hypothesis ... which, whether it be true or no, I shall not now dispute. However it serves as an illustration, which is sufficient for my present purpose.[13]

Behind this casual front of indifference, Norris in fact cherished the categories of scholastic thought. He was determined to refine and use Aquinas and Duns Scotus for example, while rejecting "those voluminous intricacies and abstrusities" with which they burdened the management of their arguments.[14]

Norris's clearest exposition of what he valued in the scholastics' art of reasoning is contained in the 1704 preface to the second part of his *Theory*. In the first place he claims that scholastic reasoning is essential to discourse:

[11] *Theory*, I, 447.
[12] *Ibid.*, I, 390.
[13] *Miscellanies*, p. 7.
[14] "An Idea of Happiness" (dated 18 April 1683), *ibid.*, p. 327.

However the physics, or natural philosophy of the Schools does not please me, ... yet I have a great value and esteem for their metaphysics, and for their theology.... Whatever their matter be, their form and method is always excellent.... And indeed I am pretty much of opinion that nothing of any moment, either in philosophy or religion, can be either distinctly stated, or well understood, without the help of their useful, I might say, necessary distinctions.[15]

He is also prepared to defend syllogistic reasoning on the grounds of clarity and conciseness:

I have thought it convenient to use great plainness and chasteness of style, and to express myself not only scholastically, but even sometimes syllogistically, as being not out of conceit with syllogism. ... And I know no better way to form a right judgment of any discourse; or to prevent our being imposed upon by the plausible flourish of a long harangue, than to reduce it to a syllogism.[16]

The last sentence is intriguing. Norris gives the impression that he is urging a renewal of scholastic discourse, not because he hankers after a past that is dead and gone, but because he sees scholastic reasoning as a weapon with which to fight the copious eloquence of Renaissance rhetoric on behalf of the brevity and conciseness of Enlightenment classicism. And indeed in the central passage of this preface, it becomes obvious that this is what Norris intended:

Those who write in the clouds, as we say, involving their sense in hard words, as the Chymists, or perplexing it with ambiguous expressions, or who keep within the sphere of loose and indefinite generalities, especially if they have such a flow of words as to draw out their periods to great lengths, that the parts of the argument may lie at a distance from one another, and are withal so much masters of style, as to give their sentences a tunable turn, a smooth movement, and a round graceful close, they have the happiness not only to hide their faults (since nobody can see very far in a mist) but are oftentimes admired for their profoundness. They walk in the night, and though for that reason they stumble ever now and then, yet it passes unobserved, and their darkness is their protection: Whereas when a man writes clearly and distinctly, and explains things of great abstrusity upon clear and intelligible principles, and in a perspicuous manner and method, he holds out a light to his reader whereby to discover his own defects, and 'tis then easy to see whether he succeeds well or no in what he undertakes: For when 'tis once conceived what 'tis a man means, 'twill not be very difficult to discern whether what he means be true. So that a man that shall write clearly, had need advance that which is true and solid, or else his own light will betray him. As a man that has a light shop had need sell good ware. Clear writing than is not always the best policy,

---

[15] *Theory*, II, Preface.
[16] *Ibid.*

but 'tis the best honesty and ingenuity, and that's better than policy, or all the false colours of a corrupt and imposing eloquence.[17]

It thus appears that, far from enjoying the suspended animation of Sir Thomas Browne's intellectual schizophrenia, Norris is claiming a place for modernised scholasticism in the framework of the Enlightenment. Although he does not eschew Ciceronian eloquence in his own style, he is upholding the Senecan ideals of the Royal Society, and making a useful contribution to the eradication of Renaissance rhetoric.

The one aspect of scholasticism which Norris consistently attacked is its commonplace way of writing. This of course was not a sin confined to the schoolmen; it was also a characteristic of the bookish side of the Renaissance, witness Hamlet's self-ironic "My tables, – meet it is I set it down." [18] Here again it would appear that Norris's attitude to scholasticism is inextricably bound up with his contribution to the Enlightenment. Disregarding the categories of medieval and Renaissance thought, he sets out, for example, on a "way of writing Ethics" that is "entirely new and unblown upon," and castigates accordingly "that narrow strait-laced humour of adhering to the dictates of those, who have nothing more to recommend them, but only the luck of being born before us." [19] He associates the commonplace writer with the previous age, and strikes an attitude of Enlightenment complacency, when he claims to be "not so much in love with Prynne's *Histrio-Mastix,* or Burton's *Melancholy,* as to affect such a common-place way of writing myself, or to think it a proper entertainment for the nicer taste of our more correct and judicious age." [20] Elsewhere he proclaims his faith in "the late improvements of reason and speculation, the strange awakenings of thought and reflection, and the modern enlargement of the world out of the servile straitness of authority and commonplacing into the liberty of meditation and good sense." [21]

It would be difficult to find in this period a more explicit confidence in intellectual progress than in Norris's campaign against the commonplace writer. His incipient complacency is held in check by a Miltonic call to action. Take, for example, his sally at Aristotle's commentators:

With the commentators of Aristotle, the truth of what he affirms is supposed, and all the question is about what the philosopher means. That's a certain argument, or at least a strong presumption of an obscure writer, as the other

---

[17] *Ibid.*
[18] *Hamlet,* I, v, 107.
[19] John Norris, *The Theory and Regulation of Love. In Two Parts. To which are added Letters Philosophical and Moral between the Author and Dr H. More* (2nd ed.; London: S. Manship, 1694), "To the Reader," and p. 2.
[20] *Theory,* I, 177.
[21] *Ibid.,* I, 2.

is of a superstitious and bigoted reader, to be so devoted to human authority as to rest and acquiesce in it with an implicit faith.[22]

Milton had contended that the only real heresy was to accept a truth on the basis of mere authority; Norris too abhors the man who cannot think for himself. Finding Aquinas guilty on this score, he notes with an amused shrug of the shoulders:

'Tis pleasant to see how that great wit is oftentimes put to 't to maintain some unlucky authorities, for the salving of which he is forced to such shifts and expedients, which he must needs (should he dare to think freely) see through and discern to be false.[23]

When however a Quaker controversialist trips him up on a point of order, he retorts with some impatience that "a man may venture to give an account of one notorious principle belonging to a certain persuasion, and to show the difference between that and another, upon the stock of his former reading, without being obliged to bring an author to attest to everything he says." [24] In calling his age to thrust off the strait-jacket of authority, Norris identifies himself with the forces of the Enlightenment.

In his *Theory* however, Norris defends his right to make one exception, that of Augustine, from whom he quotes voluminously. This relapse into a commonplace way of writing occurs in a section entitled, "Wherein is considered how far the grounds of this hypothesis are laid by the Schools, and the hypothesis itself confirmed by the authority of St Austin: With some concluding reflections upon the whole, relating to morality and religion." [25] It is in fact the last chapter of Norris's magnum opus. After a thousand pages of discourse, he writes: "Labour at once recommends and justifies the indulging one's self some ease and refreshment, and therefore after all this toil and travel of thought, let us now a little repose ourselves upon the bed of authority." [26] And he justifies this repose with the following encomium on his hero:

I take him to have been a very great, as well as a very good man, and worthy of all the reverence and high esteem which has been paid to his name, both in the School and in the Church; upon which consideration I the less admire to find him quoted so much as he is, even by those who are the least addicted to authority, I mean the modern philosophers. For indeed this Father stands

[22] *Ibid.*, II, Preface.
[23] "Of the Advantages of Thinking," *Miscellanies*, p. 119.
[24] John Norris, *Two Treatises Concerning the Divine Light. The first being an Answer to a Letter of a Learned Quaker. The second being a Discourse Concerning the Grossness of the Quakers' Notion of the Light Within* (London: S. Manship, 1692), I, 27.
[25] *Theory*, II, 519.
[26] *Ibid.*

them in great stead, some of the best foundations of the new philosophy being laid in his principles. And my opinion is, that if the Schools had followed St Austin more than they have done, and Aristotle less, they would have left us another system of both physical and metaphysical doctrine than what the world now possesses.[27]

The passage is revealing, for it registers the distance between Norris and the new philosophy, as well as their common ground. There is the same distance and closeness between Fénelon and the French Enlightenment. Fénelon shared Norris's admiration of Augustine, and said so in the same breath as he associated himself with the Enlightenment's rejection of all authorities:

Descartes, qui a osé secouer le joug de toute autorité pour ne suivre que ses idées, ne doit avoir lui-même sur nous aucune autorité. . . . Je croirais même St Augustin bien plus que Descartes, sur les matières de pure philosophie.[28]

It can hardly therefore be suggested that, by using Augustine as an authority, Norris is wholly invalidating his persistent attack on the commonplace way of writing. In isolating this besetting sin of the medieval and Renaissance mind for special consideration, Norris is pursuing the task of demystification, which the Enlightenment had set itself.

The measure of Norris's closeness to the spirit of the Enlightenment is perhaps also apparent in the one panegyric he wrote. Panegyric often expressed the Enlightenment's sense of having arrived at final and settled truths. Norris, in his panegyric on Henry More, proffered the following flourish in the current celestial style of compliment:

> There's now no work left for thy accomplished mind,
> But to survey thy conquests and inform mankind.[29]

In the first place, the choice of subject is significant; Norris addressed not Locke or Newton, but the most mystical representative of Cambridge Platonism. There is also, in the direction "inform mankind," a hint that More's work has not been vulgarised as it should, that his conquests had not been made relevant to the many. More's work was after all a personal and idiosyncratic achievement, rather than an accomplishment which affected the future of mankind. Norris, though closer to the spirit of Locke and Newton than More had been, did not indulge in the passive panegyric of the kind so frequently to be addressed to Locke and Newton in the age of the Enlightenment. He conserved a good deal of that energy, which all

---

[27] *Ibid.*, II, 526-527.
[28] Fénelon, p. 317.
[29] "To Dr More, An Ode," *Miscellanies*, p. 74.

active minds of the 17th century shared, together with a strong sense of freedom from intellectual slavery.

The form is which Norris most strongly suggests his kinship with the minds of an earlier age is in his manifesto of eclecticism, where, as a positive corollary to his attack on the commonplace writers, he describes his ideal of the independent author in these terms:

Having cast off this intellectual slavery, like one of the brave Ἐκλεκτικοὶ mentioned by Laertius, he addicts himself to no author, sect or party, but freely picks up truth wherever he can find it; puts to sea upon his own bottom; holds the stern himself. And now if ever we may expect new discoveries.[30]

Norris develops this self-styled eclecticism in such a way as to stand out in relief from the development of the Enlightenment. There is even a parting of the ways in his preference for his own private path as against the general road. Of course many of the notions he derived from his eclecticism he in fact shared with the Enlightenment. As we have seen, the commonplace writer is a slave to the road of tradition and authority. Norris abhors those who will have "posterity trudge on in the same dirty miry road after their forefathers." [31] He is annoyed that Aquinas was "such a slave . . . that he would rather lose truth than go out of the road to find it." [32] But, as often as not, the byways he takes are his own, and as idiosyncratic as Henry More's before him. Just as More preferred to follow the easy emanations of his own mind rather than a predetermined track, so Norris confesses at the end of one of his more original essays:

If sometimes I happen to be in the road, and sometimes in a way by myself, 'tis no wonder. I affect neither the one nor the other, but write as I think.[33]

This candour lies behind Norris's distaste for the cobwebs and dust of the Dark Ages; but it also lies behind his aversion to the new road of the Enlightenment. The Augustans, who followed this high road and left the byways to eccentrics and enthusiasts, were "afraid to put men to live and trade each on his own private stock of reason," because they suspected "that this stock in each man is small, and that the individuals would do better to avail themselves of the general bank and capital of nations and of ages." [34] Norris, nearer in this to Milton than to Burke, believed the opposite; and if there were no other grounds on which to distinguish him

---

[30] "Of the Advantages of Thinking," *ibid.*, p. 119.
[31] *Reflections upon the Conduct of Human Life*, Dedication (1689).
[32] "Of the Advantages of Thinking," *Miscellanies*, p. 119.
[33] "An Idea of Happiness," *ibid.*, p. 343.
[34] Edmund Burke, *Reflections on the French Revolution* (London: J. M. Dent, 1910), p. 84.

from the age which in so many other ways he heralded, this in itself would be a decisive one.

Having done Norris the justice of delineating the extent of his participation in the emerging Enlightenment, it is only fair to give some weight to his contemporary reputation in certain circles as an obscurantist visionary. In the preface to the first part of his *Theory*, Norris refers to those critics who charge that his work is "visionary and fantastic," remarking merely by way of reply, that he doubts "whether the presentialness of an Ideal World to our minds be really such Platonic gibberish." [35] Few of Norris's contemporaries can have been convinced by this luke-warm disclaimer. Thomas Durfey certainly spoke for the majority, when he seized upon Norris's magnum opus as an occasion for Rabelaisian parody. Locke's circle took a similar view. In a letter to Locke, William Molyneux wrote: "I ever looked on Mr Norris as an obscure enthusiastic man." [36] And, since Locke had done Norris the honour of a reply on the question of the nature of the human understanding, Molyneux went to the trouble of repeating himself in a later letter to Locke:

I expect nothing from Mr Serjeant but what is abstruse in the highest degree. I look for nothing else from Mr Norris; I thought that gentleman had enough on it, in his first attempt on your *Essay*: but he is so over-run with father Malebranche, and Plato, that it is in vain to endeavour to set him right, and I give him up as an inconvincible enemy.[37]

It is not surprising that, in aligning himself with Malebranche and Plato, Norris gave offence to those who represented in some sort the spirit of the Enlightenment. A contemporary of Norris, Robert South, himself less of a modernist than Tillotson, made no bones about distinguishing between obscurantism and Enlightenment, when he saw them side by side. For South, the philosophy of Malebranche was "a gibberish of things," which "may very well sort together" with "the divinity of Jacob Behmen." [38] Locke's essay on Malebranche was, in South's view, a "clear and excellent confutation of a very senseless hypothesis." [39] As the English Malebranche, Norris stood condemned out of hand; for all his modernist zeal and love of truth was wrapped up in Platonic gibberish.

In the last resort, Norris is out of joint with the emerging forces of the

---

[35] *Theory*, I, ii.

[36] The letter, dated 16 March 1697, is printed in John Locke, *Works* (9 vols.; 12th ed.; London: C. & J. Rivington, 1824), VIII, 404.

[37] *Ibid.*, VIII, 435-436. This letter is dated 4 October 1697.

[38] MS dated 6 December 1699, as quoted in Charlotte Johnston, "Locke's Examination of Malebranche and John Norris," *Journal of the History of Ideas*, XIX (1958), 553.

[39] *Ibid.*

Enlightenment. It is not so much that he is an ancient among moderns –
he went a long way with the post-Cartesian moderns; he is rather to be
seen as a man of the 17th century, whose magnum opus, delivered to the
world in the first years of a new century, could not but be a standing target
for the satirist. A work of sustained and fastidious speculation, offering a
newfangled and precise investigation into the nature of truth and knowledge, by way of an elaborate system, which sought to explain the relations
between man, God and the universe – such a work was an anachronism in
1700. To the satirist like Swift, who was using common sense as a sharp
tool to anatomise pretensions and abuses in religion, philosophy and learning, Norris was indeed "an obscure enthusiastic man." In 1707, Thomas
Durfey published a parody of Norris's *Theory*. This is worth perusal in
some detail, for it pinpoints the absurdities of Norris's system, and does so
with some gusto, by employing the techniques that Swift had developed in
A Tale of a Tub. Moreover, Durfey's parody of Norris provides further
confirmation of the impossibility of making large claims for the spirit in an
age that was becoming increasingly mechanical and scientific. The ploy of
the satirists of this age, and supremely that of Swift, was to expose the
pretensions and abuses of ancient spirit and modern science in one fell
blow, along the lines of a generalised investigation into the "mechanical
operation of the spirit." It is significant that Norris lends himself to this
sort of treatment.

Norris's *Theory* was published in two parts, in 1701 and 1704. Durfey's
parody came out with a title-page as follows:

An Essay towards the Theory of the Intelligible World
intuitively considered
Designed for Forty-Nine Parts
Part III
Consisting of a preface, a postscript and a little something between

by GABRIEL JOHN

Enriched with a faithful Account of his Ideal Voyage, and illustrated with
Poems by several hands, as likewise with other strange things not insufferably
clever, nor furiously to the purpose.
   The Archetypally Second Edition. 1707. London.

In the two hundred odd pages that follow, Durfey takes up several lines
of attack. One of the most effective is his anatomy of vision. Norris, in his
attempt to validate the claim that we see all things in God, contended that
such vision depended not on the power of individual eyesight or perception, but on the power of the light which illuminated the object or ideal
world, and that this light naturally derived from God. This enabled him

to claim superiority for his theory over any alternative, for he was raising a metaphysical theory of vision on an objective ground outside the phenomenological. Hence his haughty disparagement of his critics: "I therefore may think I see things in a better light than they do, though not with better eyes." [40] Clearly the only way to demolish such an incipiently preposterous position is that taken by Durfey, a cool raillery, based on the common-sense proposition that vision is a matter of sensory perception. Hence Durfey's parody:

I have been long conversant in this kind of studies, and therefore may see things in a better light than they do, though not with better eyes. Nay, so many thoughtful and solitary hours, so many nightly lamps and lucubrations, have these studies cost me, that indeed my poor eyes, what with age, and what with assiduous poring, have the one departed this world, and the other almost worn itself out with incessant grief for the loss of its fellow. By this I am accidentally reduced very near to that state of *Illuminating Blindness,* which F. Malebranche had at first recommended to me.[41]

Durfey does not so much twist Norris's meaning, as gently expatiate it on the literal level, until it stands in all its patent absurdity. After all, Norris and Malebranche did stand for "illuminating blindness," if the alternative was the common eyesight of men like Durfey.

Preoccupied with his defence of seeing all things in God, Norris could quote Malebranche's approval of the visionary with perfect equanimity. Malebranche "says in a certain place that he had rather be called a Visionaire, a Phantastic or Fanatic, or by any of those pleasant names which the Imagination (which is ever disposed for raillery in little wits) is wont to oppose to such arguments as it does not comprehend, or cannot defend itself against, than to grant that bodies are able to enlighten him, or that he is to himself his own master, his own reason, his own light, and that to be solidly instructed in all things he need only consult himself." [42] Durfey has only to take the opposite view (the common-sense view that man is his own master, reason and light, and sees what he sees with his own eyes), for the "little wits" to become the heroes of the passage, and the visionaries to become what they are on their own confession, enthusiasts, for whom illumination comes through blindness. Thus Durfey:

'Tis certain that a pleasant vein of raillery may sport itself with the noblest composition, and make the most sublime truths a subject of laughter; and there are a crew of little wits, the very pest of a commonwealth, that will be

[40] *Theory,* I, iii.
[41] Thomas Durfey (pseudonym: Gabriel John), *An Essay Towards the Theory of the Intelligible World Intuitively Considered. The Archetypally Second Edition* (London, 1707), p. 211.
[42] *Theory,* I, 157-158.

nibbling at everything that's great; and by these I expect to be dignified with the title of Visionist, or Enthusiast, only because the truths I deliver are *above their comprehension*.[43]

In the controversy over the merits of raillery, Durfey was on the side of the witty, with Swift and Shaftesbury, against the pious, who included Malebranche, Norris and Collier. And in Norris's anatomy of the understanding in terms of light and vision, Durfey found plenty of raw material on which to exercise his raillery.

Norris was aware of the difficulty in the task he had set himself, but he was not one to give up:

'Tis a great thing which is now taken in hand, to explain the way of our understanding. . . . The motions of the moral heart, like those of the natural, though easily felt, are very hard to be discerned in their springs and principles. And though the understanding seems to promise a discovery of itself by its own light, yet it has a dark side to usward, and that which perceives all other things cannot so easily perceive itself.[44]

For Durfey, such passages merely corroborated his sense of the absurdity of Norris's position. Norris, an unenlightened or over-enlightened 17th century metaphysician, was creating his own difficulties and abstrusities. His arguments were patently absurd to the light of common sense, and Durfey merely accentuates this absurdity, by interpreting Norris's concept of the dark side of the understanding literally:

The Father ordered me to leave my wings behind, for they would be a mighty hindrance to me in flying, and he would undertake for my safe and easy conveyance without them; only I must needs give myself up entirely to his guidance and also submit to be hoodwinked: Nay if my desire was to become a true philosopher, by seeing the ideal world to the best advantage, there was nothing so proper or expedient as to put out my eyes. . . . Upon this I immediately blinded over my eyes with my own hands, and then delivered them up to my guide, that he might pull me along behind him; treading sometimes upon his heels; and sometimes pushing him forward out of eagerness.[45]

Durfey's parody continues in this vein; man must become blind if his inward vision is to operate. Durfey journeys to the ideal world, and entertains the vision of, amongst other things, "the ideas of two eyes":

The pupil of the one just discovered itself peeping from behind the lid, like the sun half-set; but the other had turned itself quite inward. From this I concluded that if they had any sight at all, they must see things double. However, they were evidently more perfect than real eyes; for the perfection does

---

[43] Durfey, p. 210.
[44] *Theory*, II, 3.
[45] Durfey, pp. 115-117.

not consist in external seeing, but in pleasing the internal sight; now these were endued with a very shining jet, which may be esteemed the true emblem of *Illuminating Darkness*; and if they were not clearsighted themselves, that was compensated by a more rare and admirable virtue; for both of them were transparent, and might clearly be *seen through*.[46]

Durfey ends his parody with a final thrust at Norris's theory of ideal vision:

Turning accidentally my internal optics towards my ideal garret in New Barbican, what should appear to me at the window but the counterpart, or the beautiful idea, of myself.... By endeavouring to stare hard upon my idea, my eyes *burst open* and I saw myself at that instant relapsed into the sensible world.[47]

With this raillery, Durfey speaks for the common sense of the English Enlightenment. Norris's version of Malebranchian occasionalism is mockingly demolished as a preposterous absurdity; men of good sense will not stand by, while wool of this sort is pulled over their eyes.

In his raillery Durfey never loses sight of the spirit and method of Norris's treatise. As a solemn and painstaking inquiry into the nature of the understanding, Norris's work is hidebound by its scholastic categories and idealistic preconceptions. By their remoteness from the categories of human experience and the normal run of ideas, Norris's theories could not but be ridiculed as obscurantist, in an age which was finding its feet on the ground of common sense, after a century of speculative flights. Norris, for all his partial involvement with the new forces of the Enlightenment, stands out, in the synthesis of his thought, a clear anachronism and ripe for parody.

---

[46] *Ibid.*, pp. 125-126. Cf. Swift's description of the Laputans: "Their heads were all reclined either to the right, or the left; one of their eyes turned inward, and the other directly up to the zenith." *Gulliver's Travels*, Book III, Chapter 2, in Jonathan Swift, *Works*, ed. Herbert Davis (14 vols.; Oxford: Blackwell, 1939-1962), XI, 143.
[47] Durfey, pp. 197-198.

CHAPTER EIGHT

PHILOSOPHY: "PLATONIC GIBBERISH"

Norris lived in an age when the Enlightenment was in the making. It is thus hardly fair to relate his thought to an external homogeneity, which when he wrote did not exist. The byways of his eclecticism need to be explored in order to show how he built up his philosophy bit by bit in reponse to the pressures of his age. These pressures include some miscellaneous and heterogeneous concepts, which eventually became part of the fabric of the Enlightenment, but they made themselves felt above all in the influence of Plato, Descartes and Locke. In his reaction to these influences, Norris adumbrates in many ways the philosophy of the Enlightenment, chiefly by filtering elements of Cambridge Platonism through to the 18th century, and eventually to Coleridge. In this he carries on the work of More, by registering, both ideologically and aesthetically, the waning of the Renaissance and the eventual rise of Romanticism. Norris's ambivalence at the threshold of the Enlightenment means that he is particularly well-equipped to register this change. His isolation is not that of personal eccentricity. For two elements meet in him, as they met in the Cambridge Platonists, and Platonism and Cartesianism have in themselves an ambiguous relation to the Enlightenment. Under the influence of Plato and Descartes, Norris pursues philosophical byways which are both original and representative.

The ambiguity inherent in Platonism became only too evident in the latter half of the 17th century. From the 15th century, Platonism had constituted one of the chief elements in the progressive side of the Renaissance, and in the minds of the Cambridge Platonists the Dark Ages were still a sufficiently powerful reality for them to justify their claim to be on the road towards Enlightenmenment. But already in Cromwellian Cambridge, Whichcote's Platonism had been attacked with a double-edged sword. In 1651 Dr Tuckney, Whichcote's predecessor as vice-chancellor, accused him not only of deviating from Calvinist orthodoxy, but also of speaking

in "school-language . . . begot in the depth of anti-Christian darkness." [1]
Between 1650 and 1700, from being an instrument of light and progress,
Platonism became associated with the forces of darkness and obscurantism.
Tuckney may not heve been exactly an apostle of sweetness and light, but
Whichcote was at the beginning of this reversal. Cambridge Platonism
fought a losing battle. In 1682 Norris unwittingly betrays the decadence of
the Platonic tradition, and simultaneously inaugurates his own reputation
as "an obscure enthusiastic man": "I know those who are unacquainted
with the inexpressible exaltations of contemplation and seraphic love, will
think this downright raving nonsense, but without question there is such a
thing as is here described, though I confess withal 'tis a kind of divine
madness." [2] By this time Platonism was becoming ipso facto gibberish.
Accordingly it either became outrageously Hermetic and Rosicrucian, or
trimmed its wings and developed into a quaint self-conscious cult. This
second aspect of its decadence is worth consideration, because Norris, for
all his high seriousness, was closely associated with those who perpetrated
the cult.

The refinement of Platonism into a cult of Platonic love occurred towards the end of the 17th century amongst a group of bluestockings who
included Lady Mary Chudleigh (1656-1710), Mary Astell (1666-1739),
and Cudworth's daughter, Lady Masham (1658-1708). These learned
ladies were all admirers of Norris, and they appear to have received a good
deal of encouragement from the journalist John Dunton, who was not slow
in publicising their activities.

Lady Chudleigh in particular illustrates the way in which Platonism
merged into the Enlightenment. Some of her poems are direct paraphrases
from Norris, and date from 1685. In "The Resolution," published in 1703,
she writes thus of Norris: "Plato revived, we in his writings find, / His
sentiments are there, but more refined." [3] In her own poems Plato is almost totally refined into Locke. One of her couplets runs: "The understanding more sublime will grow, / We shall more accurately think, and
much more fully know." [4] In Miss Rostvig's words, "a diluted neoplatonism goes rather well with the psychology of Locke." [5] And, as Fair-

---

[1] Quoted in Henry More, *Philosophical Poems*, ed. Bullough, pp. xviii-xix.
[2] John Norris, *Hierocles upon the Golden Verses of the Pythagoreans. Translated
out of the Greek into English* (London: M. Flesher, 1682), Preface.
[3] Lady Mary Chudleigh, *Poems on Several Occasions: Together with the Song of
the Three Children Paraphrased* (2nd ed.; 2 parts, separate pagination; London: Bernard Lintott, 1709), part 1, p. 47. Quoted in Fairchild, I, 243.
[4] Lady Chudleigh, *The Song of the Three Children Paraphrased*, p. 61. Quoted in
Rostvig, I, 428.
[5] Rostvig, I, 429.

child puts it, in Lady Chudleigh Platonism parts company with Christiani-
ty and languishes into sentimental idealism.[6] In one of her essays, Lady
Chudleigh demonstrates how harmoniously she could refine Plato into
Locke:

What I would advise myself and others in relation to a course of study, should
be to endeavour to get an insight into the useful parts of learning, and to
attend more to things than words. Let languages be left to the grammarians,
and let the rhetoricians contend about the niceties of style; and while they are
quarrelling about the husk, the shell, the superficial worthless part, let us be
solicitous only for the substance.[7]

Lady Chudleigh not only contributed to the evaporation of Platonism; she
also contributed to the cult of Platonic love. In letters to Lady Wharton,
which were published in 1732, she discusses "Mr Norris's finespun metaphysical theory of love," and makes an attack on "that modern idol
Reason." [8] Like Lady Chudleigh, Mary Astell entered into discussion with
Norris on the nature of love, disputing his theory that God should be the
sole object of human love.[9] And Lady Masham, as a young woman, had
corresponded with Norris on the subject of Platonic love.[10] There can be
no doubt that in conducting these discussions Norris contributed to the
metamorphosis of Renaissance Platonism into the first manifestations of
sentimentalism and preromanticism.

This conjuncture is even more apparent when we take into consideration John Dunton's contribution to the cult of Platonic love. Dunton,
with whom Norris collaborated on the *Athenian Mercury*, transposed
these high-minded philosophical debates into the mould of journalistic
sensationalism. He treats the subject in the tone of irreverent playfulness,
announcing a "project":

The Athenian Spy: or the Secret Letters of Platonic Courtship between the
Athenian Society and the most ingenious ladies in the three kingdoms; with
the form of solemnising Platonic matrimony, invented by the Athenian
Society. To which is added, their amorous quarrels on the disputable points
relating to love and wedlock. – The copy of an act, to provide maids with

---

[6] Fairchild, I, 243.
[7] Lady Chudleigh, *Essays upon Several Subjects in Prose and Verse* (London: R.
Bonwicke, 1710), p. 9.
[8] Gwinnett, pp. 32-33.
[9] Their correspondence was published by Norris in *Letters Concerning the Love of
God, between the author of the Proposal to the Ladies and Mr J. Norris; wherein his
late discourse showing that it ought to be entire and exclusive of all other loves, is
further cleared and justified* (London: S. Manship, 1695).
[10] See Myra Reynolds, *The Learned Lady in England 1650-1760* (Boston and New
York: Houghton Mifflin, 1920), p. 101. Lady Masham's *Discourse Concerning the
Love of God* (1696) was a reply to the letters between Norris and Mary Astell.

husbands. As also a method for unmarrying those that are unequally yoked. Published to direct the bachelor and virgin in their whole amour.[11]

He prints a letter from his wife to "Mrs Singer" – i.e. the Pindaric Lady, alias Philomela, or, as she was to become, Mrs Elizabeth Rowe – dated 27 August 1695, in which she writes as follows concerning the friendship between her husband and Mrs Singer:

I ever esteemed Platonic love to be the most noble, and thought it might be allowed by all: but some wise persons are afraid lest sex should creep in for a share. Here was no danger.[12]

And Dunton does not scruple to bring up Norris's name in this sort of context:

There is no sex in souls. . . . My first wife was of this opinion; and therefore told the Pindaric Lady, that "Platonic love is the most noble, and may be allowed by all." The learned Norris published several letters which he sent to his maiden friend; and sure I am, none but such as are lewd themselves and so cannot help suspecting of others, will censure a friendship where the body has nothing to do.[13]

Here we see the condition to which the Platonism which informed Donne's "Ecstasie" ("We see by this it was not sex") has been reduced. In a sense Dunton throws as much light on the incongruity of Norris's Platonism as Durfey does on his idealism; neither will hold water in an age of common sense.

Unlike the Cambridge Platonists, Norris had no scruples about Cartesian dualism; where More found Descartes problematic, Norris found him axiomatic. The ambivalence of Norris's Cartesianism lies elsewhere, and chiefly in the fact that the English Enlightenment was turning its back on Descartes at just that time when Norris was busy modernising him. By the 1690s Locke and Newton were firmly in the saddle as leaders of the English Enlightenment. In 1692 the Athenian Society's review of Norris's attack on Locke, suggested that Norris's Cartesianism rendered him incapable of understanding Locke. Norris reacted with astonishment:

Why the being a Cartesian, and according to the way of M. Malebranche, should make me less apt to comprehend Mr Locke's book, I cannot divine. . . . I am rather apt to think that I have comprehended Mr Locke's sense well enough, but that you understand neither me, nor Mr Locke.[14]

---

[11] Dunton, p. 197.
[12] *Ibid.*, p. 198.
[13] *Ibid.*, p. 408.
[14] "A Brief Consideration of the Remarks made by the Gentlemen of the Athenian Society," in John Norris, *Practical Discourses upon the Beatitudes, Vol. 1* (4th ed.; London: S. Manship, 1699), following the appended *Cursory Reflections upon a Book called An Essay Concerning Human Understanding* (separate pagination), p. 37.

Norris must have felt this review as an affront, since he had himself taken part in the activities of the Athenian Society.[15] But his devotion to the Cartesian system was such, that it was inevitable that he should be misunderstood. The formation of the intellectual hegemony of Newton and Locke meant that Cartesianism now belonged with Platonism to the unenlightened past. To the English Enlightenment, Descartes belonged with Plato and Malebranche amongst the visionary enthusiasts beyond the pale. In the words of Walter Harte:

> Reason, like virtue, in a medium lies.
> A hair's-breadth more might make us mad, not wise,
> Outknow even knowledge, and outpolish art,
> Till Newton drops down giddy – a Descartes! [16]

Norris did not drop down giddy, but followed faithfully.

In the first place Norris bypasses the problem of dualism, by crediting Descartes with similar intentions to his own. For him Descartes

was indeed a great master in the rational way, but no magnifier or exalter of human reason. So far from that, that he seems to have had the most inward and feeling sense of its infirmities and defects, and the best to have understood what a poor little thing 'tis to be a man, of anyone in the world.[17]

But Norris goes further; he consistently embraces the Cartesian system as an all-sufficient substitute for Aristotelianism, and as capable of supporting his Malebranchian occasionalism. Compared to his English contemporaries, content with their sublunary empiricism, he appears to be strangely obsessed with finding a modern philosophy that will support a metaphysical superstructure as well as an experimental infrastructure. Hence:

When I speak of philosophy, I mean true philosophy; not that which reigns in the Schools, (which after a great deal of time and pains spent in it, I think to be a mere fantastic amusement . . .) but the Cartesian and the Experimental philosophy.[18]

Descartes then, replaces Aristotle, in physics and metaphysics: "Were I to state the general difference between the Cartesian and the Aristotelian philosophy, might I not securely place it in this, that the one offers to explain appearances of nature by forms and qualities and other such abstruse beings, which the other chooses to resolve into the more simple and intelligible

---

[15] See Dunton, pp. 189-190 for an account of Norris's introduction to the Athenian Society.

[16] Walter Harte, "An Essay on Reason," Chalmers, XVI, 353.

[17] *An Account of Reason and Faith*, p. 278.

[18] John Norris, *Spiritual Counsel: or The Father's Advice to his Children* (London: S. Manship, 1694), p. 116.

principles of figure and motion." [19] Norris, like Malebranche, builds his occasionalism on the Cartesian Cogito:

The other accounts of human understanding . . . are all of them . . . consistent with atheism. . . . This hypothesis is . . . such as no atheist can hold, . . . it being as plain a consequence . . . I think, therefore, God is; as I think, therefore I am.[20]

Hence his rejection of Locke, and hence his imperviousness to the problems of Cartesian dualism. It remains to be seen how far his Cartesianism led on into the Enlightenment, in spite of his English critics, and how far it modified the nature of his Platonism.

It needs to be shown that Norris was not only a follower of Descartes in matters of metaphysics. He spent a good deal of time expounding Descartes' mechanical theories. This he could do unreservedly, for he had no theories about the "spirit of nature" to propound. Descartes applied his mechanics to all matter, from minerals to man. In 1649 he had made the astounding assertion that "the body of a living man differs from that of a dead man just as any machine that moves of itself differs from itself when it is broken and the principle of its movement ceases to act." [21] Norris applied this theory, not as an experimental scientist, but in the spirit of 17th century philosophy, to the microcosm and the macrocosm. The passages where he develops this theory into a system of mechanical psychology deserve to be quoted at length, for they modify his reputation as an obscure Platonist, and look forward to the discoveries of Hartley and the French philosophers. Norris's tone is so enthusiastic, that what is meant as an application of the machine as analogy to explain the phenomena of the vegetable, animal, and human worlds, becomes almost an adoration of the mechanical as such.

Norris begins with an encomium on the progress of the mechanical sciences, and an application of the mechanical principle to the life of a plant:

Though the power of matter be so imperfectly comprehended by us, and we have so little force, and such unwieldy instruments to reduce that little theory which we have to practice; yet what strange things in the way of mechanism have been done by the art of man, and what stranger things yet may? And who can tell to what pitch of perfection that continually growing art will, by the constant improvement of the mechanical sciences, in future ages actually arrive? He that should have been told in some of the past ones, before the

[19] *Two Treatises Concerning the Divine Light*, I, 27.
[20] *Theory*, II, 554.
[21] Descartes, *The Passions of the Soul*, as quoted in Bullough, *Mirror of Minds*, p. 92.

invention of watches, that there might be such an instrument contrived, which by the bare mechanic structure and disposition of its parts should do what we see done by some of these machines in the state of perfection they are in at present, would have thought it incredible perhaps impossible. And should one of the best of these pieces of art be now shown to a stranger of a barbarous country . . . he would go near to think it alive. And perhaps the main reason why 'tis not thought so by more, is because we see its inward structure, the springs and wheels whereby its motions are caused and regulated. Though after all, whether that be a good reason why we should not think it alive, as truly as a plant is alive (though not in so perfect a degree) I know not, as not being able to conceive anything by what we call the life of a plant, but only a more perfect mechanism, such a structure or disposition of its parts, as enables it to receive in the juices of the earth, and to work them into its proper substance, so as to grow or be nourished by them. And when that structure is so disordered that it cannot do this, then the vegetable watch ceases to go, or the plant dies. . . . Could we see the interior of a plant, as distinctly as we do that of a watch . . . we should see by what springs and wheels its vital operations, as we call them, are carried on, and so should no more think of life in a plant than in a watch.[22]

Nothing could be more representative of Enlightenment philosophy than Norris's view of the man-made machine as the universal norm. Unlike the Cambridge Platonists, he sees no inconvenience in equating the vital with the mechanical.

Norris pursues his discourse with an analogy between animal life and the latest mechanical inventions in the art of landscape gardening:

But among the many strange and stupendous things done by the artful management of matter and motion, I chiefly mean and appeal to those which are near imitations of life and sense, and where there is a ground laid for such a train and suit of movements as resemble those which thought ordinarily produces. The grottos and water-works . . . in some great men's gardens, are a fit illustration of what I mean, where when strangers enter they cannot help treading on certain springs so disposed, that if they approach to a Diana that is bathing herself, they will make her run away and hide in the reeds or rushes; and if they offer to go further in pursuit of her, they will make come towards them a Neptune, who shall menace them with the trident, and forbid their curious progress. Here you see are movements that use to accompany the passions of shame and anger, and the occasions upon which they are done makes it seem as if they proceeded from them here, and you may easily carry on the train a great deal further if you please. But now if mechanism can rise to such things under the conduct of human art, what will it not be able to do under the direction of a divine hand? . . . One may well compare the nerves of the bodies of animals to the pipes of the machines of those fountains; their muscles and their tendons to other springs which serve to move them, their animal spirits to the water which moves them, whereof the heart is the source,

22 *Theory*, II, 83-85.

and the cavities of the brain are the heads of the conduit. In fine we may consider the external objects which, by their presence, act upon the organs of sense of beasts, as those strangers who entering into some of the grottos of these fountains, cause, without thinking of it, the movements which are there done at their presence.[25]

Apart from its implications for the aesthetics of classicism, and its contribution to the Augustan concept of nature methodised, this passage represents a remarkable development of Cartesian mechanical theory, and adds point to the vehement physiological wit of the Scriblerus school of satire.

So far Norris has confined himself to argument by analogy. When he comes to consider more specifically the little world of man and the great world of the cosmos, he appears to take the analogy literally:

The world is a great machine, and goes like a watch, and the several bodies that compose its system are ... mechanically made and laid together, and must in like manner be resolved and accounted for. And so as to the operations of Nature, as great and as strange as they are, they proceed ordinarily from mechanism, the wise disposition of matter and motion, and then do we understand them more perfectly, and philosophise upon them with best satisfaction when we can resolve them into their natural, that is, their mechanic causes. For though other principles (fit rather to amuse than instruct) have been pretended, yet I doubt not but that the true reason after all why the load-stone draws iron, or why salt preserves bodies from corruption, or why the air dissolves them, why rhubarb purges, or why the fruit of the quince tree binds, why opiates still and quiet the spirit, or why coffee disperses them, etc. ... must be such as is taken from the specific contexture of these bodies, and the different figure and motion of those parts whereof they consist. This you may call, if you please, New Philosophy, but 'tis what should have been the old; and if anyone should go about to reprehend it as injurious to piety, and should gravely say, that mechanic principles will not serve alone to account for the phenomena of Nature, but that we must needs have recourse to the being of a God for the explanation of them, he will be found to be one of those impertinent objectors that are so far from confuting the hypothesis they pretend to censure, that they do not so much as contradict it. For when the Moderns contend that there are no other principles but matter and motion etc. to be sought for in explaining the phenomena of Nature, they speak of the constituent or inherent principles of bodies, that there is nothing in the bodies themselves but the disposition, figure or motion of their parts that is the cause of their operations, in opposition to those imaginary principles of substantial forms and qualities introduced by the school of Aristotle, not in the least intending to exclude a God, neither from being, nor from operation, whom they suppose to have laid things thus mechanically together, and to conduct and direct them according to those general laws of motion which he has established, whereby the course of Nature proceeds, so that the

[23] *Ibid.*, II, 85-86.

earth itself may be said to bring forth fruit mechanically, or as a great automaton.[24]

Norris's conclusion gives some indication as to how an obscure Platonist could speak out so unreservedly on behalf of some of the more daring discoveries of the Enlightenment. His occasionalist philosophy removes his defence of God and spirit totally out of the context of matter, motion and sensory perception. The dualism which so worried the Cambridge Platonists affects Norris only in so far as it conditions the whole structure of his thought, and allows his Cartesianism and his Platonism to coexist.

The extent to which Norris's thought is conditioned by Cartesian dualism becomes only too evident when he relates his occasionalist superstructure to his mechanical base. Norris had no qualms about accepting the total alienation of mind and matter, and expressed much of his Platonic thought in terms of Cartesian dualism.[25] He is adamant that the "operation wherein our fruition of God does consist is an operation of the intellectual part and not of the sensitive . . . because the essence of God cannot be the object of any of our senses." [26] On this principle he erects his "ideal system." His eulogy of the mechanical must be seen in the light of his conviction that matter is essentially inert, and that only spirit can produce motion.

On at least two occasions he spelt out the implications of this principle at once Platonic and Cartesian. In a sermon on the text "Thou shalt love the Lord thy God with all thy heart, and with all thy soul, and with all thy mind," [27] he remarked:

The whole matter of the creation, though in continual motion, is yet as to us, that is, to our spirits, an idle, dead, unactive thing, and that of itself signifies no more to the production of our several sensations, than a company of odd figures of senseless characters do to the cure of an ague.[28]

The relevance of this theory to the development of pietism and Evangelicalism, as opposed to an Enlightenment religion based on the Newtonian argument from design, is worth noting. And when Norris expatiates at leisure, and with rhetorical indulgence, on the same theme, its relevance to

---

[24] *Ibid.*, II, 87-89.
[25] Cf. "The Refinement":

> "Did ever things so wide, so close combine
> As massy clods and sunbeams, Earth and Mind?
> . . . Unequal match!" *Miscellanies*, p. 104.

[26] "An Idea of Happiness," *ibid.*, pp. 326-327.
[27] St Matthew, xxii, 37.
[28] John Norris, *Practical Discourses upon Several Divine Subjects, Vol. 3* (2nd ed.; London: S. Manship, 1701), pp. 45-46.

the philosophy of Berkeley, and its hostility to the aesthetics of Newtonian preromanticism, become equally apparent:

Reflect . . . what a dead unactive thing matter is, and withal, how poor and empty the material is in comparison of the intellectual world. And accordingly, whether such an unactive empty being, that is so without power or force, and without form and void, can be a fit or reasonable object of thy love? What power of efficacy may be attributed to second causes, as they are called, or what force one body may have to move another, I shall not now dispute; but 'tis plain that bodies cannot act upon our souls, nor cause in them the least pleasure or the least pain, the lowest taste, or the faintest smell, or any other sensation. 'Tis not the fire that gives thee heat, nor the sun that gives thee either heat or light; nor yet the sun against a watery cloud, or as he brings back the day from the rosy east, that entertains thee with delightsome colours. The fruits of Eden, though not one of them had been forbidden, could not have obliged thee with one taste; nor can all the spices of Arabia now bestow upon thee one smell. These are but imaginary causes of real effects, fantastic powers, mere idols of our imagination. . . . Those odours, those savours, may even those colours which are imagined to be in bodies, are really not in them, but in ourselves. And yet we court them and command them, and say that one shines, and another has a fine perfume, etc. But they, poor creatures, have none of those finenesses, excellencies, or beauties which we think we see in them . . . but are . . . utterly void and destitute of all those agreeable prettinesses, those charming graces which the poetical imagination of philosophers, like the passion of lovers, has conferred upon them, and the blushes of the morning are as much a fiction as Aurora itself. Indeed 'tis all fiction, complement, fallacy, dream, imposture, and man walks in a vain show among cheats and delusions, empty representations, and false appearances, and the world is to him as some enchanted place, where he is abused by resemblances of things that are not. . . . Those beauties which he thinks he perceives without, are really in himself, and he carries about him the world that he admires.[29]

Militantly opposed to the ideological basis of preromantic aesthetics, Norris here voices an iconoclasm which, in the very temper of its protest, carries hints of his own early poetic impulse. The philosophical implications to be drawn from this passage are that, for Norris, Platonism and Cartesianism carry the same message.

Norris's combination of Platonism and Cartesianism allows him to cut the bridges between mind and matter which the Cambridge Platonists so jealousy guarded. Norris has no use for a middle ground, and on more than one occasion he expressly denounces bridge-building of this sort as an unenlightened anachronism. He is particularly concerned to explode the scholastic version of the Cambridge Platonists' middle ground, namely the

[29] *Theory*, II, 253-255.

"intellectus agens." He calls this concept a "hocus-pocus," [30] and likens his own attack on it to "fighting with windmills." [31] This does not stop him from quixotically refuting the concept at least four times.

The "intellectus agens" had been invented to bridge the gap between matter and mind. According to Norris, its function

is to purify and refine these material phantasms and to render them immaterial. A very hard task for poor Intellectus Agens, and were he not a creature of their own brain, it would move anyone's pity to think what a piece of drudgery he is condemned to.[32]

Elsewhere Norris compares this absurd operation with that of the philosopher's stone:

'Tis a sign philosophers are hard put to't when they must entrench upon the province of poets, and use fiction for the support of an hypothesis. But we have already ruined so much of this romantic system, that we need now only consider this one rare expedient, upon which they lay the great stress of it, viz. the transmutation of these sensible, and as such, by their own confession, unintelligible species, into spiritual and intelligible ideas, by the operation of Intellectus Agens. . . . The Philosopher's Stone, as they call it, whereby viler materials are pretended to be turned into gold, were it true, is but a Fool to the great Metaphysical Elixir, Intellectus Agens.[33]

Norris furnishes two further reasons for his objection to this particular form of "plastic nature." In the first place, there is no need for this go-between, since ideas do not originate in the human understanding, but in the mind of God:

The Schools might have spared this imposition upon poor Intellectus Agens. For thanks be to God, we want not ideas, nor could any faculty of ours pretend to make them if we did. Nor indeed is it the business of human understanding to make ideas, but only to contemplate them, which alone (without working at that intellectual forge which the Schools have set up) will sufficiently employ all its activity as well as capacity.[34]

Here Norris betrays the static essence of Platonism (to contemplate ideas) in contra-distinction to the dynamic essence of the European Enlightenment (to make ideas). In the second place, God needs no viceroy in either the sensible or the intelligible worlds:

We may beat the field of nature over and over for ideas, or employ Intellectus Agens to forge them for us; but still we shall find that there is nothing in the sensible, not yet in the intellectual world that can represent God.[35]

[30] *Ibid.*, II, 348.
[31] *Ibid.*, II, 351.
[32] *Two Treatises Concerning the Divine Light*, II, 28.
[33] *Theory*, II, 351, 353.
[34] *Ibid.*, II, 138.

At this point in his treatise, Norris lays down his arms, satisfied that he has dealt a death-blow to this particular windmill.

Norris is less voluble when he comes to consider the modernised version of Intellectus Agens, propounded by More and Cudworth. In one of his poems he uses the phrase "plastic nature," without disparaging it or contesting its validity.[36] But in his reply to Mary Astell's objection that his theory "renders a great part of God's workmanship vain and useless," [37] and her suggestion that he consider "that vital congruity which your friend, Dr More, will have to be between some certain modifications of matter, and the plastic part of the soul," [38] Norris is adamant that matter and spirit are too unlike to have any "sensible congruity." [31] For Norris, More's "middle life" is a notion as unenlightened and as otiose as the wretched Intellectus Agens of the Schoolmen.

Since Norris so eagerly jettisoned More's "middle life," it may well be asked whether he can be considered properly to belong to the English Platonic tradition. Does he not undermine the central pillar of mid-17th century Platonic thought? In the last resort the answer must lie in the affirmative. He may well have safeguarded values and modes of thought which were ignored in an age of Enlightenment; but the 17th century world-picture, which Cudworth in his latterday zeal had propped up with the aid of his "plastic nature," was no more susceptible to modernisation than were the waning forms and forces of the Metaphysical tradition in poetry. For all his faith in the saving grace of occasionalism, Norris, far from carrying on the work of the Cambridge Platonists, comes near to being one of those

professed theists of later times, who might notwithstanding have an undiscerned tang of the mechanic atheism hanging about them, in that their so confident rejecting of all final and intending causality in nature, and admitting of no other causes of things, as philosophical, save the material and mechanical only; this being really to banish all mental, and consequently divine causality, quite out of the world; and to make the whole world to be nothing else but a mere heap of dust, fortuitously agitated, or a dead cadaverous thing, that hath no signatures of mind and understanding, counsel and wisdom at all upon it; nor indeed any other vitality acting in it, than only the production of a certain quantity of local motion, and the conversation of it according to some general laws; which things the Democritic

[35] *Ibid.*, II, 285.
[36] "Divine Hymn on the Creation," *Miscellanies*, p. 70.
[37] *Letters Concerning the Love of God*, p. 278.
[38] *Ibid.*, p. 280.
[39] *Ibid.*, p. 305.

atheists take for granted, would be all as they are, though there were no God.[40]

Apart from his occasionalism, there is only one feature of Norris's Platonism which is not integrated into his Cartesianism; and that is is insistence on the immutability of truth and morality, independent of the will of God. On this score, Norris sides with Cudworth and More against Descartes. According to Descartes,

two and two might not have been four . . . if God had pleased so to order and decree it. A most monstrous doctrine, and I think, by far the most absurd in the notion of it, and the most dangerous and pernicious in the consequence of it, of any that can be picked out of the whole body of Cartesianism.[41]

Norris asks: "Is it not a thing astonishingly strange and surprising, that a man so mathematically disposed, and that hath made such great improvements in geometry, should advance a proposition that so directly tends to the ruin even of his own beloved and admired science?" [42] He goes on to point a moral that extends beyond the bounds of the scientific:

And yet this is not the worst of it, for it undermines also the foundations of morality and religion, as well as of natural science, and so shakes the whole frame of the intellectual world, which is a sad consideration. For if all truth be by positive order and constitution, then where are the antecedent reasons and differences of good and evil, where is the intrinsic beauty of virtue, . . . and then what excellency or advantage has the moral beyond that of the ritual or ceremonial, or any other positive law of God? . . . which immediately runs us into the very dregs of libertinism and is a very fair step towards atheism itself.[43]

This concern, which Norris shared with his Platonist predecessors, is not one which disappeared with the advent of the Enlightenment. It was modernised by Shaftesbury into the doctrine of moral sense and benevolence, and, transposed onto the aesthetic plane, became a principal ingredient of preromanticism. To associate Norris however with the origins of preromanticism would be misleading; this modernisation did not occur overnight. The evidence of Norris's work points first and foremost to the waning of Renaissance Platonism.

Norris's rejection of the "middle life" is categorical; a reflection of it can be seen in one of his poems called "Love." In the absence of Cudworth's prop, Norris feels that he can sum up the state of affairs as follows:

---

[40] Cudworth, I, 217.
[41] *Theory*, I, 339-340.
[42] *Ibid.*, I, 347.
[43] *Ibid.*

Nature's great statute law did ne'er design
That heavenly fire should kindle here below;
Let it ascend and dwell above
The proper element of Love.[44]

The bird has flown, and Cudworth's heap of dust is one step nearer. Turning his back on More's "middle life," Norris describes the coherence of things in the Enlightenment image of the watchmaker servicing his machine:

Love's the great spring of Nature's wheel,
The universe is kept in tune by Love,
Thou Nature giv'st her sympathy,
The centre has its charm from thee.[45]

The music of the spheres is being metamorphosed into the ticking of the machine. Since Norris is this close to the spirit of the Enlightenment, it becomes once more necessary to correct his image by taking stock of his controversy with Locke. This exchange throws considerable light on the stand Norris was taking against current Enlightenment philosophy.

There are at least two good reasons why Norris found himself in the position of having to object to Locke's new way of ideas. In the first place, he held that man has access to a higher order of truth than that which is susceptible to demonstration. For Norris, "demonstrative knowledge is what in the Schools is called Science," and what "I would call Reasoning"; while "intuitive knowledge" produces "principles," "demonstrative knowledge" produces "conclusions"; it follows that "intuition is clear, simple, entire." [46] In the second place, and equally contrary to the spirit of Baconian empiricism, he held that reason operated in a sphere above that of common sense. Writing "On a Musician supposed to be mad with music," he states that "his soul outflies / Not reason's bounds," but willingly allows that "Outsoars he does the sphere of common sense." [47] When Norris comes to refute Locke's theories, he does so on two principal counts.

In the first place he objects to Locke's theory of the origin of ideas:

To say with Mr Locke that we have them from our senses, gives me no satisfaction at all: for if he means that they are derived to our minds by way of a real physical emission from sensible objects: this, as I have abundantly shown, is a false account of the origin of our ideas. But if he means only that they are

---

[44] "Love," stanza 6. *Miscellanies*, p. 109.
[45] *Ibid.*, stanza 3.
[46] *An Account of Reason and Faith*, pp. 41, 46.
[47] *Miscellanies*, p. 22.

occasioned by the impressions which are made by those objects upon our organs of sense, that indeed may be ordinarily true. . . . There is nothing peculiar in this account. . . . There is nothing instructive in it. It gives no light into the main question that concerns the theory of human understanding, since, though our senses should be allowed to be the occasions of our ideas, it still remains to be inquired what those ideas are. . . . I would not be thought to slight or undervalue the performance of this ingenious author, which I allow to be very valuable and considerable in many respects, and that he has deserved well of the public for those many useful truths which he has cleared, and those many great discoveries which he has made in the intellectual way. But as to the account which he has given us of ideas (which ought to have been the great subject of his undertaking, in an Essay of Human Understanding), that, I think, is as lame and defective as anything can well be, since; in that sense, wherein it would have been to the purpose, it appears not to be true, and in that sense wherein it is true, it is not much to the purpose.[48]

In the second place he quarrels with Locke about the nature of the understanding. As early as 1684, he had written that it was "as much against the nature of the understanding to make that truth which it speculates, as 'tis against the nature of the eye to create that light by which it sees, or of an image to make that object which it represents." [49]

Twenty years later Norris indirectly accuses Locke of philosophical Pelagianism:

Notwithstanding the bold and forward offers that have been made by some men towards the setting up the creature upon a bottom of its own, I cannot but look with a very jealous eye upon all such opinions as tend to lessen that essential dependence which we have upon God; and Durandus is to me a Pelagian in metaphysics.[50]

Durandus of St Pourcain (d. 1332) had "abandoned Thomism in spite of the instruction of the General Chapter of Saragossa, which in 1309 declared it to be the official doctrine of the Dominican order," and had developed "a theory of knowing by which the soul and the intellect, far from being illuminated passively, are, on the contrary very active"; according to Durandus, "the soul's perfection is such that it need receive nothing from outside." [51] The crux of Norris's occasionalism was that, contrary to the opinions of either Durandus or Locke, "we depend as much upon God for our understanding as the greatest anti-Pelagian could suppose us to do as to our will, as being no more able to think or understand without the Divine Light, than we are to will and act what is good without

---

[48] *Theory*, II, 516-517.
[49] "A Metaphysical Essay towards the Demonstration of God," *Miscellanies*, p. 119.
[50] *Theory*, II, 557.
[51] Anne Fremantle, *The Age of Belief* (New York: New American Library, Mentor Books, 1954), pp. 199-200.

the Divine Grace." [52] Norris consequently accuses Locke and the philosophical Pelagians of trying to pull themselves up by their own shoestrings, whereas it is not in man's nature to comprehend his own understanding:

I know, or rather feel by inward sentiment that I think, and I make a shift in a rational method to find out what it is that thinks in me; but what that act of mine which I call thinking is, I want, I will not say words to express, but penetration of thought to comprehend. Sometimes my Fancy whispers me that 'tis a kind of application of the mind to its ideal or intelligible object; but then I reject that again as a figurative way of speaking. . . . Then again I say to myself, that sure 'tis an intellectual sight, a kind of vision of the mind. But here I correct myself again. . . . For either vision here is taken materially . . . and then there is nothing but a dark and confuse metaphor in the expression; or else vision is here taken formally . . . and in this sense vision is indeed the same with thought, and so can give no illustration to it. [53]

In other words, Norris defies Locke to define the Cogito. It is significant that in reply Locke challenges Norris to define the Divine Light. Each is sceptical of the other's home ground.

There may have been personal reasons for Locke's attacks on Norris and Malebranche, [54] but, whatever the pretext, the substance of his argument reflects the inevitable reaction of the Enlightenment in four respects. In the first place Locke raises the cry of "words without ideas." Anthony Collins had criticised him for paying too much attention to such "an obscure enthusiastic man"; Locke replies:

As for the rummaging over Mr Norris's late book, I will be sworn, it is not I have done that; for however I may be mistaken in what passes without me, I am infallible in what passes in my own mind; and I am sure, the ideas that are put together in your letter out of him, were never so in my thoughts, till I saw them there. What did I say, "put ideas together"? I ask your pardon, it is "put words together without ideas." . . . Men of Mr Norris's way seem to me to decree, rather than to argue. [55]

For Locke, Norris's speculations concern things outside man's mind; they are therefore words without ideas, since ideas are only valid when forged out of the infallibility of one's own mind.

In the second place Locke argues from the common sense of mankind against the extraordinary implications of Norris's occasionalism:

[52] *Theory*, II, 558.
[53] *Ibid.*, II, 109-110.
[54] See Charlotte Johnston, *Journal of the History of Ideas*, XIX (1958), 551-558.
[55] Letter to Anthony Collins, 21 March 1703-4, in Locke, *Works*, IX, 283.

A man bred up in the obscurity of a dungeon, where by a dim and almost no light, he perceives the objects about him; it is true, he owes this idea to the light of the sun; but having never heard, nor thought of the sun, can one say that the idea of the sun is his "immediate object of knowledge," or that therefore "his mind was made for the sun"? This is the case of a great part of mankind; and how many can we imagine of those, who have got some notion of God, either from tradition or reason, have any idea of him present in their minds as often as they think of anything else? [56]

Locke is saying that it simply is not true that even saints see all things in God all the time. They are not conscious of such vision, and what one is not conscious of has no certain existence.

It follows, thirdly and fourthly, that Locke resorts to the usual fideism and scepticism of the English Enlightenment. He accuses Norris of claiming that it is "impossible for the Almighty to produce anything, but by ways we must conceive, and are able to comprehend; when he that is best satisfied of his omniscient understanding, and knows so well how God perceives, cannot explain the cohesion of parts in the lowest degree of created beings, unorganised bodies." [57] Fideism is based on scepticism, and Locke includes in his remarks on Malebranche the following argument which is equally relevant to Norris:

It is not to be denied that God can enlighten our minds after a thousand different fashions; and it cannot also be denied, that these thousand different fashions may be such, as we comprehend not one of them. The question is, whether this talk of seeing all things in God does make us clearly, or at all, comprehend one of them; if it did so to me, I should gratefully acknowledge that then I was ignorant of 999 of the 1000, whereas I must yet confess myself ignorant of them all.[58]

In all these respects, Norris's philosophy is judged at the bar of the Enlightenment, and found wanting.

If Locke's refutal of Norris is decisive, it is by no means overwhelming. As we have seen, some of the Platonic and Cartesian elements in Norris's thought adumbrate the philosophy of the Enlightenment and seriously qualify his reputation as a purveyor of gibberish. The way in which Norris's Platonism prefigures the Enlightenment's sense of fulness can be perceived from the following paragraph; in this prose rhapsody Platonic ecstasy is almost ready to merge into the clockwork of the Enlightenment:

---

[56] "Remarks upon some of Mr Norris's books, wherein he asserts P. Malebranche's opinion of our seeing all things in God," *ibid.*, IX, 251.

[57] *Ibid.*, IX, 250.

[58] An Examination of P. Malebranche's Opinion of Seeing All Things in God," *ibid.*, IX, 230.

So far is the State of Nature from being (according to the elements of the Leviathan) a state of hostility and war, that there is no one thing that makes more apparently for the interest of mankind, than universal charity and benevolence. And indeed, would all men but once agree to espouse one another's interest and prosecute the public good truly and faithfully, nothing would be wanting to verify and realise the dreams of the Golden Age, to anticipate the millenial happiness, and bring down heaven upon earth. Society would stand firm and compact, like a mathematical frame of architecture, supported by mutual dependencies and coherences; and every man's kindnesses would return again upon himself, in the circle and reciprocation of love.[59]

The enthusiasm of this particular rhapsody is intriguing. It suggests a link between the literary tradition of Renaissance Utopias and the social philosophy of the Enlightenment. This rhapsody has a fresher sense of delirium about it than the similar common-sense effusions of Shaftesbury, because for Norris "society would stand," whereas for Shaftesbury it does stand. The distance between the two is not great; but whereas the age of Shaftesbury had scientific corroboration based on the nature of the universe which allowed the individual moral sense to be closely knit to the social framework, Norris speaks as in a vision, and is not yet assured that the old ruined world can be repaired by new social instincts.

Norris's contribution to idealist philosophy and to Metaphysical poetry depends on his sense of discontent, but his Platonism works towards the Enlightenment as well as against it. Thus he upheld the two Platonic conceptions of God.[60] God is not only "absolutely good and perfect in himself so as to be able to fill . . . our desires," [61] but also "the most communicative and self-diffusive of beings." [62] This Platonic theory of plenitude contributed in no small way to the Enlightenment's "chain of being" which interlocked natural and moral philosophy in one harmonious system.[63] Here

---

[59] "General Apology for the Christian Religion," *Miscellanies*, pp. 186-187.
[60] See Arthur Oncken Lovejoy, *The Great Chain of Being: A Study of the History of an Idea* (New York: Harper Torchbooks, 1960), pp. 86-88.
[61] "Contemplation and Love," *Miscellanies*, p. 251.
[62] *Ibid.*, p. 254.
[63] Cf. Henry Brooke, *Universal Beauty*, I, 217-220:
  "One is the flood which universal flows;
  And hence the reptile, hence the seraph glows:
  Still equal, though unequal, that and this;
  Since fulness bounds, and all are filled with bliss."
Chalmers, XVII, 339.
Cf. also Edward Young, *Night Thoughts*, VI:
  "Look Nature through, 'tis neat gradation all. (. . .)
  Grant the soul of man
  Eternal; or in man the series ends,
  Wide yawns the gap; connection is no more."
Chalmers, XIII, 452.

then is a measure of an obscure enthusiast's involvement in the making of the philosophy of the Enlightenment. This involvement is partial, as one would expect from a late Metaphysical poet, but the justified opposition of both Durfey and Locke does not entirely jeopardise the value of Norris's position as a transitional thinker.

CHAPTER NINE

RELIGION: THE GROUNDS OF ASSENT

Norris, like the Cambridge Platonists, was a latitudinarian. In his "Discourse concerning Heroic Piety" (1684), he writes of "those excellent degrees and eminences of religion we may fall short of without sin." [1] But Norris's religious thought is not merely transitional between the Cambridge Platonists and the Enlightenment. Although he prefigures certain elements of Enlightenment Christianity which allow scope for opposition to deism, he also consolidates several characteristics of 17th century religious experience, and transmits them to the age of 18th century religious revival.

By preserving the theological spirit of Cambridge Platonism, Norris qualifies his involvement in the development of Enlightenment natural religion. Although Christian Platonism prepared the ground for deism, Norris shares the basic assumption of More and Cudworth that true divinity had nothing to fear from truth, science or morality. And he shares their enthusiasm in proclaiming this assumption, rather than hiding it under the bushel of a luke-warm and fearful orthodoxy. Thus he is almost as adamant as Henry More in his belief that Christianity and Platonism have more in common than is generally acknowledged:

There is not one precept of Christianity so exalted and heroical but may be paralleled in a heathen. What high raised notions of virtue, what angelical precepts, what immaterial transportations are to be found in heathen writers! One would think that with St Paul they had been wrapt up into the third heaven and learnt their divinity from the immediate intuition of God. They discourse so much like seraphims and the most ecstasied order of intelligences. That wherein they were generally most defective was the notion of God. And yet even here the wiser pagans were accurate enough in their conceptions, and (except only the inconceivable mystery of the Trinity) thought as well of God as any Christian whatsoever; nay, and better than a great many of them do.[2]

[1] *Miscellanies*, p. 219.
[2] *Hierocles*, Preface.

Henry More had not even excepted the Trinity, though he might well have done had he lived as near the deist controversy as Norris.

The trend from Platonism to deism can be felt as a force which Norris is determined to resist in the following passage, where he describes the Incarnation in the language of Augustinian Platonism:

Philosophers may talk of their Verbum Mentis, the word of the mind; but there is no word of the mind that I know of, but the word of the eternal mind. For sure that word which is the wisdom of God, is fittest to be also the light of men. Even that divine word, which was incarnate, that was first with God, and afterwards with us, that became sensible, because we were not wholly intellectual, and that put on a cloud of flesh, because we could not so well endure to behold his naked glory full of grace and truth. For then it was that the great intelligible sun suffered an abatement of his splendour to accommodate his light to the infirmities of our eyes and (to allude to an expression of St Austin) became, as it were, a moon to comfort and refresh our night.[3]

The slighting reference to philosophers in the preamble to this gloss on the first chapter of St John's gospel, corresponds to his brief parenthesis on the Trinity. Neither qualification seriously detracts from Norris's confident preservation of the spirit of the Cambridge Platonists.

This spirit is perhaps nowhere so much in evidence as in the following passage, where truth, science and morality are related to divinity:

To apply one's self to the sciences, is the same as to contemplate truth, and to contemplate truth is indeed to contemplate God. Divinity then is a larger study than men are ordinarily aware of; there is something of it diffused throughout all the sciences, and a good philosopher is a natural divine as well as a lover of God; which may serve to show us, by the way, with how little true knowledge and true light (how flaming soever their zeal may be) those people would talk who should go to cry down and disparage science under the opprobrious terms of vain philosophy, and carnal reason etc. ... Nor yet are they that respect it altogether faultless, since they court it generally as a humane accomplishment, without regarding the divinity of that truth which they contemplate.[4]

The last sentence hardly modifies Norris's confidence; it constitutes a reprimand rather than a reservation. It is because Norris conceived his theology in the spirit of the Cambridge Platonists, that he both resists and contributes towards the rise of natural religion.

Norris's contribution to the trend from Platonism to deism needs to be delineated at the outset. His originality may lie elsewhere, but he was neither so original nor so eccentric as to be impervious to the prevailing religious spirit of his age. In the language of Tillotson, rather than of More,

[3] *Theory*, II, 466-467.
[4] *Ibid.*, II, 486, 488.

he wrote: "Religion is so very agreeable, both to the inclinations and discoursings of human nature, that as none is capable of being religious but a rational creature, so 'tis almost impossible for a creature to be endued with reason and not to be religious." [5] And in the spirit of Clarke and Watts, Norris made very little distinction between natural and revealed religion. Both "concentre in the happiness and welfare of mankind"; revealed religion is "a pursuance of the same excellent end, only by more close and direct means." [6] In like manner, Norris shares the Enlightenment view that the law of nature subsumes those of Moses and Christ:

The Christian law is nothing else but the law of Nature retrieved, explained, and set in a clearer light. Christ indeed, added some new precepts that were not in the law of Moses; but not any that were not in the law of Nature.[7]

In the light of these statements, Norris's defence of revelation against Toland appears to belong to the long string of half-hearted orthodox apologies for Christianity, which characterised the religious controversy of the early 18th century. But it must be remembered that Norris's "General Apology for the Christian Religion," from which these passages are extracted, was a very early work, and that the crux of Norris's religious thinking is more militantly at odds with the spirit of deism and natural religion than this essay suggests.

There is a hint of the religious spirit of an earlier age even in the precociously latitudinarian "General Apology." Side by side with the argument from the law of nature, we find the following Tertullianism: "We should discern great reason to be cautious how we set limits to the divine omnipotence; and should rather support our faith against all objections, with that universal salvo of the apostle, *I know whom I have believed.*" [8] In answer to Toland, Norris strikes an even more resounding echo of Sir Thomas Browne's "O Altitudo":

I am not against your making use of your reason. No, I would only have you reason rightly, and that you may do so, would have you by all human methods to improve and cultivate your reason as much as you can, being well persuaded that as a half-view of things makes men opinionative, disputatious and dogmatical, so a clear and thorough light makes them humble and distrustful of themselves, and that the more cultivated and improved any man's natural reason is, the easier it will be for him to captivate it to the obedience of faith.[9]

---

[5] "General Apology for the Christian Religion," *Miscellanies*, p. 176.
[6] *Ibid.*, p. 177.
[7] *Ibid.*, p. 182.
[8] *Ibid.*
[9] *An Account of Reason and Faith*, "Address to the Socinians," p. 337.

It is a rare phenomenon to find such a late example of this old 17th century voice, sweetened, measured and gentle, parleying with the spokesman of a new century.

The survival of this note is all the more remarkable, when one considers what Tillotson and Shaftesbury thought of Sir Thomas Browne's Tertullianism. Tillotson, with smooth reasonableness, reversed Browne's profession of faith:

I know not what some men may find in themselves; but I must freely acknowledge, that I could never yet attain to that bold and hardy degree of faith, as to believe anything for this reason – because it was impossible; for this would be to believe a thing to be, because I am sure it cannot be. So that I am very far from being of his mind, that wanted not only more difficulties, but even impossibilities, in the Christian religion, to exercise his faith upon.[10]

Shaftesbury asked in the playful spirit of polite banter: "But if a reverend Christian prelate may be so great a volunteer in faith, as beyond the ordinary prescription of the catholic church to believe in fairies, why may not a heathen poet, in the ordinary way of his religion, be allowed to believe in muses?" [11] The effectiveness of Norris's answer to Toland lies in his access to the insights of a previous age. Far from sharing the conceptions of Tillotson and Shaftesbury at this crucial level of Christian apology, Norris creates a tone which is utterly incommensurate with the prevailing trend towards natural religion.

Norris even has access to the medieval De Contemptu Mundi tradition, unsullied by the shades of the 18th century graveyard school. The following passage, nearer in spirit to Donne and Drummond of Hawthornden than to Gray and Dr Johnson, corroborates that aspect of Norris's religious thought which has its roots in the early 17th century:

Indeed, could a man's life be so contrived, that he should have a new pleasure still ready at hand as soon as he was grown weary of the old, and every day enjoy a virgin delight, he might then perhaps, like Mr Hobbes his notion, and for a while think himself happy in this continued succession of new acquisitions. But alas, Nature does not treat us with this variety. The compass of our enjoyments is much shorter than that of our lives; and there is a periodical circulation of our pleasures, as well as of our blood. . . . The enjoyments of our lives run in a perpetual round, like the months in the calendar, but with a quicker revolution, we dance like fairies in a circle, and our whole life is but a nauseous tautology.[12]

[10] John Tillotson, *Works*, ed. Thomas Birch (10 vols.; London: Richard Priestley, 1820), VIII, 327. Quoted in Louis G. Locke, *Tillotson: A Study in 17th Century Literature* ("Anglistica," No. 4; Copenhagen: Rosenkilde and Bagger, 1954), p. 105.

[11] Anthony Ashley Cooper, 3rd Earl of Shaftesbury, *Characteristics of Men, Manners, Opinions, Times*, ed. John M. Robertson (2 vols.; Indianapolis and New York: Bobbs-Merrill, 1964), I, 7.

[12] "An Idea of Happiness," *Miscellanies*, p. 324.

Once again then, Norris makes his bid to be considered as an interesting relic, the last specimen of a spent tradition, whether it be 17th century religious thought, or Metaphysical poetry, or Renaissance Platonism. To do Norris justice however, one has to take into account his involvement in the Enlightenment. Norris tried to defend his expression of an earlier age's religious experience in reasoned discourse as well as in lyrical description. This defence provides a valuable link between the age of Donne and the age of Watts.

The early 17th century was prepared to defend faith with the tools of human reason. Logic and rational discourse constituted an elaborate yet valid path towards truth. Thus Donne rated "those artificial lights, which ourselves make for our use and service here, as fires, tapers and such" above the mere light of nature, as instruments to discover truth; in his view,

though the light of these fires and tapers be not so natural as the moon, yet because they are more domestic, and obedient to us, we distinguish particular objects better by them than by the moon. So by the arguments, and deductions, and conclusions, which ourselves beget and produce, as being more serviceable and under us, because they are our creatures, particular cases are made more clear and evident to us; for these we can behold withal, and put them to any office, and examine, and prove their truth, or likelihood, and make them answer as long as we will ask; whereas the light of nature, with a solemn and supercilious majesty, will speak but once, and give no reason, nor endure examination.[13]

The Enlightenment on the other hand, with its preference for the axiom over the syllogism, rated the light of nature far above the artificial lights of reason. Thus Addison, Pope, Berkeley and Watts, welcomed the self-evidence that had no need to speak more than once, and eschewed that minute philosophy which relied on arguments, deductions and conclusions.

The earlier trust in the powers of human reason died hard however. Both Watts and Berkeley preached and practised a modicum of carefully constructed rational discourse, though they tended not to rely on it when the light of nature was available, or the essentials of religion at stake. Norris, whose faith in the validity of rational discourse was considerably greater than that of Watts or Berkeley, tends nevertheless to relax at times, and noticeably when under pressure from Toland. One passage of his reply to Toland can be identified as half way between Donne and Watts, in its combination of esteem for, and weariness with the demonstrative powers of human reason. He writes:

[13] John Donne, *Biathanatos*, Nonesuch Donne, p. 426.

We must assist our feeble eye by the advantage of a glass; now reason is this glass, naturally indeed a very good prospective, but which logic and especially algebra has improved into a telescope. But yet still it is but an artificial way of seeing, and all art supposes and argues defect in nature. And though it be a great help, yet we know 'tis no very great commendation to a man's eye-sight to see with spectacles. . . . And why then are we proud? . . . Our natural reason is a mark of our limitation as creatures – our reason not so much enlightening as betraying the darkness of our understandings. Some few things we know as angels do by intuition (or else we could not so much as reason like men), but still the main fund of our knowledge lies in the rational and demonstrative kind, and we are fain to use clues and chains to conduct our thoughts through the infinite mazes and labyrinths of truth, and proceed in a train from one thing to another, to walk step by step and feel our way with wariness and caution, like men that go in the dark.[14]

Here we see the Enlightenment in the making, as it tones down the extravagant claims for reason made by the earlier 17th century, and substitutes its own improved telescope in place of the anachronistic magnifying glass. But here at least Norris maintains a sense of the inadequacy of either to establish truth or the grounds of assent. He answers Toland with a combination of Enlightenment reserve and an early 17th century sense of the intricacy and labyrinthine darkness of things.

In some respects however, Norris's grammar of assent is barely distinguishable from that of the Enlightenment. His defence of religious experience on sensory and moral grounds is close to certain arguments used by the orthodox in the deist controversy. In the first place Norris accuses the deists of ignoring the testimony of sense, and claims that his own idealist philosophy does not preclude this support of the Christian faith:

Not that I would be thought hereby to insinuate any sceptical suspicion or disparagement of the testimony of sense. For though I cannot magnify it as some do, nor am so much an Epicurean as to make sense the foundation and measure of all certainty, . . . so neither am I so much a sceptic, nor yet so much an academic, as to reject absolutely the reports of sense as false, or at least uncertain. I might add, nor yet so much a friend to deism.[15]

This is of course a parenthetical disclaimer, not a main argument in the course of Norris's treatise. But central to Norris's argument is his distinction between metaphysical and moral certainty, as expressed in his view that "the certainty we now have . . . is not metaphysical . . . but . . . moral," and "such as has force enough to persuade though not enough to extort the assent." [16] On this point he is insistent:

[14] *An Account of Reason and Faith*, pp. 49-50.
[15] *Theory*, I, 186-187.

'Tis most clear that the certainty of faith can be but moral, and consequently not equal to that of science. . . . It must be said, and I hope may without any offence to such as have the light of knowledge with the heat of zeal, that faith in its present ordinary state has but a moral certainty. Which is indeed sufficient for all the purposes of Christian life, to persuade a man to renounce the present world for the glories of the next, and to make it such a faith as shall work by love. And they do no real service to the interest of religion, but rather expose it to the ridicule of the more philosophic libertines, who go to strain the matter any higher.[17]

Norris's argument here is similar to that of More's. It is not only that metaphysical certainty is impossible; it is also undesirable, for it leaves room for neither More's free spirit, nor Norris's work of love. This aspect of Norris's argument, which differentiates him from the Enlightenment proper, is also present in his preference for the term "moral certainty" rather than "probability." The latter was to be exhaustively employed by Bishop Butler. A generation earlier, Norris rejects the "diminutive term of probability, which carries not a very good signification, and by those who are not the best friends to revealed religion may be abused to a worse"; moral certainty is a "safer and more theological term." [18] These reservations illustrate Norris's position in, but not quite of, the line of those who formed the Enlightenment tradition of Christian apologetics.

Further evidence that Norris could at times stand as an exponent of Enlightenment religious thought, is to be found in his treatment of the utilitarian motive in the theory and practice of Christianity, and in his modernist attitude towards sin and evil. We have seen that from his Platonism he developed the concepts of moral sense and benevolence; these same concepts are used to describe the essential nature of religious activity. According to Norris, "the naked efficacy of self-love" is "sufficient to engage us upon religious performances," and the "principle of generosity" is sufficient "to carry us on to the higher advances, the more glorious achievements in religion." [19] This is near enough to the views of Shaftesbury, Pope and Bolingbroke, as to be indistinguishable from them. The trend from religion to moralism, which Lichtenstein traces in Henry More and the Cambridge Platonists, is here apparently accomplished. Christianity is commended as a system of utilitarian ethics; in Norris's own words, "Christian law . . . consists only of such practical maxims, which carry a natural relation to the true interest and well-being of mankind." [20]

[16] *Ibid.*, I, 219-220.
[17] *Ibid.*, I, 221.
[18] *Ibid.*, I, 222.
[19] "Discourse Concerning Heroic Piety," *Miscellanies*, p. 216.
[20] "General Apology for the Christian Religion," *ibid.*, pp. 184-185.

Norris's attitude to sin and evil is undoubtedly typical of the Enlightenment. Although he can write, "I not only freely acknowledge but contend that sin is a real entity," and although he holds that sin is "positive" and not simply "privative," he can come out on the same page as more Leibnizian than Leibniz, with "It is no absurdity to say that moral evil should be metaphysically good." [21] Norris in fact depersonalises sin and evil, and treats them as social phenomena. Of the three suggested deterrents to committing evil – the moral deterrent of internal dissatisfaction with the act, the religious deterrent of rewards and punishments in another life, and the social deterrent – Norris prefers the third; at any rate he makes it the most eloquent. Arguing that if one man sins, then all men have the right to sin, he points out that "the evil would come about again, even to him whom we just now supposed a gainer by his theft," and concludes, with a touch of bourgeois indignation: "As to the public, 'twould be all one as if there were no property." [22] Norris is not belittling sin; in one place he goes so far as to describe it as monstrous: "For however the magic of self-love may reconcile men to their own faults, yet if we set the object at a more convenient distance from the eye, and consider the nature of sin irrespectively to ourselves, 'twill certainly appear to be the most deformed monstrous thing that can either be found or conceived in nature." [23] His conclusion however is neither theological nor spiritual, but resoundingly social. The magic of self-love, i.e. sin, "justles the great wheel of society out of its proper track." [24] This is hardly the traditional Christian sense of sin. It reflects rather the Cartesian theory of monsters in nature. It is significant that Norris uses the wheel image when referring to this theory:

There was no monster to be seen at the opening of this first scene of Nature. But now in the administration of the world, God proceeds by general and stated laws of motion, and those exceeding few and simple, which is the occasion of those little aberrations which sometimes happen in the course of generation, when the wheel of Nature gives us a jog by stepping a little out of the tract, and since we will not admire the regularity of her ordinary procedure, tries to amuse and stir up our wonder by irregular births.[25]

Norris is not of course saying that sin is an occasional aberration designed to amuse us, but there is a clear analogy between monsters in the natural world and sin in the social world; neither does more than jog or jostle us as we pursue our sure and settled course. Norris even conceives that one might be able to eliminate or dispense with sin:

[21] "Considerations upon the Nature of Sin," *ibid.*, p. 303.
[22] "General Apology for the Christian Religion," *ibid.*, p. 193.
[23] "Considerations upon the Nature of Sin," *ibid.*, pp. 304-305.
[24] *Ibid.*
[25] *Theory*, I, 290-291.

He who thoroughly understands and actually attends to the nature of sin cannot possibly commit it. . . . There is a false proposition of the understanding before any misapplication of the will.[26]

Clearly there is a complete absence of any Pauline conception of sin and evil in the work of Norris.

It would not however be quite fair to Norris to imply that his belief in the elimination of sin marks him as a Pelagian on the verge of deism. After all, John Wesley stamped his brand of Arminian Evangelicalism with the doctrine of perfect love, whereby his followers who attained "those excellent degrees and eminences of religion" were counted and declared sanctified. There is evidence that Norris's belief in the eradication of sin partakes of the spirit spread by Wesley, as much as of the latitudinarianism which merged into the Enlightenment. Evangelicalism emerged out of pietism, and Norris made some contribution to the development of pietism and the religion of the heart. Thus he commends the story of the heathen philosopher, "who was baffled into Christianity by the mere warmth and heartiness wherewith the good old man addressed him." According to Norris, the philosopher was equipped to resist the arguments of the missionary, "but not the spirit and zeal wherewith he spake." [27] Norris's many discourses on practical religion have a strong tang of pietism about them. In them Norris turns his back on his elaborate epistemological foundation work, and implies that religious activity depends on something more simple than a theory of the ideal world. He strikes the tone of pietism in the following passage, where religious life is distinguished from theological wrangle:

Nor would I have you bestow much time in reading books of controversy, and disputes about religion. 'Tis a thing of great labour, and but little profit, there being not so much truth gained by it as will compensate for the loss of charity. For that which the world is pleased to call controversy, is generally little else than a litigious wrangle, proceeding upon darkness and obscurity, fallacies and equivocations, double acceptation of words and confusion of ideas; from men's mistaking and misstating the thing in question: from misunderstanding of the point, of themselves, and of one another. And while men do so, they may dispute for ever, without knowing when they agree, or when they differ. Leave then these wranglers to enjoy the dust which they raise, and while they dispute, do you learn to live.[28]

Norris goes as far as evolving a philosophical infrastructure for pietism, out of the spirit of Cambridge Platonism. Thus he commends a hypothesis,

---

[26] "Considerations upon the Nature of Sin," *Miscellanies*, p. 307.
[27] *Reflections upon the Conduct of Human Life*, p. 213.
[28] *Spiritual Counsel*, p. 114.

which "does not send us one way for the furniture of our knowledge, and another way for the cause of our sentiments, but he that causes the one, is here supposed to be the object of the other, and so all competitions are removed, and God is entirely placed upon the throne of the heart." [29] Norris may elsewhere have couched his hypothesis in the "darkness and obscurity" of "fallacies and equivocations," but its aim, as stated here, is similar to that of Schleiermacher, who, at the end of the Enlightenment, attempted to provide a philosophical basis for pietism and Evangelicalism.

The various aspects of Norris's religious thought, which we have distinguished and delineated, may appear inconsistent and contradictory. But seen in the light of Norris's prevailing spirit and the exigencies of his age, they have a certain coherence. This coherence is nowhere better expressed than in his early essay, "An Idea of Happiness," where he writes:

'Tis not all the sophistry of the cold logicians, that shall work me out of the belief of what I feel and know, and rob me of the sweetest entertainment of my life, the passionate love of God. Whatever some men pretend, who are strangers to all the affectionate heats of religion, and therefore make their philosophy a plea for their indevotion, and extinguish all holy ardours with a syllogism; yet I am firmly persuaded, that our love of God may be not only passionate, but even wonderfully so, and exceeding the love of women. 'Tis an experimental, and therefore undeniable truth, that passion is a great instrument of devotion. . . . But then as to the objection, I answer with the excellent Descartes, that although in God, who is the object or our love, we can imagine nothing, yet we can imagine that our love, which consists in this, that we would unite ourselves to the object beloved, and consider ourselves as it were a part of it. And the sole idea of this very conjunction, is enough to stir up a heat about the heart, and so kindle a very vehement passion. To which I add, that although the beauty or amiableness of God, be not the same with that which we see in corporeal beings, and consequently, cannot directly fall within the sphere of the imagination, yet it is something analogous to it; and that very analogy is enough to excite a passion.[30]

Here if anywhere there is patent corroboration of the view that Norris is not merely transitional between the Cambridge Platonists and the Enlightenment, and also justification of the analogy between his religious spirit and his Metaphysical poetry. Both his religion and his poetry belong to the tradition of the Caroline divines and lyricists. But Norris appears so late in time that his religious spirit seems to be transmitting these Caroline insights forward into the age of pietism and Evangelicalism. If the echo and the intimation constitute two strands in Norris's religious thought, they are defined and regulated by the pressures of a third; for his commendation

[29] *Theory*, II, 560.
[30] "An Idea of Happiness," *Miscellanies*, pp. 338-339.

of experimental religion is not untinged with the prudent spirit of Enlightenment orthodoxy. Norris thus not only points back to Herbert and forward to Wesley, but also qualifies the sweetness of his spirit with the cold touch of Butler's argument from analogy and probability. In registering simultaneously these three strands of the religious spirit, Norris pinpoints the metamorphosis from Renaissance to modern in a unique if eclectic way.

CHAPTER TEN

POETRY: THE LAST OF THE METAPHYSICALS

Norris wrote practically no poetry after 1687. Perhaps like Coleridge he found good poetry and good philosophy incompatible, but no more than Coleridge did he pursue poetry as a side-track while maintaining his main interest elsewhere. It may be that Norris's poetry would be less easily identifiable with the Metaphysical tradition had he gone on writing verse after 1687, but as it is, even as the last of the Metaphysicals, Norris reveals an involvement in the forces and forms of poetry which succeeded the Metaphysical tradition. This is inevitable given the date of Norris's poetry; what is remarkable is that Norris's poems are so strongly and homogeneously marked by the Metaphysical tradition.

Geoffrey Walton has suggested that, after the death of Cleveland, "a taste for specifically Metaphysical poetry survived especially among the elderly and isolated." [1] He also comments on the similarities between Cleveland's posthumous *Vindiciae* (1677) and the 1687 preface to Norris's *Miscellanies,* and finds in Norris's early work evidence of a continued admiration for Cleveland "sixteen years after Dryden's strictures on 'Clevelandisms'." [2] It is true that in *A Murnivall of Knaves* (1683), Norris remarks that the Whigs needed "the pen of a Cleveland, though never so sarcastic, to reduce them to obedience." [3] Norris seems to have Cleveland's satiric vehemence in mind here, but this could hardly be separated from the Metaphysical dress in which he served up his saeva indignatio. Cleveland was the champion of those who "felt themselves threatened by the new dictators of letters," [4] and it is no coincidence that Norris was among those who contracted out of Dryden's cultural settlement.

---

[1] G. Walton, p. 59.
[2] *Ibid.*, pp. 59, 141.
[3] John Norris, *A Murnivall of Knaves: or Whiggism Plainly Displayed and (if not grown shameless) Burlesqued out of Countenance* (London: James Norris, 1683), Dedication. Quoted in G. Walton, p. 141.
[4] G. Walton, p. 59.

There were others who contracted out, but on the whole they preserved the preciosity rather than the strength of Cleveland. And their preciosity was faintly quaint rather than fully baroque. Thus one of Norris's contemporaries, Thomas Heyrick (1649-1694), preserved an echo of the Metaphysical tradition, in his use of the figure of the microcosm. In a volume published in 1691, he wrote:

> Man is a little world ('tis said)
> And I in miniature am drawn,
> A perfect creature, but in short-hand shown.[5]

In the poems of a bluestocking of Norris's generation, there is evidence that the line of wit has not yet run out, though it verges on the whimsical and the sentimental. Thus Ephelia, in a volume published in 1682, could write, "We'll mix our souls, you shall be me, I you," and produce the following contribution to the cult of Platonic love, with its distinct if muted echo of Donne's "Extasie":

> We will forget the difference of sex
> Nor shall the world's rude censure us perplex.
> Think me all man: my soul is masculine,
> And capable of as great things as thine.[6]

If the age of Norris could still take the microcosm and the ecstasy seriously, it could also write funeral elegies in the Metaphysical tradition. The following couplets by Thomas Fletcher (1667-1713), could perhaps have been written by Lady Winchilsea, but they are certainly nearer to Marvell than to Pope:

> O happy, happy state! Why do I stay?
> Move faster, Time, how slowly dost thou fly,
> As if the weight of years had crippled thee!
> Thou, Death's procurer, quickly bring me safe
> Into the cold embraces of the grave;
> There shall I blest, at least shall quiet lie
> Till the angelic summons from on high
> Call me to bliss and real life away.[7]

---

[5] Thomas Heyrick, "On an Indian Tomineios, the Least of Birds," *Miscellany Poems* (1691). Printed in *Rare Poems*, ed. Marshall, p. 111.

[6] "To Phylocles, inviting him to friendship," in Ephelia, *Female Poems on Several Occasions, with large additions* (1682). Printed in *ibid.*, p. 60.

[7] Thomas Fletcher, "The Impatient," *Poems on Several Occasions, and Translations* (1692). Printed in *ibid.*, p. 97.

This passage reflects the evaporation of the Metaphysical tradition; the well-worn correspondence between sex and death is fairly well managed, and enlivens an otherwise insipid rhapsody. In Heyrick, Ephelia and Fletcher, the survival of a Metaphysical tradition after the death of Cleveland can be identified as a rarity. Only in Norris is its presence strong enough and homogeneous enough to resist the refining pressures of the age. The Metaphysical tradition survived on into the work of Watts, but, the phenomenon of Edward Taylor in America set aside, only Norris can be called the last of the Metaphysicals.

One of the reasons why Norris is able to inject new life into the Metaphysical tradition, and avoid anachronistic echoes, lies in his modernism. He was his own best refiner, and he did not refine his material out of all recognition. Rather than wane into incoherence, he took the Metaphysical tradition by the horns, dismissing what he considered out of date, and using what he could. The earlier Metaphysicals had dug for their conceits in the deepest mines of poetic fancy. Norris's Platonism discuraged him from such research. He turned his back on hidden knowledge, hidden definitions, hidden resemblances, hidden conceits, asking "Why then shall I with sweat and pain / Dig mines of disputable ore?" [8] And yet the ore is disputable and the temptation remains, in spite of his philosophically based resolution. Equally, in what must be a direct allusion to the aims and methods of the earlier Metaphysicals, his promise that he will "never try to catch the falling star," [9] does not mean that he has eradicated Metaphysical wit from his poetry. His Platonic rhapsodies do of course illustrate his intention to "view the bright appearance from afar," [10] but Metaphysical conceits abound none the less in his poems. He refines without extinguishing.

Because it modernises rather than rejects, Norris's poetry can span the vast gap between the techniques of the age of Donne and those of the age of Pope. Thus for example, he manages to preserve a good deal of the Metaphysicals' taste for paradox and mystery that is resolved by a trick of witty logic:

> 'Tis the grave doctrine of the Schools
> That contraries can never be
> Consistent in the high'st degree.
> But thou must stand exempt from their dull narrow rules.

[8] "The Discouragement," *Miscellanies*, p. 40. The same image occurs with similar implications in "To Himself" and "Satiety," *ibid.*, p. 28 and p. 58.
[9] "The Infidel," *ibid.*, p. 21. Cf. Donne's "Go and catch a falling star."
[10] *Ibid.*

> And yet 'tis said the brightest mind
> Is that which is by thee refined.
> See here a greater mystery,
> Thou makest us wise, yet ruin'st our philosophy.[11]

In this address to Melancholy, Norris smooths out the tone of Donne, while preserving the maximum of Metaphysical spirit and technique. Nothing, on the face of it, could be more alien to the age of Pope. And yet the 18th century did not exclude paradox as such, and in another poem, Norris gives us a sample of that sober verbal juxtaposition of opposites which constitutes the neoclassical conception of paradox as a literary figure:

> Alas, I'm over pleased, what shall I do
> The painful joy to undergo? [12]

Many of Charles Wesley's best hymns exploit this figure. By using his Platonism to polish the argumentative paradoxes of the Metaphysicals into an 18th century verbal trick, Norris comes near to achieving the couplet economy of Pope. At times indeed Norris is as Augustan in his construction and cadence as Lady Winchilsea. Consider for example:

> Tortured or tickled unto death
> As sprights and angels alike fright
> With too much horror or with too much light.[13]

or:

> Though often balked he hopes for rest,
> Sleeps on and dreams and is in error blest.[14]

It may be unwise to claim from these few examples that Norris is as striking an illustration as Lady Winchilsea of the combination of continuity and metamorphosis in the switch from Metaphysical to Augustan poetic modes, but to the extent that these extracts are incorporated into poems that are above average in unity and quality, one has to acknowledge Norris as an important participant in the line of wit which Dr Leavis has described as the significant link between Donne and Pope.

The central aspect of Norris's poetry remains its resistance to refinement. Elements of Metaphysical wit weigh heavily and consistently on the

---

[11] "To Melancholy," *ibid.*, p. 105.
[12] "The Infirmity," *ibid.*, p. 80.
[13] *Ibid.*
[14] "Against Knowledge," *ibid.*, p. 64.

best of his poems. At times they may sit uneasily on his predominantly Platonic themes, quaint lumps of dross, but more often than not, they are well worth their carriage, and integrated into the logic and life of the poems. In so far as this is the case, Norris is nearer to Marvell than to Cowley, and renews rather than diminishes the stock of the Metaphysicals. In his imagery, Norris shows some of the range and sparkle of the earlier exponents of wit. It can be homely and domestic, as when he addresses Fortune as "Thou midwife to abortive bliss," [15] or, describing the creation, writes: "First matter came undressed, she made much haste to obey." [16] These conceits are far from indigestible, but would be condemned as barbaric by the poets of the 18th century. Norris injected a gentle smoothness into the Metaphysical lyric, whereby the conceit is assimilated into the easy expressionist lilt. Thus:

> How soft and easy my new birth will be
> Helped on by Music's gentle midwifery.[17]

But in 18th century eyes, no amount of smoothness could excuse such outlandish imagery. Norris's wit could range from the domestic to the ecclesiastical. In true 17th century style, before the age of deism and occasional conformity, Norris could write the following verses:

> Some lesser Synods of the wise
> The Muses kept in Universities,
> But never yet till in thy soul
> Had they a Council Oecumenical.[18]

> Now give me leave to turn Apostate too
> Since you do from yourself depart.
> Thus the Reformed are counted free
> From Schism though they desert the Roman See.[19]

These figures in the service of panegyric and persuasion would indeed appear anachronistic in the poems of most of Norris's contemporaries; it is to Norris's credit as a poet that he has been able to use them in a living tradition.

Apart from his use of domestic and ecclesiastical allusions, Norris shared the earlier Metaphysicals' taste for conceits drawn from geography and geometry. Some vestiges of the previous age's excitement about the poetic

---

[15] "The Infidel," *ibid.*, p. 21.
[16] "A Divine Hymn on the Creation," *ibid.*, p. 70.
[17] "A Wish," *ibid.*, p. 72.
[18] "To Dr More, An Ode," *ibid.*, p. 73.

potential of circles, globes and circumferences, survive in Norris. He writes
as follows about Fame:

> Let her loud trumpet sound me far and near,
> The Antipodes will never of me hear.
> Or were I known throughout this ball,
> I've but a point, when I have all.[20]

And a compass conceit fits snugly into one of his best Platonic rhapsodies:

> How cold this clime! and yet my sense
> Perceives even here thy influence.
> Even here thy strong magnetic charms I feel,
> And pant and tremble like the amorous steel.
>
> To lower good, and beauties less divine
> Sometimes my erroneous needle does decline,
> But yet (so strong the sympathy)
> It turns, and points again to thee.[21]

Equally typical of the earlier Metaphysicals, is Norris's exploitation of the
prelapsarian theme in the meditative lyric. In one place Norris uses a
prelapsarian conceit to give a witty turn to his panegyric:

> Strange restless curiosity,
> Adam himself came short of thee,
> He tasted of the fruit, thou bear'st away the tree.[22]

In another place he draws on the prelapsarian theme to point his dispraise
of those who neglect natural science:

> What strange perversity is this of man!
> When 'twas a crime to taste the enlightening tree
> He could not then his hand refrain,
> None then so inquisitive, so curious as he.
> But now he has liberty to try and know
> God's whole plantation below,
> Now the angelic fruit may be
> Tasted by all whose arms can reach the tree:
> He is now by licence careless made,
> The tree neglects to climb, and sleeps beneath the shade.[23]

[19] "The Defence," *ibid.*, p. 96.
[20] "The Indifferency," *ibid.*, p. 78.
[21] "The Aspiration," *ibid.*, p. 95.
[22] "To Dr More, An Ode," *ibid.*, p. 73.
[23] "To Dr Plot, On his Natural History of Staffordshire," *ibid.*, p. 101.

Marvell, who had already platonised the Metaphysical tradition, had written in similar vein, and Norris is one of the last in a long line to cultivate this particular garden.

Norris's affinities with Donne, Herbert, Marvell and Vaughan are to be found as much in the informal tone of his poetry as in his use of Metaphysical wit. The Metaphysicals were masters of the colloquial and the casual. The tone of their poems implied that the reader, like the poet, could find a place in the life of the poem, whereas neoclassical formality placed the reader in the position of detached observer. A Metaphysical poem invites the reader to participate in its process, because there is a space, whether of dialogue, questioning or relationship, between the poet and his poem. In 1686 Edward Taylor began a poem with the line, "Look till thy looks look wan, my soul." [24] The twice-repeated "look," with its three-fold syntactical variation, would have offended neoclassical taste; moreover a neoclassical poet would never have started a poem with so much space between subject and object, between the protagonist and his alter ego. This combination of familiarity and direct address must have struck the 18th century as barbaric, if not schizophrenic. Norris is perhaps the only poet, apart from Edward Taylor, to have so consistently employed this tone so late in the 17th century. Like the earlier Metaphysicals, he uses the casual opening to thrust the reader in medias res, as in "Well, Fortune, do what thou wilt," [25] and "Well, 'twas a hard decree of Fate." [26] His intrusion into the life of his poems gives the reader the impression of over-hearing him, rather than being addressed in a formal manner. Thus Norris writes "Credulous and silly I," [27] or "But now the better part of me is gone," [28] and the reader feels he is catching the poet unawares. At other times the violence of direct address within the dialogue of the poem, pulls the reader in to participate, as in "Not yet convinced?," [29] "No, you misconstrue my design," [30] "Call me not Stoic," [31] and "Some courteous ghost, tell this great secrecy." [32] It is instructive to compare the last phrase, with direct addresses to spirits made by other poets. Edward Taylor, for example, retains the Metaphysical familiarity, when he writes in 1707,

[24] Edward Taylor, *Sacramental Meditations*, I, 19, in *Poems*, ed. Donald E. Stanford (2nd ed. abridged; New Haven and London: Yale University Press, 1963), p. 32.
[25] "The Defiance," *Miscellanies*, p. 88.
[26] "The Refinement," *ibid.*, p. 104.
[27] "Seraphic Love," *ibid.*, p. 18.
[28] "The Parting," *ibid.*, p. 15.
[29] "To Himself," *ibid.*, p. 28.
[30] "The Discouragement," *ibid.*, p. 40.
[31] "The Indifferency," *ibid.*, p. 78.
[32] "The Meditation," *ibid.*, p. 25.

"Will ye be neighbourly, ye angels bright?." [33] The atrabilious Blair on the other hand, although plagiarising Norris's phrase, managed to replace Norris's quaint intimacy with a pseudo-Shakespearian exclamatory rhetoric: "Oh! that some courteous ghost would blab it out; / What 'tis you are, and we must shortly be." [34] Norris's sweet insinuation has become a theatrical pose. Norris does not often sustain a Metaphysical tone throughout a whole poem, but it is a measure of his resilience to the refining pressures of his age, that he so often engages a dialogue, and entices the reader to share his lyrical spirit.

Where Norris falls short of the earlier Metaphysicals, is in his inability to sustain an argumentative lyric. He rarely rises above the semblance of an argument, and is thus deficient in that tough reasonableness which informs the lyric grace of Herbert and Marvell. When he does fuse reason and imagination, it is only for a moment, and the poem rapidly disintegrates into an average or mediocre effusion. "The Conquest," for example, opens with a quaint resilience reminiscent of Herbert:

> But yet I will not be excelled thought I
> In love, in love, I'll with my maker vie.[35]

Like Herbert, and unlike Donne, Norris does not describe a struggle the issue of which is in doubt, and any conflict within the poem is emblematic, the battle having been won before the poet puts pen to paper. Even so, the reader expects the poet to go through the motions of an argument. The musing candour and insistent tone promise at least the show of a struggle. Unfortunately the poem's promise evaporates fairly rapidly into the language of Platonic rhapsody, and the resolution, though based on the logic of Metaphysical wit, is far too explicit and hollow to do justice to the poem's beginning:

> Thus in this strife's a double weakness shown,
> Thy love I cannot equal, nor yet bear my own.[36]

This predetermined Q.E.D. is superimposed, and does not arise out of what has gone before. Poet and reader are cut adrift from the life of the poem.

There are many other ways in which Norris's poems display the evaporation of the Metaphysical tradition. Few of them are exclusively lyrical, and the other genres in which he wrote show even more clearly how the

---

[33] Taylor, *Sacramental Meditations*, II, 76, in *Poems*, ed. Stanford, p. 210.
[34] Robert Blair, *The Grave* (1743), Chalmers, XV, 66.
[35] "The Conquest," *Miscellanies*, p. 61.
[36] *Ibid.*

Metaphysical idiom broke up under the pressures of neoclassicism. His Pastorals, Pindarics and Panegyrics are on the whole long and bad. Devoid of lyricism, they tend towards the neoclassical, with a touch of incongruously decadent baroque about them. The following sample perhaps illustrates why Norris stopped writing verse while still in his thirties. A deus ex machina, redolent of the Enlightenment, is lowered to comfort the sorrow of the Virgin Mary:

> A large prospective wrought by hands divine
> He set before her first enlightened eye.
> 'Twas hewn out of the heaven crystalline,
> One of whose ends did lessen, th'other magnify.
>
> With that his sufferings be exposed to sight,
> With this his glories he did represent.
> The weight of this made th'other seem but light,
> She saw the mighty odds, adored and was content.[37]

Here one feels that Norris is registering the awkwardness of transition between a poet in the mould of Crashaw and a poet of the age of Thomson. Were a poet, basking in the benevolent complacency of the Newtonian universe, to try his hand in the manner of Crashaw, this outlandishly mechanical ease would have been the result.

The larger part of Norris's poetic work consists neither of lyrics proper, nor of Pastorals, Pindarics and Panegyrics, but of Platonic rhapsodies. These vary in quality from the repetitively mediocre to the slightly above average, and their content is not without philosophical interest. They certainly represent the principal way in which Norris registers the waning of the Metaphysical tradition. Two of these are of particular interest as being the only poems Norris published after 1687. They are incorporated into the text of his *Theory,* and may well therefore have been written as late as the early years of the 18th century. They are of critical interest in that they throw light on the development of the hymn out of the late Metaphysical lyric. The first stanza of the first poem points to the love-lyric as a source of the hymn:

> Lay down proud heart they rebel arms,
> And own thy conqueror divine,
> In vain thou dost resist such charms,
> In vain the arrows of his love decline.[38]

[37] "The Passion of the Virgin Mother, beholding the Crucifixion of her Divine Son," *ibid.,* p. 75.
[38] *Theory,* I, 175.

The diction and syntax are remarkably pure and simple to have been written by a late Metaphysical. They suggest that Norris is learning to abandon the cul-de-sac of his earlier Platonic rhapsodies, and is moving in the direction taken at exactly this time by Isaac Watts, who published his *Horae Lyricae* in 1706, and his *Hymns and Spiritual Songs* in 1707. The conclusion to this poem is even more hymn-like:

> Sun of my soul, what shall I do
> Thy beauties to resist, or bear?
> They bless, and yet they pain me too,
> I feel thy heat too strong, thy light too clear.
>
> I faint, I languish, I almost expire,
> My panting heart dissolving lies,
> Thou must shine less, or I retire,
> Shade thou thy light, I cannot turn my eyes.[39]

Such use of antithesis and paradox, and such willingness to skirt the edges of bathos, constitute not merely a refinement of the techniques of the Metaphysical religious lyric, but also a contribution to the development of the neoclassical hymn. Norris joins the wide extremes of Crashaw and Wesley.

Corroboration of this slender continuity between the late Metaphysical lyric and the early neoclassical hymn can be found in two anthologies of divine poems which appeared in 1709 and 1735. The first contains several of Norris's poems and, in a "Hymn on the Sacrament by an Unknown Hand," the following eloquent lines:

> No, let 'em parcel out the earth
> While heaven and thou art mine.[40]

This morsel of hymn is a perfectly balanced combination of personal and public modes of expression, at once Metaphysical and Augustan. It demonstrates how the private passion of the 17th century lyric could be modified and sunk to meet the needs of 18th century congregational enthusiasm. The 1735 anthology contains contributions by Mr Westley (sic), as well as by Norris and others. The preface contains this brief and eloquent sentence: "Piety and elegance are not inconsistent, and a man may be a wit without being an atheist." [41] The compiler of the anthology is laying claim to some sort of continuity between the line of wit as repre-

[39] *Ibid.*
[40] *A Collection of Divine Hymns and Poems on Several Occasions* (London: J. Baker, 1709), p. 33.

sented by Norris, and the new departure in lyrical pietism as represented by Wesley. His words no longer appear as cliché or wishful thinking when we consult the work of Watts, and additional support for his claim can be drawn from Norris's last published poem:

> Sing, then ye bless'd attendants on his throne,
> Hymns as immortal as your joys above;
> The fountain of your bliss and knowledge own,
> And as you shine with light, so burn with love.
>
> Praise the great author of your brighter day,
> To us below a star, to you a sun:
> With never silent harps this tribute pay,
> And hallelujahs that are still begun.
>
> You see the rising springs of life and light,
> Which with a double tide your breasts o'erflow,
> O praise the beatific object of your sight,
> Whose good's your life, and by whose light you know.
>
> You need not fear the exhausting of your lays,
> While you in song exalt your heavenly king,
> He has a boundless theme to employ your praise,
> As you a whole eternity to sing.[42]

In this Platonic rhapsody, Norris moves towards Watts's achievement of sinking his Metaphysical lyricism into the new idiom of the hymn. The quality may not be much above mediocre, but at least its Parnassian smoothness and syntactical clarity enable it to avoid the pitfalls of Metaphysical decadence.

The discrepancy between Norris's lyrical best, his rhapsodic average, and his Pastoral, Pindaric and Panegyric worst, has led one critic to suggest that Norris was the "victim of a theory" and "attempted too much." Powicke goes on to remark that Norris "is never so happy as when he stops trying to teach the age or be sublime, and lets the genuine lyrical impulse which often came to him have its way." [43] There is a good deal of truth in this, for the majority of his poems are variations on the Platonic vision, where the sublime and the didactic smother the incipient lyricism. And yet the Platonist design, however palpable, did not have a wholly detrimental effect on Norris's poetry, for it could be combined with both the

---

[41] *The Christian Poet, or Divine Poems on the Four Last Things* (London, 1735), Preface.

[42] *Theory*, II, 561.

[43] Powicke, *A Dissertation on John Norris*, pp. 31-32.

spirit of the Metaphysical lyric and a neoclassical purity of diction. In the preface to his translation of Robert Waring's *Amoris Effigies,* he gives a hint of his own taste in aesthetic theory. He praises Waring as follows:

His thoughts are so numerous, sublime and depending, his images of things so fine wrought and pathetical, his method so secret and lurking, yet withal so accurate, that they require as much advertency of mind as a mathematical demonstration. Nay there are some such mystical and exalted conceptions in him, as can scarce be reached but by a reader almost dieted into a Platonist.[44]

The heights of Platonism are thus associated with the "secret and lurking" processes of the Metaphysicals, and with the "mathematical" accuracy of neoclassicism. More explicitly Norris confesses that what he values in Waring is his "sweetness of fancy, neatness of style and lusciousness of hidden sense." [45] There can be little doubt that Norris's poetry reflects these three strands of aesthetic theory. The sweetness of the lyric goes hand in hand with a classical neatness, and is seasoned with the lusciousness of Platonic rhapsody and Metaphysical wit. Norris set himself a difficult task in attempting to harmonise these ingredients. If he was a victim of a theory, then this theory was "to make substantial massy sense yield to the softness of poetry." [46] He was convinced that "without this mixture, poetry is nothing worth." [47] With this mixture, poetry "has all it can have and is withal so divine a thing, that even Plato, I fancy, would give it entertainment in his commonwealth." [48] Many of Norris's rhapsodic poems pay mere lip-service to "massy sense," while in the Pindarics and Pastorals the massy sense does not "yield to the softness of poetry." In a handful of lyrics however, he achieved what he set out to do.

Norris's lyricism inevitably inserts itself into the wide gap between Marvell and Blake. Yet his work no more fills this gap than do those critics and anthologisers who have unearthed the skeleton of a continuous tradition. Doughty's *English Lyrics in the Age of Reason* and *Forgotten Lyrics of the 18th Century* confirm rather than bridge the chasm.[49] Miss Rostvig's painstaking documentation indeed shows that "it is possible to trace a direct line of development from the 17th century mystic motif of nature as a divine hieroglyph to the 18th century physico-theological motif

[44] John Norris, *The Picture of Love Unveiled. Made English from the Latin of Amoris Effigies. To which are prefixed, 1. A. brief account of the author and translator. 2. Some reflections upon love and beauty* (4th ed.; London, 1744), Preface. Waring's work was published in 1649 and Norris's translation in 1682.

[45] *Ibid.*

[46] *Miscellanies,* To the Reader.

[47] *Ibid.*

[48] *Ibid.*

[49] Oswald Doughty, *English Lyrics in the Age of Reason* (London: D. O'Connor, 1922), and *Forgotten Lyrics of the 18th Century* (London: H.F. & G. Witherby, 1924).

of the glory of God's planned creation." [50] But her claim that "nothing could be more erroneous" than that "the ecstatic note suffered a total poetic eclipse with the advent of 18th century rationalism," is hardly borne out by the quality of the lyrics she refers to.[51] If the "ecstatic note" means anything in terms of lyrical achievement as opposed to philosophical content, then it must refer to that combination of sweetness, neatness and lusciousness, which disappeared with the last of the Metaphysicals.

On the one hand, there is Edward Taylor, who wrote in 1688, "My shattered fancy stole away from me, / ... / And in God's garden saw a golden tree," [52] and who in 1693 struck the following ecstatic note:

> Like to the marigold, I blushing close
> My golden blossoms when thy sun goes down:
> Moistening my leaves with dewy sighs, half froze
> By the nocturnal cold, that hoars my crown.[53]

And on the other hand, there is the spirit of the 18th century, as epitomised in Savage's completely opposite ecstatic note:

> More than poetic raptures now I feel,
> And own that godlike passion, Public Zeal! [54]

Nothing could be further from the spirit of the lyric. Norris could still write lyrics because, for him, poetic raptures were more important than public zeal. In "Sitting in an Arbour," he writes:

> How calm, how happy, how serene am I!
> How satisfied with my own company.[55]

With the advent of the 18th century view that social instincts held priority over private foibles, he who chose to sit in his arbour would not be taken seriously. Even a man like Savage, who lived on the edge of the social pale, would find a certain obscenity in Norris's lyrical self-possession.

As a lyric poet, Norris insists on his detachment from social responsibility. Even if he depends for his livelihood on the local aristocrat and likens himself to a caged bird, he has more grounds for enjoying himself than does the landowner:

---

[50] Rostvig, II, 157.
[51] *Ibid.*, II, 156.
[52] Taylor, *Sacramental Meditations,* I, 29, in *Poems,* ed. Stanford, pp. 46-47.
[53] *Ibid.*, II, 3, p. 85.
[54] *The Wanderer,* II, 379-380. Savage, p. 119.
[55] "Sitting in an Arbour," *Miscellanies,* p. 32.

> I can enjoy what's yours much more than you.
> Your meadow's beauty I survey,
> Which you prize only for its hay.
> There can I sit beneath a tree
> And write an ode or elegy.
> What to you care, does to me pleasure bring,
> You own the cage, I in it sit and sing.[56]

Such indulgence was condemned by the 18th century until the early Blake wrote:

> He caught me in his silken net
> And shut me in his golden cage.
>
> He loves to sit and hear me sing,
> Then laughing sports and plays with me,
> Then stretches out my golden wing
> And mocks my loss of liberty.[57]

Between Norris and Blake, serious lyrics were out of the question. There was no room for the genuine ecstatic note.

If the ecstatic note survives at all, then it survives in the shape of a highly self-conscious literary exercise, as in the cult of the Laplander song. Thus Mrs Rowe's contribution to the Lapland cult reminds one of the classically controlled sunk ecstasy of which her contemporary, Isaac Watts, was so eminently capable:

> Should she in some sequestered bower
> Among the branches hide,
> I'd tear off every leaf and flower
> Till she was there descried.
>
> .   .   .   .
>
> Should bars of steel my passage stay,
> They could not thee secure:
> I'd through enchantments find a way
> To seize my Orramoor.[58]

---

[56] "My Estate," *ibid.,* p. 60.

[57] William Blake, "Song," *Poetry and Prose,* ed. Geoffrey Keynes (London: Nonesuch Press, 1956), p. 9.

[58] Elizabeth Rowe, "A Laplander's Song to his Mistress," *Poems on Several Occasions, To which is prefixed An Account of the Life and Writings of the Author* (London: D. Midwinter, 1767), p. 188. For a detailed account of the history of the Lapland Cult, see Frank Edgar Farley, "Three Lapland Songs," *Publications of the Modern Language Association,* XXI (1906), 1-39.

In the 18th century forceful and serious lyricism could only persist in the framework of this highly artificial convention, and under the pretext of revealing a remote and quaint cultural phenomenon. The taste for Chevy Chase ballads and Lapland lyrics hardly constitutes an underground link between the ages of Marvell and Blake; it rather defines the nature of the gap.

Norris's lyricism contributes to the gap to the extent that it is tainted with the sublime. A lyric must have a particular local habitation. Norris's Platonism often spills out of the individual context into the general and vague, as when he writes:

> While you a spot of earth possess with care
> Below the notice of the geographer,
> I by the freedom of my soul
> Possess, nay more, enjoy the whole.
> To the universe a claim I lay.[59]

The antithetical figure is unbalanced by the incipient didacticism, and this decline in quality applies generally to the transition from 17th century loco-descriptive verse to 18th century cosmic verse. The lyric flourished in the confines of the 17th century walled garden, not in the vast prospects of 18th century landscape gardening. It was too slender a flower to be noticed by those poetic geographers who mapped out the Newtonian universe.

A sample of the way in which Norris diminishes the gap between Marvell and Blake will show that he does this by making massy sense yield to the softness of poetry in a style that renews the Metaphysicals' combination of sweetness and neatness. In "Plato's Two Cupids," Norris wrote a philosophical lyric after the manner of Blake's "The Clod and the Pebble." It contains the following stanzas:

> The heart of man's a living butt,
> At which two different archers shoot,
> Their shafts are pointed both with fire,
> Both wound our hearts with hot desire.
>
> In this they differ, he that lies
> A sacrifice to his mistress' eyes,
> In pain does live, in pain expire,
> And melts and drops before the fire.
>
> But he that flames with love divine,

59 "My Estate," *Miscellanies*, p. 60.

> Does not in th' heat consume, but shine.
> He enjoys the fire that round him lies,
> Serenely lives, serenely dies.[60]

This antithesis does not topple over into a rhapsody, but forms a diptych within its own four walls. A similar combination of sweet lyricism and neat argument occurs in "Superstition." This is an elegiac lyric after the manner of Marvell's "The Picture of Little T.C.," and contains the following stanzas:

> I care not though it be
> By the preciser sort thought Popery;
> We poets can a licence show
> For everything we do,
> Hear then my little saint, I'll pray to thee.
>
> Let not the blest above
> Engross thee quite, but sometimes hither rove,
> Fain would I thy sweet image see,
> And sit and talk with thee,
> Nor is it curiosity, but love.
>
> I would not long detain
> Thy soul from bliss, nor keep thee here in pain.
> Nor should thy fellow saints ere know
> Of thy escape below,
> Before thou'rt missed, thou shouldst return again.[61]

Such a poem, like many of Marvell's, is sustained by a happy conjunction of the quaint and the classical, and as such represents the peculiar forte of the later Metaphysicals.

When justice has been done to the various facets of Norris's lyricism, to its limitations and its evaporation, to its sources and its aftermath, there is left its one redeeming quality, which is the way it injects new life into the Metaphysical tradition. Against the monotone of Platonic rhapsody, the sudden image, combining personal feeling and symbolic form, stands out. Such is the ecstatic line, "The soul stands shivering on the ridge of life." [62] This particular relic of the Metaphysical sensibility was sufficiently striking to become a cliché for the preromantics. It became the hall-mark of those who cultivated the ecstatic note after Norris. Thus Thomas Fletcher published the following in 1692:

[60] "Plato's Two Cupids," *ibid.*, p. 71.
[61] "Superstition," *ibid.*, p. 90.
[62] "The Meditation," *ibid.*, p. 25.

> O Ecstasy Divine! I cannot hold!
> Farewell, dull Earth! See where my ravished Soul
> Stands shivering on the edge of its slow clay!
> With the next rising note, 'twill fly away.
> I faint; I faint.[63]

In 1709 these lines were echoed in "Thoughts on Death. By a Young Lady":

> Methinks I have Eternity in view
> And dread to reach the edges of the shore.[64]

And in 1743, Blair, with an unerring eye for the well-worn phrase, described the soul which could "frolic on Eternity's dread brink / Unapprehensive," until "forced at last to the tremendous verge / At once she sinks to everlasting ruin." [65] The lyricism of Norris's ecstasy has been squeezed out, leaving a husk of histrionic effect.

In the sweetness and the neatness of his lyrical genius, Norris at his best is worlds apart from Blair. There is the easy compression of his tightly epigrammatic

> Let my sand slide away apace,
> I care not so I hold the glass.[66]

There is the tough reasonableness beneath the sweetly elegiac

> I've used all spells and charms of art
> To lay this troubler of my heart.[67]

And there is the calm resolution of his refusal to be disquieted:

> I stand upon the shore and view
> The mighty labours of the distant main:
> I'm flushed with silent joy and smile to see
> The shafts of fortune still drop short of me.[68]

These touchstones are palpably alien to the ways of 18th century poetry. They not only belong to the line of Herbert and Vaughan, but also look forward prophetically to Wordsworth's "Immortality Ode," Arnold's

---

[63] Thomas Fletcher, "Song," *Poems on Several Occasions and Translations* (1692). Printed in *Rare Poems*, ed. Marshall, p. 96.
[64] *A Collection of Divine Hymns and Poems* (1709), p. 119.
[65] Blair, *The Grave*, Chalmers, XV, 66.
[66] "Freedom," *Miscellanies*, p. 113.
[67] "To the Memory of my Dear Niece M.C.," *ibid.*, p. 83.
[68] "The Retirement," *ibid.*, p. 20.

"Dover Beach" and Meredith's "Modern Love." [69] They raise the ghost of a link between the Metaphysical tradition and the Romantic mode, a link which has usually been confined to the work of Lady Winchilsea and Isaac Watts.

Such affinities cannot easily be dismissed. The persistence of the ecstatic note after Norris, suggests that the disappearance of the Metaphysical tradition coincides with the rise of an aesthetic which has the hues of Romanticism. Consider for example the preface to the 1709 anthology, which contained several of Norris's lyrics:

Now the great business of poetry (as everyone knows) is to paint agreeable pictures on the imagination, to actuate the spirits, and give the passions a noble pitch. All its daring metaphors, surprising turns, melting accents, lofty flights, and lively descriptions serve for this end. While we read we feel a strange warmth boiling within, the blood dances through the veins.[70]

However one interprets the question of possible continuity between the late Metaphysicals and the early Romantics, there can be no doubt that Norris, in his poetry as in his thought, does more than merely register the transition from Metaphysical to Augustan.

[69] Cf. in particular, Wordsworth's "Our souls have sight of that immortal sea . . . and hear the mighty waters rolling evermore" ("Immortality Ode"), Arnold's "melancholy long withdrawing roar" ("Dover Beach"), and Meredith's "yonder midnight ocean's force" ("Modern Love" no. 50).

[70] *A Collection of Divine Hymns and Poems* (1709), Preface.

PART THREE

THE RESULT: ISAAC WATTS

CHAPTER ELEVEN

INTRODUCTION: CLASSICISM AND THE ENLIGHTENMENT

The value of interpreting the work of More and Norris in relation to such problematic terms as Metaphysical, Classical and Romantic on the one hand, and Renaissance, Enlightenment and Modern on the other, depends largely on assigning some meaning to the middle term in each of these series of abstractions. Since the field of inquiry is principally that of religious lyricism, there can be little difficulty about choosing the work of Isaac Watts as the embodiment of both classical aesthetics and the English Enlightenment.

Traditionally Addison holds this position; but this is largely because Addison appealed to the Victorians, who restored so many 18th century reputations, while Watts was discredited as a precursor of the nonconformist conscience, and hence for the Victorians not entirely of another age. But as J. W. Draper points out:

Probably Steele and Watts could claim as many readers in the reign of Queen Anne as could Addison. Their public was of a lower social degree; but it was growing with the increase in wealth and education, and in a few years its opinions, by the sheer weight of its numbers, were to dominate English taste.[1]

Unfortunately no attempt has been made to relate Watts's thought to his poetry, largely because his reputation as a philosopher did not outlive the Augustan period.

In 1753 Watts's editors made a claim that did not at that time appear in any way extravagant. They questioned "whether any author before him did ever appear with reputation on such a variety of subjects, as he has done, both as a prose writer, and a poet," and they believed "that there is no man now living of whose works so many have been dispersed, both at home and abroad, that are in such constant use, and translated into such a variety of languages." [2] Later in the century, Dr Johnson echoed these

---

[1] Draper, p. 241.
[2] Watts, ed. Jennings and Doddridge, Preface, p. vii.

sentiments in his generous encomium:

He has provided instruction for all ages, for those who are lisping their first lessons to the enlightened readers of Malebranche and Locke; he has left neither corporeal nor spiritual nature unexamined; he has taught the art of reasoning, and the science of the stars.[3]

Dr Johnson also gave what amounted to high praise, when he exclaimed of Watts's efforts in sacred verse: "It is sufficient for Watts to have done better than others what no man has done well." [4]

Since Dr Johnson's day however, no critics have treated Watts's work as a whole, and 20th century interest in Watts has been confined to his poetry, with the result that he has been taken out of context and attached either to the late Metaphysical tradition, or to the earliest stage of pre-romanticism.[5] It is time that attention was paid to Watts's work as it reflects the associated aims of classicism and the Enlightenment. The classical moment in English culture may be difficult to define, but there is a watershed between late Metaphysical and early preromantic, and there is evidence in the literature of this period to substantiate Lovejoy's parallel between deism and classicism. Watts, like other members of his generation, whether formal deists or not, gives meaning to this parallel, and thus to the middle terms in our problematic series of abstractions.

One of the rambling essays that Bolingbroke composed in the first instance for his friend Pope, contains a staggeringly explicit demonstration of Lovejoy's parallel. Indeed Bolingbroke erects a sustained analogy between the philosophy and the aesthetics of the Enlightenment. He begins with the axiomatic proposition that "the simplicity of true theism could never subsist in the figures of poetry." [6] Before the age of classicism and Enlightenment, "affected inspiration passed for real, hyperboles were understood literally, and the machinery of an ode was taken for matter of fact." [7] "True theism" is equated with "naked truth," and is at loggerheads with both metaphysical speculation and Renaissance rhetoric:

If naked truth, passing through many hands, came to be disguised, what must have happened to truth, wearing a mask at her first appearance? The hiero-

---

[3] Samuel Johnson, "Life of Watts," *Lives of the Poets* (2 vols.; London: Oxford University Press, 1906), II, 384.

[4] *Ibid.*, II, 385.

[5] See notably, T. A. Birrell, "Sarbiewski, Watts and the Later Metaphysical Tradition," *English Studies,* XXXVII (1956), 125-132; and Vivian de Sola Pinto, "Isaac Watts and the Adventurous Muse," *Essays and Studies,* XX (1935), 86-107, and "Isaac Watts and William Blake," *Review of English Studies,* XX (1944), 214-223.

[6] Bolingbroke, IV, 17.

[7] *Ibid.*

glyphic and the symbol remained, and the fable continued in tradition, when the signification of the one, and the moral of the other, were forgot.[8]

Pursuing the analogy with aesthetics, Bolingbroke sets out to demystify the uses and abuses of allegory:

An allegory may be contrived to puzzle and perplex the understanding, or to hold out nothing to us but itself. In the first case it is impertinent, in the second it is fraudulent, and in both it perverts the sole use it should be employed for, in the didactic, or even in the poetic style.... Allegory, in the true intention of it, is designed to make clearer as well as stronger impressions on the mind.[9]

The grounds of truth and beauty, once cleared of cant, are revealed as identical.

Bolingbroke is chiefly concerned to pursue the Baconian critique of religious superstition, but he does so with the support of arguments and vocabulary that invite the reader to pursue the Baconian critique of Renaissance rhetoric. According to Bolingbroke, Bacon did not go far enough; in his view, Bacon

makes parables and allegories so essential to religion, that he affirms, that to take them away is to forbid almost all commerce of things divine and human. Whatever reasons this great author had to make such a declaration, it was rashly made. The expression is allegorical, but the meaning of it is obvious; and therefore I say, that as far as man is concerned in carrying this commerce on, we are justified in suspecting it of enthusiasm or fraud; since allegory has been always a principal instrument of theological deception. The chancellor admits, that it serves to involve and conceal, ... which is in direct contradiction to its proper use, for that is to enlighten and illustrate.... He chose to say nothing of the former, rather than to be engaged in disputes, ... and we may add, rather than offend the clergy. For me ... who have no cavils nor invectives to fear, when I confine the communication of my thoughts to you and a very few friends, as I do in writing these essays; I shall repeat what I have said already, that the philosopher or divine, who pretends to instruct others by allegorical expressions without an immediate, direct and intelligible application of the allegory to some proposition or other, has nothing in his thoughts but the supposed allegory.... If he has anything there which he distrusts, and dares not venture to expose naked and stripped of allegory to the undazzled eye of reason, it is too much even to insinuate in such a case, and especially on subjects of the first philosophy. We may compare such theology to those artificial beauties, who hide their defects under dress and paint.[10]

The aesthetics of classicism are thus seen to be inextricably bound up with

---

[8] *Ibid.,* IV, 19.
[9] *Ibid.,* IV, 52.
[10] *Ibid.,* IV, 54-55.

the philosophy of the Enlightenment. In the work of Watts, philosopher and poet, this parallel is eloquently embodied.

Bolingbroke's explicit insistence might suggest that Lovejoy's parallel can be easily substantiated in a variety of places over a period of years. Unfortunately the Enlightenment was not coextensive with deism, and its identity in England is especially blurred against the background of the decay of rationalism and the rise of sentiment. It is important to bear in mind at least one basic ambiguity in the nature of the philosophy of the Enlightenment. As Fairchild suggests,

the Enlightenment regarded reason as a universal faculty lodged within the human breast, a sort of Inner Light, which enabled all men easily to comprehend the few simple axiomatic truths which constituted the groundwork of nature. Hence the line between reason and feeling was extremely thin, and for men of emotional rather than cerebral temper there was nothing to prevent rationalism from collapsing into sentimentalism.[11]

Such a view is both illuminating and confusing. It is difficult to maintain that the Enlightenment comprehends two opposites, and yet one of the functions of the Enlightenment was to prevent rationalism from collapsing into sentimentalism.

It is significant that Bolingbroke was aware of this ambiguity, and equally concerned to dispel it. He thus confirms Fairchild's definition of the Enlightenment, while vigorously opposing its implications. Bolingbroke traces the source of this ambiguity to the Cartesian Cogito and to the French word "sentiment"; in his view the Enlightenment must distinguish, as Descartes did not, between reason and inner light:

The French philosopher, . . . made clear and distinct ideas the necessary materials of knowledge. But then as he left this important article too general and too loose, so whilst he built up truth with one hand, he laid a foundation for infinite error on the other. He disarmed the scholastics; but he furnished arms to the mystics. Besides clear and distinct ideas, he admits a certain inward sentiment of clearness and evidence. The word sentiment is applied in the French language so variously and so confusedly, that it becomes often equivocal. But since it is distinguished, on this occasion, from idea, it must be meant either to signify that immediate perception which the mind has of some self-evident truth, in which case it is not a principle of knowledge, but knowledge itself, intuitive knowledge; or else it must be meant to signify that apparent evidence wherewith notions and opinions enter into the mind of one man, that are not accompanied with the same evidence, nor received in the same manner, in the mind of another. Now in this case the lively inward sentiment of Descartes is nothing better than that strong persuasion, wherewith every enthusiast imagines that he sees what he does not see. . . . If any-

[11] Fairchild, II, 9.

thing else be meant by sentiment, thus distinguished from idea, I confess myself unable so much as to guess what it is.[12]

Bolingbroke thus traces the thin line between reason and feeling. That other exponents of the Enlightenment were less scrupulous is evident if one refers to Fénelon and Rousseau at either end of the period under discussion.

Fénelon establishes a definition of Enlightenment which is coextensive with pietism, and yet his main ground is the same as Bolingbroke's. According to Fénelon,

c'est donc à la lumière de Dieu que je vois tout ce qui peut être vu. Il ne faut point la chercher cette lumière au dehors de soi: chacun la trouve en soi-même; elle est la même pour tous.[13]

Similarly Rousseau defines the Enlightenment in terms of sentiment, without abandoning ground common to both Fénelon and Bolingbroke. According to Rousseau, "le culte que Dieu demande est celui du coeur; et celui-là, quand il est sincère, est toujours uniforme." [14] A concept of the Enlightenment, which excluded Fénelon and Rousseau on the grounds that they blurred Bolingbroke's thin line, would be an impoverished one; and yet between pietism and sentimentalism, both historically and philosophically, there is room for a central phase of Enlightenment, which is concerned to prevent the collapse of rationalism. And in England, Berkeley, Hume, Gibbon and Watts, at least, as well as Bolingbroke, belong to this phase. At the moment of Enlightenment they stand, sandwiched between the long and pervasive latitudinarian movement, and the equally long and pervasive development of a religion of sentiment.

Corresponding to this transitional moment of Enlightenment, one can identify a similarly transitional moment of classicism. As Draper suggests,

to call the age of Queen Anne a transition period is perhaps too bold a paradox; but in the broader sweep of culture-history, it seems scarcely more than a momentary rest in the rapid evolution from the intellectualistic and aristocratic world of the Renaissance to the modern world of emotionalism and democracy; it is a truce between contending forces, as was the Elizabethan age, and, like every truce, a period of deep-laid preparation for ensuing conflict.[15]

Watts's poetry makes good these sweeping statements. As a religious lyricist, he provides valuable evidence concerning the nature of this large-scale evolution from Renaissance to modern. Classicism, if it was anything

---

[12] Bolingbroke, IV, 162.
[13] Fénelon, pp. 152-153.
[14] Jean-Jacques Rousseau, *Profession de foi du vicaire savoyard* (Paris: J. J. Pauvert, 1964), p. 130.
[15] Draper, p. 249.

homogeneous, was an attempt to prevent Renaissance literature from collapsing into modern and inferior ways. It attempted to bolster a collapsing
aesthetic by purifying poetic diction and strengthening the sinews of syntax. Few English poets interpreted classicism in this way. For most, classicism meant slavish imitation of classical models; but not for Watts.

The following chapters are an attempt to give an account of Watts in
terms of the above outline. His thought is related to what can be identified
as the Enlightenment, and to trends in philosophy and religion that lie
outside. His aesthetic theory and poetic practice are similarly related to
classicism, and to the Metaphysical and preromantic trends which run
into and out of the classical phase.

CHAPTER TWELVE

THE ENGLISH ENLIGHTENMENT

Watts's thought provides an insight into the peculiar nature of the English Enlightenment. It is fair to say that the European Enlightenment was the cultural expression of an age of absolutism. The German Aufklarung flourished under the enlightened despotism of Frederick the Great; the French Siècle des Lumières grew out of, if in reaction to, the reign of Louis XIV. Such nationalist absolutism fostered the spirit of intellectual and spiritual absolutism, which was the hall-mark of the Enlightenment mind.

The English Enlightenment presents an interesting contrast; it expressed itself in the context of social, political and religious compromise. Absolutism, national or intellectual, was out of the question. The 1688 revolution had got rid of Sancroft, Jeffreys and James II. The cultural revolution was hence confined to the established channels of social and political change; it had no brief to flourish in and for itself, as it had in France and Germany.[1] Hume and Gibbon were notable exceptions, but in both the European influence was dominant.[2] The temper of insular Enlightenment can better be gauged from the work of Watts and Addison, which keeps to the via media and eschews the absolute.

The via media of the English Enlightenment was followed even by Bolingbroke, for all his anti-clericalism and continental contacts. The spirit of compromise is evident in his aversion to both Cudworth and Hobbes:

I cannot soar so high as Plato and Cudworth. I will not sink so low as Protagoras and other ancients; as Hobbes and other moderns. The former amaze,

[1] For a stimulating and original account of the absolutism of the European Enlightenment, see Karl Barth, *From Rousseau to Ritschl* (London: Student Christian Movement Press, 1959), Chapter 1, "Man in the 18th Century."

[2] Hume pushed certain tendencies of the English mind to their logical conclusions, but the English mind itself has a tendency to shun logical conclusions. If Hume was a Scot, and thereby open to Europe, Gibbon was a European, conditioned by continental Calvinism and continental Catholicism.

instead of instructing me; and if I understand the latter, I only understand them, to know that they impose on themselves, and would impose on me, the grossest absurdities. Strange extremes! When Cudworth holds up the metaphysical glass to my eye, I see something, I know not what; something that glitters at an immeasurable distance from me. When Hobbes holds it up, he changes the position: and I see something monstrous at the very end of the glass.[3]

Addison shared Bolingbroke's philosophical conservatism. Reporting on the French intellectual scene, he claimed that the "French don't care for following" Malebranche, "and look upon all the new philosophy as visionary or irreligious." [4]

Addison of course cultivated the via media in all fields. His political journalism was based on the view that the principles of Popery and Republicanism "are respectively disclaimed and abhorred by all the men of sense and virtue in both parties, as they now stand." [5] Watts also cultivated the via media over a wide spectrum. As his latest biographer has pointed out,

Watts . . . was often inconsistent in his various beliefs, for he was an ingrained compromiser. He confided too often in the pragmatic explanation to rescue him from a philosophical dilemma. But his impulses were usually right, even if he failed on occasion to justify them rationally. Watts accepted Locke's philosophy, but he also clung to the theory of "innate ideas"; he wrote a *Guide to Prayer* to tone down dissenter enthusiasm in prayer, but he published *An Exhortation to Ministers* to arouse more warmth in nonconformist preaching; he rejected the Trinity of the Athanasian Creed because it was illogical; yet he refused to be classed with the Unitarians; he exalted reason in his non-religious essays and depreciated the sufficiency of reason in the religious; he has the usual neoclassic horror of enthusiasm, but he spent a lifetime trying to infuse it into the religion of his age; he believed in the certain election of a chosen few, but at the same time he insisted that all men have free will.[6]

Watts and Addison were indeed kindred spirits.

Addison claimed to "have brought philosophy out of closets and libraries . . . to dwell in clubs and assemblies," [7] and Watts thought he could "assume this pleasure of being the first who hath brought down" the Hebrew Psalmist "into the common affairs of the Christian life." [8] It is

---

[3] Bolingbroke, V, 13-14.
[4] Letter to Bishop Hough, December 1700, Addison, V, 332.
[5] *The Freeholder*, No. 54 (25 June 1716), *ibid.*, V, 97.
[6] Arthur Paul Davis, *Isaac Watts, his Life and Works* (New York: Dryden Press, 1943), p. 222.
[7] *The Spectator* (12 March 1711), Addison, II, 253.
[8] Preface to *The Psalms of David*, Watts, IV, xxi.

not surprising that Watts considered Addison to be "the most authentic judge of fine thoughts and language that our age has produced." [9] Addison was of course something of an aesthete, and Watts was something of a pietist; but both embody, over a wide range of activity and enquiry, the spirit of the English Enlightenment.

Prudence and reserve govern intellectual and spiritual operations. Reason and inner light are held in balance, so as not to disturb the uniformity of Enlightenment available to all men. Fairchild's account of the poet Young suggests that this compromise was shortlived. According to Fairchild, Young "saw in Addison a perfect equilibrium of elements which he desired to reconcile in himself: reason and feeling, wit and piety, aristocratic urbanity and bourgeois earnestness." But Young was unable to attain this equilibrium, since his emotions were stronger than his character, and "running through Young's life we can see the crack caused by imperfect juxtaposition of the two sides of the Addisonian compromise." [10] It may be useful to equate the English Enlightenment with the Addisonian compromise, but only if the work of Watts is placed alongside that of Addison.

The belief that truth can be expressed axiomatically is characteristic of the English Enlightenment. This belief reflects a timidity and prudence with regard to the intellect, and a common refusal to raise the ghost of 17th century controversy. Indeed one could argue that England had had her Enlightenment under Cromwell, when Hobbes and Milton had written for and about the absolutist mind, and the foundations of the Royal Society had been laid. But England had thrown overboard the political and religious dimensions of this Enlightenment, and severely reduced the scope of its cultural and intellectual implications. The 18th century suffered accordingly, and Watts voices its ethos.

In an essay on the nature of space, Watts writes: "It would be a great happiness, if we could all unite in some settled and undoubted opinion of this subject." [11] It is ironic that intellectual uniformity should have been the end-product of the latitudinarian tradition. Watts's motives are clear; he starts off with a Miltonic attitude towards truth, then clips his wings, and out of the absolutist premise draws a prudential conclusion. Consider for example this passage from *The Improvement of the Mind*:

[9] *A Guide to Prayer*, Watts, III. 141.
[10] Fairchild, II, 133.
[11] *Philosophical Essays*, Watts, V, 501.

Truth does not always go by the lump, nor does error tincture and spoil all the articles of belief that some one party professes.

Since there are difficulties attending every scheme of knowledge, it is enough for me in the main to incline to that side which has the fewest difficulties; and I would endeavour as far as possible, to correct the mistakes or the harsh expressions of one party, by softening and reconciling methods, by reducing the extremes, and by borrowing some of the best principles or phrases from another.[12]

With this spirit, the 18th century chose to soften its intellect, in the interests of political and religious compromise.

Watts's aim, in all his prose works, is to arrive at settled and undoubted opinions concerning obvious and known truths. Since obvious and known truths are arrived at axiomatically, it follows that they are not subject to the scrutiny of scholastic disputation. Watts makes the point with some concern:

Let not obvious and known truths, or some of the most plain and obvious propositions be bandied about in a disputation, for a mere trial of skill: For he that opposes them in this manner will be in danger of contracting a habit of opposing all evidence, will acquire a spirit of contradiction, and pride himself in the power of resisting the brightest light, and fighting against the strongest proofs: This will insensibly injure the mind, and tends greatly to an universal scepticism.[13]

The 18th century relied on the bright lights of evidence, and Watts helped them shine by modernising the art of logic. And yet one cannot help feeling that the rather worried suggestion that scepticism is a form of mental illness, betrays a sense of vulnerability, which Watts's patronising assurance does not quite overcome. What are these obvious and known truths? Are they truths? Or are they the comforting myths of his age, the untested clichés of social and political compromise? One thing appears certain; the English Enlightenment relied on, and abused, the methods of Ramist logic, according to which, in Perry Miller's words,

truth does not need proof, but only assertion. Hence true doctrine is a series of axioms, and correct propositions are so self-evident that in almost all cases doubt can be resolved by the mere statement of alternatives in the disjunctive syllogism.[14]

English classicism, as well as the English Enlightenment, thrived on such theory.

Watts was zealous in his mission of modernisation. The 18th century

---

[12] *The Improvement of the Mind,* Watts, V, 293.
[13] *Ibid.,* V, 253.
[14] Perry Miller, *The New England Mind: The 17th Century* (Cambridge, Mass.: Harvard University Press, 1939), p. 151.

compromise encouraged the golden mean in all things, and Watts worked hard to reduce the extremes in various fields. His constant preoccupation is to establish an incontrovertible via media, in which the opinions of all men may unite. His principal effort was directed towards logic and metaphysics:

An unknown heap of trifles and impertinences have been intermingled with these useful parts of learning, upon which account many persons in this polite age have made it a part of their breeding to throw a jest upon them. . . . But this is running into wide extremes; nor ought these parts of science to be abandoned by the wise, because some writers of former ages have played the fool with them. True logic teaches us to use our reason well, and brings light into the understanding.[15]

As this passage suggests, Watts's argument for Enlightenment is not so much based on the clarifying energy of intellectual vision, as on the axiomatic propositions of a social and religious compromise.

The polite age, with all its breeding, needed to be reminded that the body of Dissenters, raised in their Academies on Ramist logic, had something to offer their unenlightened university-trained Anglican brethren. As Samuel Wesley, the elder, remarked – and he had himself been trained in an Academy before turning Anglican –, the Academies operated an effective brain-drain on those who would otherwise have gone to the universities. Wesley challenged the Dissenters "to persuade the world that it has been no injury to the University to drain away such considerable numbers, several of the nobility, many of the gentry, who would have sought their education there, had they not been intercepted by these sucking Academies." [16] Watts made a decisive contribution towards the enlightenment of the Dissenters. Through his efforts, as well as through those of Defoe, they came to be associated with the via media of English society.

The wide extremes of puritan and polite were joined in the religious compromise of the Enlightenment. That the age was conscious of this compromise can be seen in Savage's poem on the Baptist preacher, James Foster:

> Foster well this honest truth extends;
> Where mystery begins, religion ends.
>
> .   .   .   .
>
> His faith, where no credulity is seen,

---

[15] *The Improvement of the Mind,* Watts, V, 305.
[16] Samuel Wesley, *A Defence of a Letter* (London, 1704), p. 14.

'Twixt infidel, and bigot, marks the mean.

.   .   .   .

But should some churchman, aping wit severe,
The poet's sure turned Baptist say, and sneer?
Shame on that narrow mind so often known,
Which in one mode of faith, owns worth alone.

.   .   .   .

Thee boast **Dissenters**; we with pride may own
Our Tillotson; and Rome her Fénelon.[17]

Watts, like Foster, believed that puritan peculiarities should be sunk. In
his ars poetica of prayer, he advised dissenting preachers to abandon the
outward signs of ranting enthusiasm: "Let your words be all pronounced
distinct, and not made shorter by cutting off the last syllable, nor longer,
by the addition of hems and o's, of long breaths, affected groanings, and
useless sounds, of coughing or spitting." [18]

Watts was not however prepared to surrender what was valuable in the
dissenting tradition, and in the matter of preaching style he called for a
via media between puritan and polite, eschewing the extremes of both:

Our fathers formed their sermons upon the model of doctrine, reason and
use, . . . but the very names . . . are become nowadays such stale and old-
fashioned things, that a modish preacher is quite ashamed of them. . . . The
address . . . must not be named . . . lest it should be hissed out of church, like
the garb of a round-head or a puritan. . . . Some of our fathers neglected
politeness perhaps too much, and indulged a coarseness of style; . . . but we
have such a value for elegancy, and so nice a taste for what we call polite that
we dare not spoil the cadence of a period to quote a text of scripture in it,
nor disturb the harmony of our sentences to number or to name the heads of
our discourse.[19]

For all his bitterness about the polite elegance of 18th century preachers,
Watts clearly modernised more than he conserved. Otherwise his preaching style would not have earned the praise of Dr Johnson, who noted, with
characteristic frankness, that Watts "did not endeavour to assist his eloquence by any gesticulations; for as no corporeal actions have any correspondence with theological truth, he did not see how they could enforce
it." [20] Once again, as in Bolingbroke's essays, the Enlightenment settlement
is described in terms which identify its philosophical and aesthetic interests.

---

[17] "Character of the Rev. James Foster," lines 17-18, 27-28, 47-50, 55-56. Savage,
pp. 189-190.
[18] *A Guide to Prayer*, Watts, III, 149.
[19] *The Improvement of the Mind*, Watts, V, 350-351.
[20] Johnson, *Lives of the Poets*, II, 382.

But the via media of social and religious compromise is not always in evidence. At times philosophy itself is seen to have appropriated the law of the golden mean, independent of the social motive. Thus Watts on space: "It is strange that philosophers . . . should run into such wide extremes in their opinions concerning space; that while some depress it below all real being, and suppose it to be mere nothing, others exalt it to the nature and dignity of Godhead." [21] The extent to which 18th century minds confined philosophy and its principle operative tool, reason, to a golden mean, whereby neither too much nor too little would be claimed, can be seen in John Wesley, who wanted to find an even more secure via media for reason than either Locke or Watts were able to provide.

Watts was strongly committed to using "our reason well" and bringing "light into the understanding." [22] He was equally strongly committed to the view that "in vain our haughty reason swells." [23] Wesley was not satisfied with this state of affairs:

Is there then no medium between these extremes, – undervaluing and over-valuing reason? Certainly there is. But who is there to point it out? – to mark down the middle way? That great master of reason, Mr Locke, has done something of the kind, something applicable to it, in one chapter of his Essay concerning Human Understanding. But it is only remotely applicable to this: he does not come home to the point. The good and great Dr Watts has wrote admirably well, both concerning reason and faith. But neither does anything he has written point out the medium between valuing it too little and too much.[24]

Wesley of course gives the game away; the philosophical via media becomes a means of justifying his own particular brand of Enlightenment religion. Wesley's success in imposing his classical vocabulary on an essentially romantic movement, was the final blow to any absolutist integrity the English Enlightenment may previously have claimed. The philosophical via media was a nominal cover for a social and religious conservatism, which became so strongly instilled into the English mind in the course of the century, that the challenge of the French Revolution was weathered.

Wesley's attempts to improve on Watts were not confined to the use of reason. He also undertook the task of abridging the writings of the great abridger. This activity expresses the spirit of the Enlightenment in no uncertain fashion; it is part and parcel of the campaign to reduce extremes. Of Watts, Dr Johnson remarks: "His method of study was to impress the

---

[21] *Philosophical Essays,* Watts, V, 501.
[22] *The Improvement of the Mind,* Watts, V, 305.
[23] "The Infinite," *Horae Lyricae,* I. Watts, IV, 354.
[24] John Wesley, *Works* (14 vols.; Grand Rapids, Michigan: Zondervan, 1958-1959), VI, 354.

contents of his books upon his memory by abridging them, and by inter-
leaving them to amplify one system with supplements from another." [25]
Watts is perhaps partly responsible for that methodical and utilitarian ap-
proach to knowledge which Bentham was to champion and from which
J. S. Mill and many another Victorian child were to suffer. The rapidity
with which this attitude became a tradition can be seen in this entry from
Wesley's *Journal*: "I abridged Dr Watts' pretty *Treatise on the Passions*.
His 127 pages will make a useful tract of four and twenty." [26]

Wesley's other abridgements of Watts include 44 pages from Watts's
Ruin and Recovery (1740), which Wesley incorporated in his *Doctrine of
Original Sin* (1757), and *Serious Considerations concerning the Doctrine
of Election and Reprobation extracted from a late Author* (1778).[27] The
spirit of the Enlightenment lies behind this passion for abridging. In Bolingbroke's telling words:

The phenomena of the human mind are few, and on those few a multitude
of hypotheses has been raised, concerning mind in general, and soul and
spirit. So that in this part, the improvement of real knowledge must be made
by contraction, and not by amplification.[28]

One could not wish for a more succinct description of one of the principal
distinctions between the Renaissance and the Enlightenment.

These curious instances in which Wesley saw fit to improve on Watts
do not invalidate the general principle that Watts's contribution to the
English Enlightenment was considerably more valuable than Wesley's.
Behind Wesley's veneer of progressive vocabulary, lay an essentially conservative spirit, which no amount of sentimental religion could transform.
Watts on the other hand, as Dr Johnson points out, "taught the art of
reasoning." By doing this in an age which trembled to commit itself to any
positive intellectual method, he helped prepare the ground for those later
expressions of the Enlightenment mind, namely utilitarianism and
positivism.

Watts's method drew principally on Ramist logic as taught in the
Dissenting Academies. He deplores the decay of rationalism, and claims
that "methods of disputation should be learned in the schools in order to
teach students better to defend truth, and to refute error, both in writing
and conversation, where the scholastic forms are utterly neglected.[29] The
utilitarian application is essential; Watts is not urging the revival of dis-

---

[25] Johnson, *Lives of the Poets,* II, 379.
[26] John Wesley, *Journal* (17 February 1769), *Works,* III, 353.
[27] See Davis, p. 44.
[28] Bolingbroke, IV, 8-9.
[29] *The Improvement of the Mind,* Watts, V, 254.

putation for disputation's sake. Indeed he suggests one important change in the traditional method:

Might it not be a safer practice if the opponents were sometimes engaged on the side of truth, and produced their arguments in opposition to error? ... I confess in this method there would be one among the students ... always engaged in the support of supposed error; but all the rest would be exercising their talents in arguing for the supposed truth.[30]

The proposed change is indicative of the way in which the English Enlightenment jealously sought to guard truth from too precise a scrutiny. But for Watts at least, the exercise is more than a game or tactical ploy; it has the strategic function of training the mind in the art of reasoning.

Watts is concerned to rescue the art of logic from its gothic past. Like the 17th century puritan thinkers, he believed that the Fall had only impaired our reasoning powers, and that logic was a powerful restorative:

The great design of this noble science is to rescue our reasoning powers from their unhappy slavery and darkness; ... to diffuse a light over the understanding in our enquiries after truth, and not to furnish the tongue with debate and controversy. True logic is not that noisy thing that deals all in dispute and wrangling, to which former ages had debased and confined it; ... true logic doth not require a long detail of hard words to amuse mankind and to puff up the mind with empty sounds.[31]

The echo of the Pauline eulogy of charity emphasises the value Watts set on the art of logic. With Milton and Ramus, he believed in "natural logic." Milton had defined natural logic as "the very faculty of reason in the mind of man"; "reason or logic" is thus identified as "first the natural reason, ... then trained reason." [32] Much of Watts's energies were devoted to the cultivation of natural logic. This involved the simplification of the language of logic, and as A. P. Davis has pointed out, "perhaps the best commentary on Watts's success in this attempt ... is that literally hundreds of examples and definitions in Johnson's Dictionary are taken from Watts's Logic." [33]

The contribution of Ramist logic to the break-up of scholasticism was considerable. The various branches of knowledge were detached from their interlocking positions in the medieval hierarchy, and logic, no longer the cement of an immutable structure, was liberated to become a flexible

---

[30] Ibid.
[31] Logic (1724), Preface. Watts, V, iii.
[32] Milton, The Art of Logic (1672), Works, XI, 9.
[33] Davis, p. 87. In Johnson's copy of Watts's Logic, at least one word is marked on each page, and some of the 365 pages have as many as 11 words marked for quoting. Students at Oxford and Cambridge, as well as at the Academies, used the Logic as a textbook. See also, Thomas Gibbons, Memoirs of the Rev. Isaac Watts, D.D. (London: J. Buckland and T. Gibbons, 1780), p. 305.

and useful tool. Milton's emphasis on the utility of logic expresses the spirit of the Enlightenment as well as the spirit of puritanism:

The form or true cause of an art is not so much the methodical arrangement of those precepts as it is the teaching of some useful matter; for an art is what it is rather because of what it teaches than because of its method of teaching.[34]

The complaint against logic had always been that it set itself up as the queen of sciences, a sort of linguistic theology, and dictated the way in which the various sciences should proceed. Milton followed Ramus in seeking to rescue logic from the all-embracing and all-confusing function which it had occupied under the medieval dispensation.

Milton credits Ramus with having initiated this rescue operation, but as a man of the Renaissance, he feels that Ramus has overvalued brevity, at the expense of the "copiousness of clarity." He observes that,

though many of the philosophers, trusting to their own native abilities, are said to have contemned the art of logic, others naturally less keen and penetrating, judge that it is very useful and that they should study it diligent-ly; of the latter, as I hold with our countryman Sidney, Peter Ramus is be-lieved the best writer on the art. Other logicians, in a sort of unbridled licence, commonly confound physics, ethics, and theology with logic. But our author in seeking too earnestly for brevity seems to have fallen short not exactly of clarity but yet of copiousness of clarity.[35]

Watts, as a man of the Enlightenment, did not have Milton's scruples in this respect; indeed he would have considered "copiousness of clarity" to be a contradiction in terms. And yet he resisted the Enlightenment trend of assigning to mathematics the place reserved by the scholastics for logic. In terms strongly reminiscent of Milton's attack on "the unbridled licence" of "other logicians," he writes:

Some have been tempted to cast all their logical, their metaphysical, and their theological and moral learning into the method of mathematicians, and bring everything related to those abstracted, or those practical sciences under theo-rems, problems, postulates, scholiums, corollaries etc., whereas the matter ought always to direct the method. . . . Neither the rules for the conduct of the understanding, nor the doctrines or duties of religion and virtue can be exhibited naturally in figures and diagrams.[36]

Watts sees no point in replacing one panacea by another. What he does wish to preserve is the utility of logic as an aid to reason.

Watts's chief argument in favour of the Ramist interpretation of logic is his belief that truth is not always self-evident:

---

[34] Milton, *The Art of Logic, Works,* XI, 9.
[35] *Ibid.,* XI, 3.
[36] *The Improvement of the Mind,* Watts, V, 258.

There are several things which make it very necessary that our reason should have some assistance in the exercise or use of it. The first is the depth and difficulty of many truths, and the weakness of our reason to see far into things at once, and penetrate to the bottom of them. It was a saying among the ancients, *Veritas in puteo,* truth lies in a well; and to carry on this metaphor we may very justly say, that logic does, as it were, supply us with steps whereby we may go down to reach the water; or it frames the links of a chain, whereby we may draw the water up from the bottom. Thus, by the means of many reasonings well connected together, philosophers in our age have drawn a thousand truths out of the depths of darkness, which our fathers were utterly unacquainted with.[37]

The function of logic is to overcome the weakness of reason. Watts uses Ramus to steer a path between Donne's sense of the overwhelming difficulty of tackling truth, and Bolingbroke's sense that truths are few, easy and obvious. His argument for logic informs his campaign for the improvement of the mind. He urges young minds to overcome their laziness and timidity:

Nor yet let any student on the other hand fright himself at every turn with unsurmountable difficulties, nor imagine that the truth is wrapt up in impenetrable darkness. These are formidable spectres which the understanding raises sometimes to flatter its own laziness. Those things which in a remote and confused view seem very obscure and perplexed, may be approached by gentle and regular steps, and may then unfold and explain themselves at large to the eye. The hardest problems in geometry, and the most intricate schemes or diagrams may be explicated and understood step by step.[38]

Watts is not saying that all branches of knowledge aspire to the condition of geometry. He is saying that logic can methodise the mind, just as geometry can methodise matter.

In the context of 18th century thought, Watts's defence of logic did a lot to counteract the softening of the mind that accompanied the decay of rationalism. On the whole, the 18th century no longer believed that truth lies in a well. The relics of 17th century reason were rapidly eradicated with the rise of preromanticism and evangelicalism. James Hervey, in whom these two movements are so closely associated, explicitly rejected "the laborious method of long-deduced arguments or close connected reasonings," and chose to convey his religious and aesthetic effusions "by forming agreeable pictures of nature." [39] There is no doubt that on this issue Watts was in a minority. But he was not alone in resisting the prevailing mood. Swift, Pope and Berkeley shared his misgivings.

[37] *Logic,* Watts, V, 2.
[38] *The Improvement of the Mind,* Watts, V, 256.
[39] James Hervey, *Meditations and Contemplations* (1746-7), p. 184.

Berkeley in particular was concerned to rescue logic from abuse and disuse. His defence of logic follows in the tradition laid down by Milton and Watts. Thus he writes:

Surely it would be no such deplorable loss of time if a young gentleman spent a few months upon that so much despised and decried art of Logic, a surfeit of which is by no means the prevailing nuisance of this age. It is one thing to waste one's time in learning and unlearning the barbarous terms, wire-drawn distinctions, and prolix sophistry of the Schoolmen; and another to attain some exactness in defining and arguing – things perhaps not altogether beneath the dignity even of a minute philosopher. There was indeed a time when Logic was considered as its own object: and that art of reasoning, in-stead of being transferred to things, turned altogether upon words and abstractions; which produced a sort of leprosy in all parts of knowledge, corrupting and converting them into hollow verbal disputations in a most impure dialect. But those times are past; and that, which had been cultivated as the principal learning for some ages, is now considered in another light, and by no means makes that figure in the universities, . . . which is pretended by those admirable reformers of religion and learning, the minute philo-sophers.[40]

The view that there was nothing in the Enlightenment to "prevent ration-alism from collapsing into sentimentalism" [41] has therefore to be modified. Watts and Berkeley at least considered that logic could be an important prop.

If Watts, in his concern for the art of reasoning, displays an attitude of cautious optimism, there is, in his writing generally, a certain veneer of diction and imagery, which betrays a rather more confident complacency. Watts's snobbery – his distinction between the "politer" and the "plainer" part of mankind, for example [42] – was held in check by his background. But this was a background full of aristocratic figures, the descendants of Cromwell's entourage, and Watts held as a social ideal the "well bred gentleman in polite conversation." [43] He believed that a great deal of pro-gress, intellectual as well as social, had been made since the age of Crom-well. His works are liberally scattered with the catch-phrases of conscious enlightenment. He speaks of "this enlightened age, this age of juster reason-ing." [44] He looks upon the writings of his youth "as things afar off, and which have passed in another century." [45] He grants that "the movements of sacred passion may be the ridicule of an age which pretends to nothing

[40] George Berkeley, *Alciphron,* ed. T. E. Jessop (London: Thomas Nelson, 1950), pp. 202-203.
[41] Fairchild, II, 9.
[42] *Hymns,* 2nd ed. (1709), Preface. Watts, IV, 149.
[43] *The Improvement of the Mind,* Watts, V, 253.
[44] *Philosophical Essays,* Watts, V, 501.
[45] *Ibid.,* V, 504.

but calm reasoning." [46] And he claims that "the improvement of reason has raised the learned and prudent of the European world almost as much above the Hottentots and other savages of Africa, as those savages are by nature superior to the birds, the beasts and the fishes." [47]

Such language can of course be accounted for in terms of the society in which Watts moved. The clichés are harmless enough, although one cannot help regretting that, in the English Enlightenment generally, the social background and exigencies of patronage counted for so much, and the intellectual energy and independence for so little. On balance however, it is true that the spiritual successors of Cromwell's entourage had much to be thankful for in the social and political set-up of Hanoverian England. Watts could afford to rejoice at the gradual disappearance of Latin, for example. It was a symbol of ecclesiastical tyranny; "but we thank God the world is grown something wiser." [48] And in Watts's lifetime, the world continued to grow wiser; thus in Northampton, from 1729 onwards, Philip Doddridge arranged that all lectures in the Dissenting Academy should be given in English.[49] Watts then had some justification for proclaiming his belief in intellectual as well as social progress. Few of his generation contributed so much to the maintenance of intellectual standards.

The veneer of conscious enlightenment is seen at its shiniest in Watts's use of imagery. This is the archetypal Enlightenment imagery of light and darkness, with the sunbeams of man's mind piercing through the clouds of ignorance and superstition.[50] Here it is that Watts comes nearest to being an exponent of the Enlightenment à l'état pur. There was something of the nominalist, even the positivist, about Watts; words had meaning only if they stood for things. It was in this spirit that he abandoned the term

---

[46] *Sermons*, vol. 1, Dedication (1721). Watts, I, xxi.
[47] *Logic*, Watts, V, 1.
[48] *The Improvement of the Mind,* Watts, V, 309.
[49] See Herbert McLachlan, *English Education under the Test Acts: Being the History of the Nonconformist Academies 1660-1820* (Manchester: University Press, 1931), p. 21.
[50] Watts's German contemporary, Christian Wolff, made emblematic use of this imagery in a work which Karl Barth takes as the manifesto of the German Enlightenment. Barth, in the first paragraph of *From Rousseau to Ritschl* (p. 11), writes:

"In 1720 there appeared the famous work *Reasonable Thoughts on God, the World and the Human Soul, and All Things in General, Communicated to the Lovers of Truth by Christian Wolff*. Its frontispiece shows a sun whose powerful rays pierce a mass of black clouds, and spread light upon mountains, forests, towns and villages. The aureole of this sun is obviously not considered to be insupportable to the human gaze, for it takes the form of an exceedingly friendly and pleasantly smiling human face, whose owner seems to be extremely pleased to see the clouds in the heavens and the shadows on the earth dissipate everywhere."

"metaphysics" for the less speculative "ontology." [51] Any imagery that he uses consistently must therefore indicate a well-considered and serious preoccupation; idle flights of fancy were out of the question. It is significant that such imagery does in fact crop up at key moments in his discourse, when the central argument has to be clinched.

It is with Enlightenment imagery that Watts puts the case for the modernisation of liturgical psalms. He wishes to lighten our darkness:

When we are just entering into an evangelic frame by some of the glories of the gospel presented in the brightest figures of Judaism, yet the very next line perhaps which the clerk parcels out unto us, hath something in it so extremely Jewish and cloudy, that darkens our sight of God the Saviour. Thus by keeping too close to David in the house of God, the veil of Moses is thrown over our hearts.[52]

Introducing the first book of his hymns, he notes: "You will always find in this paraphrase dark expressions enlightened, and the Levitical ceremonies and Hebrew forms of speech changed into the worship of the gospel, and explained in the language of our time and nation." [53] In these two cases one feels that the imagery is not redundant, for it symbolises a practical reform. Watts worked hard and successfully to purify the language of the tribe in the field of liturgical singing. It is in such achievements that the correspondence between classicism and the Enlightenment is most strikingly displayed; the image reflects a substantial enterprise.

All of Watts's principal interests are liable to find occasional expression in Enlightenment imagery. There is the case of toleration, Locke's letter on which "led me into a new region of thought, wherein I found myself surprised and charmed with truth. There was no room to doubt in the midst of sunbeams." [54] There was the space controversy:

O, say our opponents, Space is a mere mode, but the substance that supports it is utterly unknown, as all substances are. Happy asylum for the learned to retreat to! This shelter of darkness! This invented idea of an unknown and unknowable thing called substance! How well does it screen and hide a modern disputant from light and argument, when they pursue him so close that he has no other refuge! Yet even this dark shelter I have endeavoured to break open and demolish in the next essay.[55]

There is the defence of the reasoning process:

---

[51] "A Brief Scheme of Ontology," Preface. *Philosophical Essays*, Watts, V, 638.
[52] *Hymns*, 1709 Preface. Watts, IV, 147. Until Watts's innovations were accepted, the clerk read out each line before it was sung.
[53] *Ibid.*, IV, 149.
[54] *Philosophical Essays*, Watts, V, 503.
[55] *Ibid.*, V, 509.

Use no subtle arts to cloud and entangle the question: hide not yourself in doubtful words and phrases; do not affect little shifts and subterfuges to avoid the force of an argument; take a generous pleasure to espy the first rising beams of truth, though it be on the side of your opponent; endeavour to remove the little obscurities that hang about it, and suffer and encourage it to break out into open and convincing light.[56]

And finally there is the sense of his own progress, since he first put pen to paper in another century:

Perhaps I might be a little pleased with some of these philosophemes in the warmer years of life; but I look upon them now with much indifference. . . . What darknesses hang about them, I should be glad to see scattered by the rays of truth.[57]

In all his work, Watts tried to live up to his motto, that "it is not reasonable to put out our candle and sit still in the dark, because we have not the light of sunbeams." [58] At times he advances with the caution of a candle-bearer, at times with the haste of a sunbeam; but at all times he works for enlightenment.

[56] The Improvement of the Mind, Watts, V, 241.
[57] Philosophical Essays, Watts, V, 504.
[58] The Improvement of the Mind, Watts, V, 338.

CHAPTER THIRTEEN

"FREE PHILOSOPHY"

It would be misleading to suggest that the fulness of the English Enlightenment sprang fully armed from the mind of Watts. Behind Voltaire there lay Bayle and the Dutch Arminians. Behind Wolff there lay Francke and the German pietists.[1] In like manner, behind Watts lay the philosophical and religious tradition of latitude. But for Watts this tradition was more than something in the air; it was embodied in the educational system of Dissent.

Watts drew his concept of Free Philosophy from the educational programme of the Dissenting Academies. The Renaissance had been first and foremost a revolution in education, and the universities had purveyed its spirit and methods. A similar educational revolution occurred in the latter half of the 17th century, as the Enlightenment replaced the Renaissance at the centre of European culture.[2] Free philosophy meant of course freedom from the authority of Plato and Aristotle, and Watts suggests that this liberation is not difficult to achieve. One has but to think a little about the new mechanical philosophy and the scales will fall from one's eyes:

Let the one believe his universal soul and the other go on with his notion of substantial forms, and at the same time teach them how by certain original laws of motion . . . allowing a continued divine concourse in and with all, the several appearances in nature may be solved, and the variety of effects produced, according to the corpuscular philosophy, improved by Descartes, Mr

---

[1] German Pietism was a more specific and homogeneous movement than either Dutch Arminianism or English Latitudinarianism. The founder of the school of German Pietism was P. J. Spener (1633-1705). His *Pia Desideria* (1675) inaugurated the attack on Lutheran scholastic theology. By 1727, when Francke died, Pietism was the dominant force in German religious life. See Arthur Cushman McGiffert, *Protestant Thought Before Kant* (London: Duckworth, 1911), Chapter 9.

[2] Karl Barth notes that in Germany in the early 18th century "there was a divergence of opinion between the educators of the pietistic and those of the enlightened school." The two schools were agreed however that education "was a matter over which they were quite capable of taking control." Barth, p. 38.

Boyle, and Sir Isaac Newton. . . . Then . . . the peripatetic forms will vanish from the mind like a dream, and the Platonic soul of the world will expire.[3]

In England however, Free Philosophy had more formidable enemies than Plato or Aristotle.

There was on the one hand the traditional zeal of the Dissenters, who were suspicious that philosophical freedom would lead to libertinism; and on the other hand there was the conservative orthodoxy of those who feared a rapid descent into Arianism, deism, Socinianism and atheism. Watts therefore had to defend the principles of Free Philosophy against the charges of lukewarmness and apostacy:

For the most part people are born to their opinions, and never question the truth of what their family or their country or their party profess. They clothe their minds as they do their bodies, after the fashion in vogue, nor one of a hundred ever examine their principles. It is suspected of lukewarmness to suppose examination necessary, and it will be charged as a tendency to aposta- cy if we go about to examine them. Persons are applauded for presuming they are in the right, and (as Mr Locke saith) he that considers and inquires into the reasons of things is counted a foe to orthodoxy.[4]

Watts wrote a poem entitled "Free Philosophy," in which he castigates

> Custom, that tyranness of fools,
> That leads the learned round the schools,
> In magic chains of forms and rules.[5]

This poem, dedicated to his teacher, Thomas Rowe, expresses the energy and enthusiasm which raise Watts's thought above the level of mediocre plagiarism.

Watts was a student at the Newington Green Academy from 1690 to 1694. He clearly profited from the liberal atmosphere which reigned there. It was from his education that he derived his treasured habit of giving his "thoughts a loose," and letting "them rove without confinement." [6] Tho- mas Rowe took over the Academy in 1678. It appears that he was re- sponsible for introducing the Free Philosophy as a basis for education around 1680.[7] The central innovation was the teaching of Cartesian prin- ciples at a time when the Aristotelian philosophy was dominant in the universities; to this was later added the teaching of mental science ac-

---

[3] *The Improvement of the Mind,* Watts, V, 340-341.
[4] *Ibid.,* V, 288.
[5] *Horae Lyricae,* II. Watts, IV, 393.
[6] Watts, IV, 532. Quoted in Harry Escott, *Isaac Watts Hymnographer* (London: Independent Press, 1962), p. 19.
[7] *DNB* (Thomas Rowe).

cording to the new ideas of Locke.[8] Cartesian physics was still being taught when Watts was at the Academy, so that his education, though far more modern than that obtainable in the universities, did lag behind the latest findings of Newton and the Royal Society. But the rivalry between Cartesian and Newtonian systems of natural science is of small account when one considers the ramifications of the Free Philosophy purveyed by the Academy.

Ramist logic, as we have seen, provided a modern method of tackling knowledge.[9] But logic had no priority over free enquiry as the way to truth; nor did ontology, by its own laws, dictate a synthesis to which all the parts of knowledge should be subject. In the first place, science was taught along experimental lines, as it was not in the universities.[10] Samuel Wesley the elder, who had himself attended Newington Green Academy before absconding with his grant and turning high-flyer, could not resist admiring the apparatus which was used for teaching experimental science. According to Wesley, the special features of Newington Green included "a fine garden, bowling green, fishpond, and within a laboratory, and some not inconsiderable rarities, with air pumps, thermometers, and all sorts of mathematical instruments." [11] In the second place – and Wesley notes this with rather more scorn than admiration –, the Academy was organised and disciplined along democratic lines, "we having . . . for what order we had, a sort of democratical government among us, anyone having power to propose a law, and all laws carried by the ballot." [12] In the third place, as Defoe, another distinguished ex-student of the Academy, notes, politics was taught as a science.[13] In the fourth place, there was a good deal of toleration between the dissenting sects, so much so that Wesley complained with high-church pique: "But do the Presbyterians and In-

[8] Locke's *Essay* was on the index at Oxford at the end of the century, and in 1703 the heads of Oxford colleges met to arrange a ban on the reading of his works. See H. McLachlan, *English Education under the Test Acts*, p. 28.

[9] Ramus was apparently unknown in Oxford in 1678. He was almost invariably studied in the Dissenting Academies, many of whose teachers in the early days were ex-Cambridge men. See *ibid.*, p. 20, and Irene Parker, *Dissenting Academies in England* (Cambridge: University Press, 1914), pp. 74-75.

[10] Cf. John Ray in 1691: "I am sorry to see so little account made of real experimental philosophy in this University, and that those ingenious Sciences of the Mathematics are so much neglected by us." Ray, p. 126.

[11] Samuel Wesley, *A Letter from a Country Divine to his Friend in London Concerning the Education of the Dissenters in their Private Academies* (London, 1703), p. 7.

[12] *Ibid.*, p. 8.

[13] Defoe was also taught 5 languages, mathematics, natural philosophy, logic, geography and history – all in English. See Escott, p. 27. Cf. Swift's ironic reference to the "ignorance" of the Brobdingnagians in "not having hitherto reduced politics into a science, as the more acute wits of Europe have done." Swift, XI, 119.

dependents hear none but such as have been ordained? I'm well assured of the contrary; for I remember several of us, if not all our pupils went to hear Friend Bunnian, when he preached at Newington Green." [14] And lastly, and for our purposes most significantly of all, the Academy put into educational practice the principles of language reform which Wilkins and others had laid down as the declared policy of the Royal Society.[15] Watts spent a great deal of energy cultivating his diction. In this respect, as in others, he was drawing on ideas he had imbibed at the Academy.

Thus Watts's Academy education embraced within a common outlook attitudes in politics and religion, methods in logic and experimental science, and practice in language and morality. It is therefore not surprising to find Watts using the slogans of Baconian and Cartesian revolution, not only to hit out at Aristotle, but also to express his own comprehensive vision.

The first slogan is the attack on "words without ideas." Watts held that "Descartes, Newton, Gassendi, Bacon, Boyle" all "carried on the noble design of freeing the world from the long slavery of Aristotle and substantial forms, of occult qualities, and words without ideas. They taught mankind to trace out truth by reasoning and experiment." [16] This is commonplace enough, though not everyone placed reasoning and experiment in the same bracket. The slogan takes on the colour of more energetic diatribe, when Watts uses it to expose the pretensions of ecclesiastical tyranny:

For many ages all truth and all heresy have been determined by . . . senseless tests, and by words without ideas; such Shibboleths as these have decided the secular fates of men; and bishoprics, or burning mitres or faggots have been the rewards of different persons, according as they pronounced them. . . . A thousand thank-offerings are due to that Providence which has delivered our age and our nation from these absurd iniquities.[17]

In such a passage, the final panegyric sentence aside, Watts, by drawing on one of the driving-forces of Dissent, attains a tone which would not disgrace the pages of Gibbon.

The second slogan is the Baconian distinction between words and things. Here Watts is faithful to a long tradition, but he is particularly concerned to apply this slogan to the field of language reform:

---

[14] Samuel Wesley, *A Defence of a Letter,* p. 48.
[15] One of Wilkins's companions at Oxford was Charles Morton who held a fellowship there in the days before the Act of Uniformity and who founded Newington Green Academy in 1667. He used Wilkins's books for tutorial work. See Escott, p. 27.
[16] *Philosophical Essays,* Watts, V, 502.
[17] *The Improvement of the Mind,* Watts, V, 255.

The first direction for youth is this, "learn betimes to distinguish between words and things." Get clear and plain ideas of the things you are set to study. Do not content yourselves with mere words and names, lest your laboured improvements only amass a heap of unintelligible phrases, and you feed upon husks instead of kernels.[18]

Here Watts is drawing on the Baconian doctrine of things, the Cartesian doctrine of clear and plain ideas, and, as a link between the two, the Royal Society insistence on simplified and utilitarian language.

The English mind in Watts's generation enjoyed this traditional inter-penetration of Cartesian and Baconian attitudes. Descartes was used to give metaphysical or ideological justification to Baconian inspired ex-perimental science, and Bacon was used to reinforce the solidity and un-alterability of the Cartesian superstructure of ideas. This interpenetration lies behind the achievement and reputation of Samuel Clarke, hailed by most in Watts's generation after the death of Locke as England's greatest living philosopher. Both Clarke and Watts approach metaphysics or on-tology as they approach physics. Ideas are as immutable and static as things. And, in Watts's words,

things are to be considered as they are in themselves; their nature is inflexible, and their natural relations unalterable; and therefore in order to conceive them aright, we must bring our understandings to things, and not pretend to bend and strain things to comport with our fancies and forms.[19]

This Cartesian application of the Baconian slogan is a characteristic feature of Watts's Free Philosophy. Mere experiments are not enough; the mind must "conceive them aright." Bacon's empirical and conserva-tive critique of the Renaissance has been transformed into an enlightened modernism, through the addition to it of Descartes' rational and radical critique of the Renaissance.[20]

The aspect of Watts's Free Philosophy which most closely reflects the ethos of Dissent is its marked individualism. Various critics have pointed out that, in the early 18th century, uniformity and individualism were no more mutually exclusive than were rationalism and sentimentalism.[21]

---

[18] *Ibid.*

[19] *Ibid.*, V, 258-259.

[20] This distinction between the work of Bacon and the work of Descartes is made by Michel Foucault in *Les Mots et les Choses,* pp. 65-66.

[21] Arthur Oncken Lovejoy, "The Parallel of Deism and Classicism," *Essays in the History of Ideas* (Baltimore: John Hopkins Press, 1948), pp. 78-99. Lovejoy's first two paragraphs are on what he calls Uniformitarianism and Rationalistic Individualism. Cf. Thomas A. Hanzo, *Latitude and Restoration Criticism* ("Anglistica" 12; Copen-hagen: Rosenkilde and Bagger, 1961), p. 48. Hanzo points out that "the individual could follow his heart or mind, assured that the rest of mankind would do the same with the same result." Cf. also Fairchild, II, 9.

Watts however emphasises the strand of individualism more strongly than others of his generation. In "The Indian Philosopher" (1701), which like "Free Philosophy" (1706) tries to provide a satisfactory basis for philosophical freedom, Watts not only specifically rejects "the schools," but also the "wide fields of Nature's Laws." He finds his ground of certainty "deep in thought, within my breast." [22] The later poem arrives at a similar conclusion; the guarantee and justification of Free Philosophy is that "knowledge invites us each alone." [23]

Watts was by and large a man of his age, and yet he was sufficiently near to his 17th century puritan roots to be able to assert a rousing individualism: "When we are arrived at manly age, there is no person on earth, no set or society of men whatsoever, that have power and authority given them by God . . . absolutely to dictate to others their opinions and practices in the moral and religious life." [24] The individualism of Watts's Free Philosophy meant that he did not have to choose between Ancients and Moderns, or a variety of theoretical systems. The Dissenting Academy had seen to it that "from the infancy of my studies I began to be of the Eclectic Sect." [25] Consequently,

it is not often that I divert out of my way to tell the world particularly what the Moderns or the Ancients have said on these subjects, nor how far I agree with them or differ from them; but in the main I directly pursue my own track of thoughts, and range this infinite variety of ideas collected from the universe of beings in such a method as appears to me the most comprehensive and natural, plain and easy.[26]

Henry More and John Norris had defined their eclecticism in very similar terms. But Watts, as befits a Dissenter, puts the emphasis not so much on easy indifference as on jealous individualism. Thus when asked where he stands in relation to the Stoics, the Platonists, Gassendi, Descartes, Newton, Tycho, Copernicus, Arminius, Calvin, Episcopacy, Presbyterianism and Independency, Watts replies:

I think it may be very proper in such cases not to give an answer in the gross, but rather to enter into a detail of particulars, and explain one's own sentiments. Perhaps there is no man, nor set of men upon earth whose sentiments I entirely follow. God has given me reason to judge for myself.[27]

In this declaration Watts appears as a mediator between the individualism which men in the 17th century strove to attain with strenuous rigour, and

[22] "The Indian Philosopher," *Horae Lyricae,* II. Watts, IV, 407.
[23] "Free Philosophy," *ibid.,* IV, 393.
[24] *The Improvement of the Mind,* Watts, V, 336.
[25] *Philosophical Essays,* Watts, V, 501.
[26] "A Brief Scheme of Ontology," *ibid.,* V, 638.
[27] *The Improvement of the Mind,* Watts, V, 293.

the individualism which the modern consciousness takes for granted as a received commonplace.

Perhaps the most striking contribution made by Watts's generation towards the evolution of the modern consciousness was Shaftesbury's idea of the moral sense. Like Watts's Free Philosophy, Shaftesbury's moral sense had its roots in the latitude of the Cambridge Platonists. Like Watts, Shaftesbury sought his ground of certainty inside man's consciousness. Both men were liberal-minded Whigs, disciples of Locke, and lovers of freedom political and philosophical. It is therefore interesting to find in Watts's fourth philosophical essay, "Of Innate Ideas," a fifth section entitled "Of the Foundations of Moral Virtue, and of Moral Sense or Instinct," which begins as follows: "There has a controversy risen long since these papers were written, ... whether the soul of man judges of moral good and evil by an inward principle or instinct, which is called the moral sense, antecedent to all reasonings; or whether ... it judges of them by reasoning." [28] Watts is willing to admit that "there is such a thing which may be called a moral sense"; [29] "but this moral sense is still the same thing, is the very nature and make of the mind; it is intelligence or reason itself." [30] This may be begging the question, but obviously Watts sees no need for there to be any other faculty than conscience, active at times as a moral sense, at times as a reasoning power.

It is clear that Watts was less worried than either Berkeley or Bolingbroke about the possibility of Shaftesbury's moral sense accelerating the decay of rationalism. Berkeley hit out at Shaftesbury with considerable vigour. Through the mouthpiece of his devil's advocate, Alciphron, he condemns the whole idea of moral sense, on the grounds that it seeks by its very nature to escape the scrutiny of reason. When pressed to define moral sense, Alciphron "declared that such exactness was to no purpose; that pedants, indeed, may dispute and define, but could never reach that high sense of honour which distinguished the fine gentleman, and was a thing rather to be felt than explained." [31] With heavy irony Berkeley embroiders on this theme:

Moral beauty is of so peculiar and abstracted a nature, something so subtle, fine and fugacious, that it will not bear being handled and inspected, like every gross and common subject. You will therefore pardon me if I stand upon my philosophic liberty, and choose rather to entrench myself within the general and indefinite sense, rather than, by entering into a precise and

[28] *Philosophical Essays,* Watts, V, 550.
[29] *Ibid.,* V, 551.
[30] *Ibid.*
[31] Berkeley, p. 114.

particular explication of this beauty, perchance lose sight of it, or give you some hold whereon to cavil, and infer, and raise doubts, queries and difficulties, about a point as clear as the sun, when nobody reasons upon it.[32]

Euphranor states Berkeley's own position in terms that brand the idea of moral sense with the mark of enthusiasm:

Should it not seem a very uncertain guide in morals, for a man to follow his passion or inward feeling? And would not this rule infallibly lead different ways, according to the prevalency of this or that appetite or passion.[33]

Bolingbroke offers an identical interpretation when he writes:

There are those who ... affirm that they have ... a moral sense, that is an instinct by which they distinguish what is morally good from what is morally evil, and perceive an agreeable or disagreeable intellectual sensation accordingly, without the trouble of observation and reflection. They bid fair to be enthusiasts in ethics, and to make natural religion as ridiculous, as some of their brothers have made revealed religion, by insisting on the doctrine of an inward light.[34]

This critique of the idea of moral sense is partly applicable to Watts, who on this issue is nearer to Shaftesbury and Locke than he is to Berkeley and Bolingbroke. Watts, to a lesser extent than Shaftesbury, was prone to abuse his cherished philosophic liberty by shying away from rational scrutiny; and, as a Dissenter, he was not innocent of the charge of ethical enthusiasm. On other grounds however, Watts took exception to the implications of Shaftesbury's interpretation of the idea of moral sense, and could be as scathing as Berkeley in demanding an "explication of this beauty" which had become so fashionable among the polite part of mankind.

Watts has no real quarrel with Shaftesbury's moral sense as such; it is the use to which it is put which gripes him. In practice, Shaftesbury equated moral sense with aesthetic sense; and his own aesthetic sense was that of a dilettante who indulged his taste and paraded his politeness. Thus Watts, who was far from deficient in classical taste and polished diction, questioned

whether several of the rhapsodies called the Characteristics would ever have survived the first edition, if they had not discovered so strong a tincture of infidelity. . . . I have sometimes indeed been ready to wonder, how a book in the main so loosely written, should ever obtain so many readers amongst men of sense. . . . There are few books that ever I read, which made any pretence to a great genius, from which I derived so little valuable knowledge as from these treatises. There is indeed amongst them a lively pertness, a parade of

---

[32] *Ibid.*, pp. 119-120.
[33] *Ibid.*, p. 120.
[34] Bolingbroke, V, 86.

literature, and much of what some folks nowadays call politeness; but it is hard that we should be bound to admire all the reveries of this author, under the penalty of being unfashionable.[35]

It is significant that Watts does not attack Shaftesbury for being a free-thinker or deist. The brunt of his attack is fair criticism in the light of Shaftesbury's inflated reputation.

But Watts has not yet finished with Shaftesbury. Forty pages later he reveals that his basic quarrel with Shaftesbury is a moral one. For Watts, intellectual effort and aesthetic achievement meant nothing apart from the moral use to which they were put. "Let me ask our rhapsodist," he writes:

How many have you actually reclaimed by this smooth soft method, and these fine words? . . . Perhaps now and then a man of better natural mould has been a little refined. . . . But have the passions of revenge and envy, of am-bition and pride, and the inward secret vices of the mind been mortified merely by this philosophical language? Have any of these men been made new creatures, men of real piety and love to God? Go dress up all the virtues of human nature in all the beauties of your oratory, and declaim aloud in the praise of social virtue, and the amiable qualities of goodness, till your heart or your lungs ache, among the looser herds of mankind, and you will ever find, as your heathen fathers have done before, that the wild passions and appetites of men are too violent to be restrained by such mild and silken language.[36]

One feels that Watts appears in his true colours when he confronts Shaftes-bury's enlightened optimism. Watts does not share Shaftesbury's con-ception of philosophical freedom. In Watts's view philosophy must not only be freed from its gothic chains; it must also be freed to be useful.

Watts's utilitarianism constitutes an important contribution to the modern consciousness. To those who looked on experimental science as a game or hobby, Watts pontificates:

Inquiries even in natural philosophy should not be mere amusements, and much less in the affairs of religion. Researches into the springs of natural bodies and their motions should lead men to invent happy methods for the ease and convenience of human life.[37]

If Norris entitled himself to the epithet "ingenious," then Watts equally well deserves that of "useful." Indeed, in one of his essays, he extracts from "the ingenious Mr Norris's little discourse of religious conversation" certain "excellent and valuable hints for our use." [38] Such an operation exemplifies Watts's approach.

[35] *The Improvement of the Mind*, Watts, V, 214.
[36] *Ibid.*, V, 243.
[37] *Ibid.*, V, 260.
[38]*An Humble Attempt Towards the Revival of Practical Religion Among Christians* (1729), Watts, III, 31.

This utilitarian approach is present in the midst of his intricate speculations on the doctrine of the Trinity. In his first treatise on the subject, he prefaces his inquiries as follows:

I imagined . . . that it would be an acceptable service to the Church of Christ, if this sublime and important doctrine were brought down to a practical use, and our particular duties to the sacred three, were distinctly declared and vindicated out of the holy scriptures; which is of far greater moment to our piety and salvation than any nice adjustment of all the mysterious circumstances that relate to this article in the theory of it.[39]

If the Trinity can be shown to be of practical use, then the more so religion in general. Watts was not above describing the usefulness of religion as a means to prevent suicide, alcoholism and duelling, and in his *Defence against Temptation to Self-Murther* (1726), he even gathers together some statistics from the weekly newspapers: "59 are known to have destroyed themselves the year past; besides 74 who were drowned, and 43 who were said to be found dead." [40]

The usefulness of religion was a theme that Berkeley treated with considerable eloquence along similar lines. Thus he declared that, "for my own part I had rather my wife and children all believed what they had no notion of, and daily pronounced words without a meaning, than that any of them should cut his throat, or leap out of a window." [41] Berkeley points the same moral as Watts when he opines, with all the good-humoured weight of Augustan common sense:

Errors and nonsense, as such, are of small concern in the eye of the public, which considereth not the metaphysical truth of notions, so much as the tendency they have to produce good or evil. Truth itself is valued by the public, as it hath an influence, and is felt in the course of life. You may confute a whole shelf of Schoolmen, and discover many speculative truths, without any great merit towards your country.[42]

As a corollary to Berkeley's distinction, it may be granted that Watts's own brand of utilitarianism had at least as much influence on succeeding generations as did Shaftesbury's doctrine of moral sense.

Watts gives the impression of being somewhat obsessed with the utility of things, from the art of shorthand,[43] to card-games,[44] and the association of ideas.[45] But in all this, he expresses the spirit of Enlightenment philoso-

[39] *The Christian Doctrine of the Trinity* (1722), Preface. Watts, VI, 416.
[40] Watts, II, 355.
[41] Berkeley, p. 105.
[42] *Ibid.*, p. 106.
[43] *The Improvement of the Mind,* Watts, V, 281.
[44] *Ibid.*, V, 386-387.
[45] *Ibid.*, V, 284.

phy, and provides an interesting link between the 17th century puritans and the 19th century utilitarians. His position in the tradition of Dissent qualifies the nature of his thought. His Free Philosophy is not merely derivative from Descartes and Locke, but arises out of the special nature of his education, has its roots in the past, and has its consequences for the future.

CHAPTER FOURTEEN

SUNK RELIGION

Watts's theology, in so far as it impinges on his thought in general, deserves special notice. Since it lies at the centre of his thought and activity, it cannot be overlooked. He himself regarded other fields of thought as peripheral, claiming that "as every man has some amusements for an hour of leisure, I have chosen Mathematical Science, Philosophy and Poesy for mine." [1] His views on latitude, natural religion, pietism and mysticism indicate ways in which religious thought contributed to the Enlightenment. His general approach can be summed up in the titles of some of his sermons. Three are entitled "The Inward Witness to Christianity," three are entitled "A Rational Defence of the Gospel," and another is entitled "The Doctrine of the Trinity and the Use of it." [2] "Inward witness," "rational defence" and "use" constitute three aspects of Watts's religious thinking which do not always blend as well as they do in the lay-out of his collected sermons.

Watts's religious outlook, half way between 17th century Calvinism and late 18th century Unitarianism, corresponds not only to the via media of the English Enlightenment, but also to the moment of classicism. As a classicist, Watts cultivated what can only be called the art of sinking in prose and poetry; his theology appears to be the product of the same art. The only difference is, that whereas in his prose and poetry he practised the art of sinking with confident single-mindedness, he felt unable to be so thorough as a theologian. Thus his only direct application of the art of sinking to theology, occurs in an attack on Locke's *Reasonableness of Christianity*. This he takes as an example of over-sinking. [3] Watts suffered

---

[1] *Reliquiae Juveniles: Miscellaneous Thoughts in Prose and Verse* (1734), Preface. Watts, IV, 457.

[2] *Sermons on Various Subjects Divine and Moral* (1721-1729), Watts, I, 1-510.

[3] *Philosophical Essays*, Watts, V, 503. Cf. a note to one of his poems on Locke: "He was no Socinian, though he has darkened the glory of the gospel, and debased Christianity in the book which he calls the Reasonableness of it." Watts, IV, 396.

from theological scruples all his life. This was partly because he was aware that Calvinism in his generation was sprouting Unitarian wings. However, the hesitancy and confusion to which such scruples gave rise, do not override the basic trend in Watts's theology towards sunk religion. Watts credited Locke on his deathbed with possessing the Christian faith.[4] In a personal sense this was certainly so. But Locke's writings on Christianity became the thin end of the wedge to sink that religion, in the sense of capsizing it, whereas Watts's aim, and the achievement of later generations, was to sink Christianity to the level of every man's understanding and capacity.

Behind the art of sinking in religion lay the spirit of latitude which, for Watts, was an important component of Enlightenment thought. He believed that "free converse with persons of different sects . . . will soften the roughness of an unpolished soul, and enlarge the avenues of our charity towards others, and incline us to receive them into all the degrees of unity and affection which the word of God requires." [5] Watts's latitudinarian spirit found expression in his proposal "to unite the Independents and Baptists by surrendering the doctrine of infant baptism, if the Baptists would give up immersion." [6] His belief in religious freedom stems from the tradition of puritan Dissent, even when it is expressly related to the influence of Locke's *Letter of Toleration*:

These leaves triumphed over all the remnant of my prejudices on the side of bigotry, and taught me to allow all men the same freedom to choose their religion, as I claim to choose my own. Blessed be God that this doctrine has now taken such root in Great Britain, that I trust neither the powers nor the frauds of Rome, nor the malice, pride and darkness of mankind, nor the rage of hell shall ever prevail against it.[7]

To the influence of Milton, Bunyan and Locke, must be added that of the Cambridge Platonists and the latitudinarian divines. Watts was averse to "making anything in religion heavy or tiresome," and was "persuaded that there is a breadth in the narrow road to Heaven, and persons may travel more than seven abreast to it." [8] Watts is not content to polish only the Dissenter's soul; he sought to cater for as wide a public as that served by the *Spectator*.[9] He wrote his hymns and spiritual songs with this public in

    [4] Watts, IV, 384, 396.
    [5] *The Improvement of the Mind,* Watts, V, 268.
    [6] *DNB* (Watts).
    [7] *Philosophical Essays,* Watts, V, 503.
    [8] Quoted in Pinto, *Essays and Studies,* XX (1935), 91-92.
    [9] Watts contributed a paraphrase of Psalm cxiv to *The Spectator* (No. 461, 19 August 1712), and in an accompanying letter, following Steele's introduction, noted

view, sinking the language to find the lowest common denominator not only of intellectual capacity, but also of religious tradition.

Thus, in the preface to his *Divine Songs Attempted in Easy Language for the Use of Children,* he writes:

You will find here nothing that savours of a party: the children of high and low degree, of the Church of England or Dissenters, baptised in infancy or not, may all join together in these songs. . . . I hope the more general the sense is, these composures may be of the more universal use and service.[10]

In the preface to the second edition of his *Hymns,* he writes in similar vein of religious latitude as the basis and motive of the art of sinking in poetry:

I have avoided the more obscure and controverted points of Christianity. . . . The contentions and distinguishing words of sects and parties are secluded, that whole assemblies might assist at the harmony, and different churches join in the same worship without offence.

If any expressions occur to the reader that savour of an opinion different from his own, yet he may observe these are generally such as are capable of an extensive sense, and may be used with a charitable latitude. . . . Where any unpleasing word is found, he that leads the worship may substitute a better; for . . . we are not confined to the words of any man in our public solemnities.[11]

In other writers of the Enlightenment, there is a combination of religious latitude and classical diction; but it would be difficult to find any writer who combined them so closely.

Latitudinarianism was a 17th century movement which became redundant as its aims were realised. Before Watts, the argument for latitude had been an argument for progress and liberty; after Watts, it became an argument for conservatism and uniformity. Once all parties and opinions had been permitted, it was only a matter of time before they came to an agreement. Watts's art of sinking in religion contributed to the redundancy of the argument for latitude, even though he was writing in the 17th century tradition. It is important to measure the rapidity with which the dynamic movement for latitude developed into the static call for uniformity. One is tempted to draw a parallel between Watts's position at the end of the latitudinarian tradition, and his position at the end of the Metaphysical tradition, since it is arguable that classicism corresponds to the conservative instinct for religious uniformity. In this sense Watts was the last latitudinarian. Assuming that liberation from the gothic past was an

with obvious approval that "persons of every party, sect and humour, are fond of conforming their taste to yours." *The Spectator* (8 vols.; London: Tonson and Draper, 1753), VI, 255.

[10] Watts, IV, 296.
[11] Watts, IV, 148-149.

acquired characteristic of his age, he set about the task of vulgarising the latitudinarian achievement, by sinking it to the level of a uniform piety accessible to the lowest capacity.

John Wesley's criticism of Watts's theology reveals how much further the 18th century pursued the art of sinking in religion. Wesley paints Watts in gothic colours. In 1780 he advises his brother Charles that the monster is dangerous:

I would not read over Dr Watts's tract for an hundred pounds. You may read it, and welcome. I will not, dare not, move those subtle, metaphysical controversies. Arianism is not in question: it is Eutychianism, or Nestorianism. But what are they? What neither I nor anyone else understands. But they are what tore the Eastern and Western churches asunder.[12]

Wesley's sensitivity may appear exaggerated. He was no doubt partly provoked by his own fears of causing schism. But, the rhetoric of passion aside, Wesley is here voicing a common 18th century complaint against intellectualism, and against those who refuse to accept the lowest common denominator of what is plain and obvious.

Eight years later, Watts irritates Wesley into a further profession of 18th century faith:

I believe just what is revealed, and no more. But I do not pretend to account for it, or to solve the difficulties that may attend it. Let angels do this if they can. But I think they cannot. . . . Some years since, I read about fifty pages of Dr Watts's ingenious treatise upon the "Glorified Humanity of Christ." But it so confounded my intellects, and plunged me into such unprofitable reasonings, yea dangerous ones, that I would not have read it through for five hundred pounds. It led him into Arianism. Take care that similar tracts (all of which I abhor) have not the same effect on you. Pursue that train of reasoning as far as it will go, and it will surely land you either in Socinianism or Deism.[13]

The useful Watts who found Norris so ingenious is himself damned as immoderately ingenious by the even more useful Wesley. One is left with quite a precise impression of the ground covered between two generations of religious consciousness. On the one hand there are the achievements of a latitude which is open to inquiry and the pursuit of truth, and on the other hand there are the consequences of a latitude which has shrunk into the jealously guarded area of prudent uniformity.

[12] Letter to Charles Wesley, 8 June 1780. John Wesley, *Works,* XII, 147. The tract in question is probably Watts's *The Glory of Christ as God-Man Unveiled* (1746), in which there is considerable disquisition on the pre-existent soul of Christ.

[13] Letter to Joseph Benson, 17 September 1788. John Wesley, *Works,* XII, 431. The last sentence of this extract ("Pursue . . . Deism.") does not appear in this edition; it is included in an extended version of this letter to be found in John Wesley, *Letters,* ed. John Telford (8 vols.; London: Epworth Press, 1931), VIII, 90.

Wesley's criticism of Watts's theology does not take into account its development. There can be few clearer illustrations of the theological revolution by which the 18th century chose to distinguish itself from the 17th century, than in a juxtaposition of the early and the late Watts. What could be more typical of the 17th century consciousness than the energetic confidence of the youthful Watts?

When I have given my thoughts a loose, and let them rove without confinement, sometimes I seem to have carried reason with me even to the camp of Socinus; but then St John gives my soul a twitch, and St Paul bears me back again . . . almost to the tents of John Calvin.[14]

This outburst dates from 1696. It belongs to an age which was rapidly coming to an end. In 1695 Cotton Mather could still quote with relish from an earlier puritan, John Cotton (1584-1652), who had remarked: "I love to sweeten my mouth with a piece of Calvin before I go to sleep." [15] But whereas the New England orthodoxy of Cotton and the Mathers made them immune from the temptations of Socinianism, Watts is able to follow his latitudinarian instincts and indulge in what amount to theological opposites.

In time however the wings of Watts's latitude were clipped. In his attempts to modernise the doctrine of the Trinity, he was forced to retreat into an impoverished orthodoxy. He no longer felt able in 1722 to give his thoughts a loose, and wrote by way of preamble to his treatise on the Trinity: "I confess my thoughts sometimes ran out too far in a defence of some occasional positions, or incidental truths; but upon a review I have cut them all off from the body of this discourse." [16] So changed was the spirit of the age between 1696 and 1722 that, in spite of these mutilations to his discourse, he was still suspect in the eyes of the orthodox. His attempt to reconcile, by means of redefinition, the view of orthodox Trinitarians with those of Arians, Socinians and Sabellians, was doomed to failure. Inevitably he came under attack from all sides.

Fifty years after leaving Newington Green Academy, he was still unable to effect a truce in the Trinitarian controversy, and in exasperation wrote "A Solemn Address to the Great and Ever Blessed God" (1745). What could be more typical of the 18th century consciousness than his resigned complaint?

---

[14] "To Pocyon. The Mischief of Warm Disputes and Declamations on the Controverted Points of Christianity," *Reliquiae Juveniles,* No. 49. Watts, IV, 532. Quoted in Escott, p. 19.
[15] Quoted in Cotton Mather. *Johannes in Eremo* (1695), and in Edward Taylor, *Poetical Works,* ed. Thomas H. Johnson (Princeton: University Press, 1966), p. 19.
[16] *The Christian Doctrine of the Trinity,* Preface. Watts, VI, 418.

How shall a poor weak creature be able to adjust and reconcile these clashing ideas, and to understand this mystery? Or must I believe and act blindfold, without understanding? . . . I want to have this wonderful doctrine . . . made a little plainer. . . . I cannot find thou hast anywhere forbid me . . . to make these enquiries. . . . But how can such weak creatures ever take in so strange, so difficult, and so abstruse a doctrine as this; in the explication and defence whereof, multitudes of men, even of learning and piety, have lost themselves in infinite subtilties of dispute, and endless mazes of darkness? . . . Forbid it, O my God, that ever I should be so unhappy as to unglorify my Father, my Saviour, or my Sanctifier. . . . Help me . . . for I am quite tired and weary of these human explainings, so various and uncertain.[17]

Watts's theological development is not merely a reflection of a temperamental discrepancy between youth and old age; it corresponds to the change from 17th century latitude to 18th century uniformity, and registers the decay of rationalism in the religious consciousness of the age.

All his life Watts was, for a Calvinist, remarkably attracted to the "camp of Socinus." Even in *The Improvement of the Mind*, a work of vulgarisation and unimpeachable orthodoxy, he is unable to avoid paying the Socinians an oblique compliment:

Truth in this world is not always attended and supported by the wisest and safest methods; and error though it can never be maintained by just reasoning, yet may be artfully covered and defended. An ingenious writer may put excellent colours upon his own mistakes. Some Socinians, who deny the atonement of Christ, have written well.[18]

Throughout his life Watts cherished the respect for reason with which he credited the Socinians. He can only safeguard his orthodoxy under the cover of a tautological axiom – that error cannot be maintained by just reasoning. This axiom covered a multitude of sins and was strained to breaking point in the 1745 outburst.

Watts was unable to sustain Berkeley's eloquent confidence. Berkeley had considered this problem and had proffered his own axiomatic front to meet the challenge of Spinoza and the Socinians. He makes Crito speak of

Spinoza, the great leader of our modern infidels, in whom are to be found many schemes and notions much admired and followed of late years: such as undermining religion under the pretence of vindicating and explaining it; the maintaining it not necessary to believe in Christ according to the flesh; the persuading men that miracles are to be understood only in a spiritual and

---

[17] Isaac Watts, *A Faithful Enquiry after the Ancient and Original Doctrine of the Trinity* (reprint of 1745 suppressed edition; Bath: R. Cruttwell, 1802), "A Solemn Address to the Great and Blessed God," pp. ii-vii. This address was incorporated in *Remnants of Time Employed in Prose and Verse*, No. 21, Watts, IV, 640-643.
[18] *The Improvement of the Mind*, Watts, V, 213.

allegorical sense; that vice is not so bad a thing as we are apt to think; that men are mere machines impelled by fatal necessity.

I have heard, said I, Spinoza represented as a man of close argument and demonstration.

He did, replied Crito, demonstrate; but it was after such a manner as anyone may demonstrate anything.[19]

Thus Berkeley slips out of the responsibility of taking Spinoza seriously. Clearly both Watts and Berkeley wanted rationalism to function within the limits of a consensus of common sense. Socinians were outside this consensus, and yet their respect for reason had to be acknowledged.

It must be remembered that the prevailing view of Socinianism was hysterical rather than reasoned. Robert South's fulminations illustrate the ordinary attitude of the established order towards the camp of Socinus:

The Socinians are impious blasphemers, whose infamous pedigree runs back (from wretch to wretch) in a direct line to the devil himself; and who are fitter to be crushed by the civil magistrate, as destructive to government and society, than to be confuted as merely heretics in religion.[20]

The attitude represented by Berkeley and Watts lies half way between South's harsh condemnation and Tillotson's generous tolerance.

In a previous generation Tillotson had paid considerably less oblique compliments to the Socinians' art of reasoning than those that can be squeezed from the pen of Watts or Berkeley. Tillotson's considered assessment of the Socinians runs as follows:

Generally they are a pattern of the fair way of disputing and of debating matters of religion, without heat and unseemly reflections upon their adversaries. . . . For the most part they reason closely and clearly, with extraordinary guard and caution, with great dexterity and decency, and yet, with smartness and subtilty enough; with a very gentle heat, and few hard words. . . . In a word, they are the strongest managers of a weak cause, and which is ill-founded at the bottom, that perhaps ever yet meddled with controversy. . . . Even . . . the Jesuits themselves . . . are in comparison of them but mere scolds and bunglers.[21]

Tillotson chose his words carefully, and his tone is measured. Although he gives more credit to the Socinians than Watts felt able to, he is at least as decided as Watts about their heterodoxy. Moreover, the via media of Tillotson's age was considerably wider than it became in Watts's day. As Archbishop of Canterbury, Tillotson maintained his contacts with Socinians and Unitarians.[22] There was less pressure for theological orthodoxy

[19] Berkeley, p. 324.
[20] Quoted in L. G. Locke, p. 74.
[21] Tillotson, III, 310-311. Quoted in L. G. Locke, pp. 73-74.
[22] See L. G. Locke, p. 93.

laid on him than there was on Watts. It is thus noteworthy that Watts allows credit to be given to the art of reasoning, even when it is practised by such arch-heretics as the Socinians.

Watts was not only up against the decay of rationalism; he was also up against the decline of Dissent. His concern about this decline accounts in large measure for his theological scruples. A. P. Davis pinpoints certain features which characterised this decline after 1715. In the first place, the decline in spiritual integrity became evident in the Salter's Hall controversy of 1719, when

a reactionary group led by Thomas Bradbury tried to force subscription to the Athanasian Creed on dissent. The effort failed, but after the debates the power of dissent both politically and spiritually waned appreciably. Both ministers and members left the movement.[23]

A second eloquent symptom of decadence appeared in 1723, when

Walpole gave £ 500 to help the widows of dissenting pastors and to augment the salaries of the poorer dissenting ministers. The money came from the private purse of the king, and Walpole used it as a bribe to silence nonconformist agitation for the repeal of the Test and Corporation acts. The bribe worked.[24]

Compromised politically and spiritually, the Dissenters administered themselves a third blow, with the publication in 1730 of Strickland Gough's *An Enquiry into the Causes of the Decay of the Dissenting Interest*. According to Gough, "dissent had lost its spiritual heritage. It had become bigoted, and 'of all Tories, dissenting Tories are the most inconsistent.' " [25] In 1731 a survey of London nonconformity was made; it showed that

fifty ministers had conformed since 1714. There were fewer meeting houses than in 1695; yet the population of London had increased by one sixth. . . . Of thirty-nine Presbyterian churches surveyed in 1731, eleven were Arminian, twelve were unwilling to declare themselves, and only sixteen were orthodox Calvinist.[26]

This state of affairs was not confined to England. In New England a similar movement away from Calvinism, towards Arminianism, and thence to Unitarianism, was beginning to make itself felt; and the Calvinists who engaged in the controversy were seen to be on the losing side by 1728.[27]

[23] Davis, p. 39.
[24] *Ibid.*
[25] *Ibid.*, p. 26.
[26] *Ibid.*, p. 40.
[27] See Norman S. Grabo, *Edward Taylor* (New York: Twayne, 1961), pp. 34-39.

In a period when Independents were abandoning Calvinism, and whole Presbyterian congregations were turning Unitarian, there was little that Watts could do to stem the tide. In 1718 he took part in a conference called by the Independents, Presbyterians and Baptists, to check the growth of Arianism in their midst.[28] In 1731 he published *An Humble Attempt towards the Revival of Practical Religion among Christians*. This was a companion pamphlet to Doddridge's *Free Thoughts on the most probable means of reviving the Dissenting Interest, occasioned by a late enquiry into the causes of its decay* (1730). Both were attempts to provide answers to Gough's gloomy analysis of the situation. Watts considered that "the great and general reason is the decay of vital religion in the hearts and lives of men." [29] In an attempt to revive and modernise the spirit of puritanism, Watts compares the "advantages of Dissenters" with "the peculiar practices of the ancient nonconformists." [30] But no amount of outward signs and practices will resurrect the old spirit, and Watts's comparison is an academic exercise.

The trouble was that Watts himself experienced the symptoms of theological and ecclesiastical disintegration. His crisis of conscience over the issue of Arianism aggravated his ill-health, and opinions vary as to the outcome of the crisis.[31] Whatever may have been his final theological position, and however seriously one takes his 1745 palinode, it remains true that Watts had first-hand knowledge of the break-up of Calvinism, and resisted to his utmost the decline of Dissent and the flight from reason, both of which characterised the mood of 18th century religious orthodoxy.

By 1745 Watts must have felt that the contacts he had with the traditions of 17th century puritan humanism were meaningless. Certainly the puritan insistence on the uses of reason was obsolete in an age which formulated its truths in axioms; and Watts himself spent a lot of time speaking the language of axiomatic theology. Puritanism was decaying and beginning its decline to what it became in Victorian England. But Watts, for all his fathering of 19th century nonconformity, had been born in an age when Bunyan and Marvell were puritans. It is his puritan orthodoxy, with its insistence on making the best use of the "ruinous remains"

---

[28] See Draper, p. 238. In 1719 James Pierce was expelled from the Presbyterian ministry for denying that Christ was equal to God the Father.

[29] Watts, III, xi.

[30] Watts, III, 50 ff., 75 ff.

[31] See *DNB* (Watts): "Lardner affirmed that in his last years ... Watts passed to the Unitarian position and wrote in defence of it; the papers were, as Lardner owned, unfit for publication, and as such were destroyed by Doddridge and Jennings, the literary trustees." Lardner's assertion has never been proved or disproved.

of a divine, prelapsarian reason, which lingers on in his qualified acceptance of the Enlightenment doctrine of moral sense.

The Enlightenment, in its will to form an absolute man, seized on the
idea of instinctive virtue. Watts does not treat this idea with Calvinistic
diatribe, but welcomes it to the extent that it corroborates his puritan
orthodoxy:

In human nature there are some few instances of it [moral sense] in most
persons, which appear chiefly in the workings of benevolence, and com-
passion in us towards sensible creatures, with some inward aversions to
cruelty, and perhaps also some sort of natural reverence towards the almighty power, whom we call God when we come to know him. These things
are some ruinous remains of that goodness, virtue, or piety which was
natural to innocent man, and are partly wrought perhaps, into his animal
nature, as well as in his soul. These instincts are certain relics of a spur to
duty.[32]

By interpreting the traditional religious views of Calvinism in terms of a
new generation's philosophical taste, Watts reveals his theological modernism. It is his modernism which makes him in many respects, in spite
of his puritan background, a cogent spokesman for 18th century religious
orthodoxy. Watts never tired of relating revealed religion to natural religion in his attempt to establish solid grounds for piety.

Watts was as keen as Clarke to state the case for Christianity in terms of
natural religion, and to subject his faith to the light of nature. The whole
tenour of *The Improvement of the Mind* reflects Watts's concern to clear
himself of any possible charge of bigotry or enthusiasm. He accepted, with
the majority of Hanoverian divines, that "what Puffendorf calls the law
of nature and nations" should be applied to theology, and that the "law
of God" was in no way exempt.[33] Revealed religion only makes sense when
built on the "firm foundations" of the "light of nature or mere reason";
its function is to raise these foundations "to more exalted degrees," and its
value resides in "building so glorious a superstructure upon them." [34] This
sounds dangerously like saying that revelation depends on natural religion,
the building imagery is clear enough, and in a sense this is what Watts
believed. As a modernist, he was prepared to begin with the pursuit of
truth, but even the most extreme modernist must leave himself something
to modernise. Watts's argument is that from the pursuit of truth "we arrive at the knowledge of natural religion and learn to confirm our faith in
divine revelation, as well as to understand what is revealed." [35] And he

[32] *Philosophical Essays,* Watts, V, 551.
[33] *The Improvement of the Mind,* Watts, V, 308.
[34] *Ibid.,* V, 307.
[35] *Logic,* Watts, V, 1.

goes on to qualify his view of revelation as superstructure, by saying that even in the infrastructure all cannot be explained:

There are some mysteries in religion, both natural and revealed. ... We must believe what revelation plainly dictates, though the ideas be obscure. Reason itself demands this of us; but we should seek the brightest evidence.[36]

The irrational nature of such a compromise was hardly questioned in the early 18th century.

Bolingbroke was one of the few who analysed the modernist's dilemma. For him, the modernism of Watts and Clarke was all of a piece with the modernism of Malebranche and Berkeley. The more one modernised, the more one exposed the absurdity of the thing or position to be modernised. For Bolingbroke, those who speculated at the level of metaphysical superstructure were purveyors of cant:

In a word, can he be less than mad, who boasts a revelation superadded to reason, to supply the defects of it, and who superadds reason to revelation, to supply the defects of this too, at the same time? This is madness, or there is no such thing incident to our nature: and into this kind of madness the greatest genii have been the most apt to fall. A St Paul, profound in cabalistic learning; a St Austin, deep read in Plato; a father Malebranche and a bishop of Cloyne. Elevation of genius makes them giddy: and these men, like those who are born in the purple, imagine they can do everything they have a mind to do, because they can do more than others. The mistake has been fatal to both; to these heroes in philosophy, as well as to the others. Though all men are not placed on the same level, there is a level above which no man can rise: and he who compares the nature of his mind with the nature of things, will be sure to find it.[37]

Bolingbroke, with his Baconian formula, is merely pushing to its logical conclusion his age's deep-seated mistrust of the intellectual faculty. Man should bend his mind and stoop to understand the nature of things, rather than pretend to erect viable fabrics in the field of metaphysics. Philosophical heroism was frowned upon, and the average 18th century religious mind tended to shun even the ruinous fabrics erected by Clarke and Watts. Thus Wesley minimised the mysteries of religion by insisting that the dictates of revelation are plain, while Bishop Butler contented himself with his theory of probability. Where doubt cannot be sealed out, virtue is made of necessity, and the diminished brightness of the evidence is welcomed on the grounds that too bright an evidence would blind man's reason.

[36] *Ibid.*, V, 162-163.
[37] Bolingbroke, IV, 172-173.

Watts moves deliberately in this direction, claiming that the "bright and growing witness to our inward and real Christianity"

is such a gentle sort of evidence, that though it may work conviction in the hearts of spectators, yet it does not strike the sense with so glaring a light as to dazzle the weaker sort who behold it into superstitious folly: nor does it give such provocation to the envy of the malicious, as if the saints had borne the sign of their high dignity in some more surprising manner in their figure or countenance.[38]

In the last resort, Watts falls back on the argument from probability:

There are a hundred things wherein we mortals in this dark and imperfect state must be content with probability, where our best light and reasonings will reach no further. We must balance arguments as justly as we can, and where we cannot find weight enough on either side to determine the scale with sovereign force and assurance, we must content ourselves with a small preponderation. This will give us a probable opinion, and those probabilities are sufficient for the daily determination of a thousand actions in human life, and many times even in matters of religion. . . . The God of nature and reason has bound us to assent and act according to the best evidence we have.[39]

English theology relied on this theory for over a century. It reflects the 18th century compromise, and the ardent wish of Watts and others no longer to have their souls twitched by a capricious and arbitrary God who encouraged violent extremes of doctrine. For Watts, as for Addison, "God is a God of light and truth, a God of reason and order." [40]

It is from this standpoint that Watts views the kindred tendencies of pietism and mysticism, which flourished on the edges of the Enlightenment consciousness. The God of the pietists and mystics may have been a God of light and truth, but he was certainly not a God of reason and order. Consequently Watts is forced into uttering the well-worn cry of "Enthusiasm!", albeit with considerably less vehemence than most of his contemporaries. He condemns any zeal which is not subordinate to the understanding.[41] This amounts to a denial of one of the chief characteristics of puritanism, and reveals that the Dissenters were aligning themselves with the dominant trend of Anglican theology, which claimed that the Enlightenment somehow dispensed Christians from their supernatural sources. Referring to Christ's disciples, Watts remarks that "this supernatural inspiration carried sufficient evidence with it to them, as well as to the ancient prophets, though we who never felt it are not so capable to judge

---

[38] *Remnants of Time Employed in Prose and Verse,* No. 17. Watts, IV, 627-628.
[39] *The Improvement of the Mind.* Watts. V. 259-260.
[40] *Ibid.,* V, 290-291.
[41] *Ibid.,* V, 290.

and distinguish it." [42] To coin a distinction, pietism heroically availed itself of this supernatural inspiration, while common piety dispensed with it.

Watts was no pietist, but he was sufficiently pious to impress Dr Johnson, who, on reading Watts, commented: "He that sat down only to
reason is on a sudden compelled to pray." [43] The passages which moved
Dr Johnson to prayer must have been those resembling the following:

It is happy for us, that this [i.e. the problem of the unknowable] does not
affect our moral and more important concerns. . . . This does not . . . make
any inroad upon our divine and everlasting interests.[44]

Let our reason blush and hide its head, and lie abased for ever at the foot
of the divine majesty. This strange theatre of argument, this endless war of
words and ideas, throws a world of confusion and abasement upon the
proudest powers of mankind. . . . Show us thyself, O God our Maker, and
teach us what thou art, that we may adore thee better; nor suffer us to
wander in this thick mist, wherein we can scarce distinguish thee from that
which has no being.[45]

Watts himself was careful to draw the distinction between this sort of piety,
with which he and Dr Johnson sustained themselves in many a dark
moment, and the unnatural excesses of pietism.

Thus, in his "Sermon on the Inward Witness of Christianity," Watts
writes:

It is a witness that dwells more in the heart than in the head. It is a testimony known by being felt and practised, and not by mere reasoning; the
greatest reasoners may miss of it, for it is a testimony written in the heart;
and upon this account it has some prerogative above all the external arguments for the truth of Christianity.[46]

Watts is prepared to place the heart above the head, the inward feeling
above the outward argument. But his sense of a via media is so strong,
that he immediately adds the following qualification:

Though this inward evidence of the truth of Christianity be a spiritual
nature, and spring from pious experience, yet it is a very rational evidence

---

[42] *Ibid.*, V, 295. Cf. Samuel Wesley's ironic complaint on the state of Anglicanism
at the turn of the century: "Alas poor Church of England! we have no visions, no
miracles, no exorcisms, resisting-invisible-flying-black-cats, or casting out devils: . . .
These are prerogatives only reserved for the Catholics and Dissenters: the Church of
England has nothing to plead for itself besides Scripture, Antiquity, and Reason."
Defence of a Letter (1704), p. 53. Cf. also Addison's comment on the martyrs who
were "either of another make than men are at present, or had such miraculous supports
as were peculiar to those times of Christianity." *Of the Christian Religion* (1717),
Addison, V, 131.

[43] Johnson, *Lives of the Poets*, II, 384.
[44] *Philosophical Essays*, Watts, V, 504.
[45] *Ibid.*, V, 515.
[46] Watts, I, 20.

also, and may be made out and justified to the strictest reason. It is no vain, fanciful, and enthusiastic business.[47]

In this way Watts measures out his rational brand of piety; on these terms the heroic piety of the mystics can still be branded as enthusiasm.

For both Watts and Dr Johnson, piety was essentially a moral attribute. Dr Johnson would have warmly applauded Watts's warning to those "in quest of intellectual gain," that they should never under-estimate the importance of "moral character." [48] As Watts puts it, in one of his rare metaphors, "no wise man would venture into a house infected with the plague, in order to see the finest collections of any virtuoso in Europe." [49] It is because Watts puts morality above intellectual and aesthetic considerations, that he issues such severe strictures on that pietism which attempts to transcend, by-pass or short-cut the natural moral process.

Watts displayed considerable irritation with what Bolingbroke called "the irradiations of mystic theology." [50] In the 17th century, puritanism was by no means hostile to certain aspects of mysticism. As Grabo and Martz have pointed out, the practice of ratiocinative meditation belonged to the puritan tradition.[51] In Watts's one reference to Jacob Boehme, there is no trace of hostility; Watts simply notes that "Bohemus was a German divine of various knowledge and sedate judgment, of admirable temper and uncommon piety." [52] Watts is equally open to the appeal of the Catholic mystical tradition, singling out Thomas à Kempis and Fénelon for special praise.[53] Watts was, however, highly suspicious of mystical irradiations which were not subject to the discipline of the ratiocinative processes. Hence his criticism of Fénelon and Malebranche, and of the mystical divinity of the Papists in general.

Watts describes Malebranche as "an admirable writer in the last age," praises the "many excellent chapters in his *Search after Truth*," but goes on to complain that he

has vented a strange opinion, that we see all our ideas in God. It is the known and distinguishing character of this rational author, that he falls into a sort of enthusiasm in his doctrine concerning our ideas of things.[54]

[47] Watts, I, 22.
[48] *The Improvement of the Mind,* Watts, V, 236.
[49] *Ibid.*
[50] Bolingbroke, V, 539.
[51] See Grabo, pp. 40 ff., and also Louis Lohr Martz, *The Poetry of Meditation: A Study in English Religious Literature of the 17th Century* (rev. ed.; New Haven: Yale University Press, 1962).
[52] "Devotional Writings," *Reliquiae Juveniles,* No. 52. Watts, IV, 537.
[53] *An Humble Attempt Towards the Revival of Practical Religion* (1731), Watts, III, 46-47.
[54] *Philosophical Essays,* Watts, V, 536.

Similarly of Fénelon he writes:

The writings of that excellent man are not all of a piece.... There are many... sections which are very weakly written, and some of them built upon an enthusiastical and mistaken scheme, akin to the peculiar opinions of father Malebranche.... There are many admirable thoughts in practical and experimental religion, and very beautiful and divine sentiments in devotion; but sometimes in large paragraphs, or in whole chapters together, you find him in the clouds of mystic divinity, and he never descends within the reach of common ideas or common sense.[55]

It is significant that Watts's anatomy of the irradiations of mystic theology takes the form of a critique of linguistic indecorum. In his attacks on Fénelon and Malebranche, he is chiefly concerned to expose their "dark and unintelligible way of thinking and speaking," and his motive for conducting such an enquiry is that "such preachers as have read much of the mystical divinity of the Papists, and imitated their manner of expression, have many times buried a fine understanding under the obscurity of such a style." [56]

In another place Watts specifies what he has in mind:

By the language of mystical divinity, I mean such incomprehensible sort of phrases, as a sect of divines among the Papists have used, and some few Protestants too nearly imitated. Such are of the deiform fund of the soul, the superessential life, of singing a hymn of silence. That God is an abyss of light, a circle whose centre is everywhere, and his circumference nowhere. That hell is the dark world made up of spiritual sulphur, and other ingredients not united or harmonised, and without that pure balsamic oil that flows from the heart of God. These are great swelling words of vanity, that captivate silly people into raptures, by the mere sound without sense.[57]

Watts's ideal was a plain style in religion and in poetry. He worked hard and consistently to sink metaphysical quirks in both spheres. A non-mystical piety went hand in hand with purity of diction. Watts's work in the fields of aesthetics and prosody provides eloquent confirmation of the moral premise which informs his religious thinking.

[55] *The Improvement of the Mind,* Watts, V, 218.
[56] *Ibid.,* V, 327.
[57] *A Guide to Prayer,* Watts, III, 144-145.

CHAPTER FIFTEEN

AESTHETICS

One could argue for a long time as to whether Watts was more of a late Metaphysical than an early preromantic poet. But to conclude, as in all reason one would have to, that he was a bit of both, raises more questions than it solves. What is the connection between Metaphysical and Romantic? Does Watts in some special way reveal the missing link in a long-term evolutionary process? Does Watts, in his aesthetic theory and poetic practice, illustrate a transitional moment between the old and the new, in the same way as the body of his thought marks the end of the Renaissance and the beginning of the modern consciousness? If it is Watts's classicism which constitutes this transitional moment, how is this part and parcel of a body of poetry at once Metaphysical and Romantic?

One answer to such questions must be that what has been detected as preromanticism is in fact nothing of the sort, but rather that aspect of the break-up of the Metaphysical tradition which occurs in More and Norris, namely, a movement towards the aesthetics of sublimity, expressed in a taste for aspiration, infinity, rhapsody, and egotistical introspection. Such a movement has obvious affinities with Romanticism, and certainly opened up some of the vistas of the modern consciousness which the Romantics were to exploit. It is primarily, however, an emphasis which is parallel to corresponding movements in the cultural sphere at large. It constitutes one expression of the widespread shift from the letter to the spirit, from the Reformation to Pietism, and from the Renaissance to the Enlightenment.

These affinities are far from specious or concocted. They inform, for example, Farquhar's defence of the sublime in poetry. According to Farquhar, Homer

was too much a poet to give rules to that, whose excellence he knew consisted in a free and unlimited flight of Imagination; and to describe the Spirit of Poetry, which alone is the true Art of Poetry, he knew to be as impossible, as for human reason to teach the gift of prophecy by a definition.[1]

The cult of the sublime is associated with a devotion to the spirit of poetry and a rejection of its art. It is not therefore surprising that it coincides with the disintegration of the Metaphysical tradition and the disuse of Renaissance rhetoric, as well as with the 18th century's refusal to rely on reason as an instrument for theological or philosophical definition. Sublimity must be seen in this context before it can be pounced on as a miraculous intimation of things to come a century later.

Sublimity was not the only expression of the Enlightenment's flight from the baroque. As a classicist, Watts came to terms with the Metaphysical tradition, not so much seeking to eradicate it, as to refine it and polish it, much as Pope sought to do with Wycherley. It may be that the flight to the sublime corresponded to the 18th century distrust of reason and resort to fideism, and that Watts's cultivation of syntax and diction corresponded to the opposing tendency to rely on logic and the reasoning process. At any rate, Watts appears to be exploring both paths. He contributes to the cult of the sublime with great gusto, encouraged no doubt by his puritan background and his faith in Free Philosophy. But his originality lies in his acceptance of diction and syntax, and his attempt to sink the idiosyncrasies and quirks of the Metaphysical tradition without abandoning its aesthetic roots.

Watts's poetry, therefore, can be divided stylistically into three parts: that which refines itself out of the Metaphysical tradition by an elevation into the sublime; that which retains identifiable relics of the Metaphysical tradition; and that which sinks the Metaphysical tradition into classicism by a methodical cultivation of diction and syntax. It is in relation to this three-fold achievement that Watts's aesthetic theory must be interpreted.

It is possible to distinguish two determining factors in Watts's aesthetic theory: on the one hand Cartesian dualism, on the other the concept of divine poetry. Watts insisted in his *Philosophical Essays* that "the two worlds of matter and mind stand at an utter and extreme distance from each other." [2] Watts held this as an axiomatic truth, but he is not content with a bare statement. He embroiders on his dualism in terms which militate specifically against the aesthetics of Metaphysical poetry:

---

[1] George Farquhar, *Discourse upon Comedy,* in *Works* (2nd ed.; London: Bernard Lintott, 1711), p. 69.
[2] Watts, V, 502.

You cannot make space think, or will, or act, as a spirit does; for join thinking and space, which are two distinct ideas, as near as possible in your mind, yet you cannot unite them into one being, nor conceive of space as having any share in thinking, or as exerting a thought. So you may join iron and joy together in your mind as two neighbouring ideas, but they will be two ideas for ever distinct: No force can squeeze, melt, or weld them together, and make them unite in one: You can never make iron become joyful: There is an utter inconsistency in their ideas, and they are eternally incompatible. Space can no more exert a thought, than iron can exert joy.[3]

Watts's analogy provides a very clear illustration of how the classical taste for antithesis grew out of an aversion to the correspondences of Metaphysical poetry. Watts multiplies his analogies, adding "green" and "violin," "red" and "cucumber," and listing as "metaphysical impossibilities": "a bitter colour," "a blue smell," "a purple sound," "a cubical circle," "a thinking statue," "a purple smell," and "a bushel of souls." [4] The examples are so far-fetched that the argument becomes crude. But that Watts felt such argument necessary is a sign of the strength of gothic unenlightenment in art and thought at the end of the 17th century. Once the argument was won, it became a commonplace in European culture until it was challenged by the French symbolists and surrealists.

In 1700 poetry and philosophy were still affected by the old habits of analogy and correspondences. Behind Locke's attack on Malebranche lies the premise that God and things are for ever distinct and separate. In taking issue with the language of occasionalism, Locke is also condemning the consciousness that informs Metaphysical poetry. Thus one of the arguments he developed against Malebranche's idea of seeing all things in God runs as follows:

It shows a little too plainly the absurdity of that doctrine, if he should say we smell a violet, taste wormwood, or feel cold in God; and yet I can find no reason why the action of one of our senses is applied only to God, when we use them all as well as our eyes in receiving ideas. If the figure, colour and smell are all of them "sentiments," then they are none of them in God, and so this whole business of seeing in God is out of doors.[5]

To a Metaphysical poet it was conceivable to "feel cold in God." The strength of the Metaphysical idiom was such that in 1683 Edward Taylor could write of his soul as God's "conduit," and complain that his "pipes" were "stopt . . . with mud." [6] As late as 1696 Taylor could write: "Mine

---

[3] *Philosophical Essays*, Watts, V, 518.
[4] *Ibid.*, V, 553, and "Brief Scheme of Ontology," *ibid.*, V, 642.
[5] Locke, *Works*, VIII, 233.
[6] Edward Taylor, *Sacramental Meditations*, "The Reflexion," *Poems*, ed. Stanford, p. 14.

heart's a park or chase of sins: Mine head / 'S a bowling alley. Sins play ninehole here." [7] Taylor in fact exemplifies the power of far-fetched analogy and crude correspondences, while at the same time demonstrating the origins in the Metaphysical idiom of classical antithesis. Thus in 1699 he wrote:

> O matchless Love, laid out on such as he!
> Should gold wed dung, should stars woo lobster claws,
> It would no wonder, like this wonder, cause.[8]

Here the crudity is deliberately emphasised, and antithesis replaces analogy, as it does in Watts's list of metaphysical impossibilities. This technique persisted only in devotional poets, like Watts and Wesley, who needed some way of illustrating that God's incarnation and man's salvation were metaphysical impossibilities which nevertheless occurred.

Taken as a whole however, these barbarous relics, which can be found on every page of Taylor's verse, belong to an age which was not yet sure how enlightened it was. Scientists believed in the growth of metals as late as 1695.[9] The problems of extended spirit and plastic nature were still debated, and the chain of being had not yet been so rationalised as to exclude all possibility of microcosmic correspondence. Watts subjected such traditional attitudes to ironic scrutiny. In one passage the tone and intention are Swiftian:

I have known a man of peculiar skill in music, and much devoted to that science, who found out a great resemblance of the Athanasian doctrine of the Trinity in every single note, and he thought it carried something of argument in it to prove the doctrine. I have read of another who accommodated the seven days of the first week of creation to seven notes of music, and thus the whole creation became harmonious.[10]

Written in 1741, this passage is clearly influenced by the Swiftian ironic mode, such as practised by Berkeley who, in the previous decade, had written with identical tone and intention:

I have known a fiddler gravely teach that the soul was harmony; a geometrician very positive that the soul must be extended; and a physician, who, having pickled half a dozen embryos, and dissected as many rats and frogs, grew conceited and affirmed there was no soul at all, and that it was a vulgar error.[11]

[7] *Ibid.*, II, 18, p. 111.
[8] *Ibid.*, II, 33, p. 139.
[9] See John Dryden, *Works*, Vol. 1., ed. E. N. Hooker and H. T. Swedenberg (Berkeley: University of California, 1956), p. 263.
[10] *The Improvement of the Mind*, Watts, V, 258.
[11] Berkeley, p. 247.

It is no accident that Watts attaches himself to a tradition established by Swift and Berkeley. The views of these men are firmly set against Metaphysical cant in art and thought. Watts certainly played his part in correcting abuses of reason in religion and learning. Clearing the mind of cant was the central enterprise of the Enlightenment. Watts participated vigorously in this unfinished task.

The aesthetic implications of this enterprise are three-fold. In the first place, the spirit and techniques of Metaphysical poetry must be eradicated. In the second place, since mind and matter are utterly separate, the poet's mind feels most at home uncluttered in space, soaring to the sublime. And in the third place, the obsession with clear and distinct ideas gives rise to the art of classicism, with its techniques of antithesis and bathos, clarity and strength.

If one takes Watts's theory of divine poetry at more than its face value, it can be seen to have a bearing on his aesthetic position exactly corresponding to the impact made by Cartesian dualism. The very idea of setting up divine poetry as a separate genre, with its own criteria and its own rules, marks a step out of the Metaphysical mind, with its precious connections and resemblances, into the modern mind, with its Baconian compartments. In the second place, the theory of divine poetry developed at a time when the taste for the sublime was being cultivated. It would be difficult to say which came first, but divine poetry was obviously the genre most demanding sublimity, and sublimity would not have flourished for so long without a theory of divine poetry to sustain it. In the third place, Watts is in the special situation, among those who upheld the theory of divine poetry, of having toned down his initial taste for the sublime to meet the needs of a stringent classicism.

Watts's theory of divine poetry coincides with the aesthetics of classicism on several scores. In the first place, it seeks to disarm the imagination by reducing it to the controllable form of fancy. Watts condemns the "silly wandering mind" which "sits at Fancy's door,"

> Calling shapes and shadows to her,
> Foreign visits still receiving,
> And to herself a stranger living.[12]

In his *Hymns,* he aims to sink the gay and fleeting light of fancy in the steady and sober "fire of divine affection." [13] And in the preface to "The Indian Philosopher," a poem in which the ornaments of fancy almost take

---

[12] "True Riches," *Horae Lyricae,* II. Watts, IV, 398.
[13] *Hymns,* 1709 Preface. Watts, IV, 150.

on the interpretative hue of imagination discovering truth, he feels it necessary to excuse the presence of "visions, images, parables and dreams," by calling them "the fabulous dress of this poem," and pointing out that beneath the dress the "narrative is grave" and the "moral just and obvious." [14]

In the second place, Watts's religious attack on Shaftesbury's idea of ridicule as a test of truth, is also a classical attack on the aesthetics of Metaphysical wit:

However an argument on some subjects may be sometimes clothed with a little pleasantry, yet a jest or witticism should never be used instead of an argument, nor should it ever be suffered to pass for a real and solid proof.[15]

Watts adds that raillery and wit "serve only to cover nonsense with shame, when reason has first proved it to be mere nonsense," and that they are the "talents of a vile animal, that is grin and grimace." [16] Wit, like imagination, is denied any part in the body of poetry; it is reduced to the level of a piece of clothing, the dress of "a little pleasantry."

In the third place, Watts's views on rhetoric corroborate his views on wit and imagination. The sense is all-important. Persuading the will and raising the passions are aids to the fundamental task of communicating sense.[17] Like Ray, who compared oratory to cooking, claiming that both were "voluptuary arts," Watts was concerned to preserve the "wholesome meats" from being spoiled by "the variety of sauces." [18] Classicism was essentially a functional aesthetic, and it is not surprising that Watts, who put the health of the body above the pleasure of taste, abstained from rhetoric.

The theory of divine poetry met with little success when it was applied to the stuff of poetry. Dr Johnson pronounced its demise in the same breath that he praised Watts as a poet:

His ear was well-tuned, and his diction was elegant and copious. But his devotional poetry, like that of others, is unsatisfactory. The paucity of its topics enforces perpetual repetition, and the sanctity of the matter rejects the ornaments of figurative diction. It is sufficient for Watts to have done better than others what no man has done well.[19]

Victorian nonconformity being what it was, it was left to A. E. Housman to rescue Watts from the "clutches of the devout," and exorcise the "curse

---

[14] *Horae Lyricae,* II. Watts, IV, 407.
[15] *The Improvement of the Mind,* Watts, V, 253.
[16] *Ibid.,* V, 291.
[17] *Ibid.,* V, 311-312.
[18] Ray, p. 124.
[19] Johnson, *Lives of the Poets,* II, 385.

of sanctity" which lay on him.[20] Watts had asked his readers to "lay aside the humour of criticism and enter into a devout frame." [21] Housman was the first Victorian to appreciate Watts without exercising Christian discrimination. In his celebrated attack on 18th century poetry, he quoted Watts as an example of true poetry "beyond Pope." [22] In the same year another critic, concurring with Housman, declared that "Watts seems to forget he was living in an age of periwigs, and powder, and politeness, and bounds over the everlasting hills like the maddest of the young Romantics." [23] In this way the theory of divine poetry is declared impoverished and redundant, and replaced by the fecund aesthetic of preromanticism, in an attempt to account for Watts's poetic qualities. This claim, similar to the interpretation of Lady Winchilsea as a precursor of Wordsworth, deserves to be closely examined.[24]

It is suggested that Watts stands half way between the 17th century puritans and the 19th century Romantics, between religious enthusiasm and poetic enthusiasm.[25] This may be true in a long-term and philosophical sense, but Watts's own career does not illustrate any such movement. On the contrary, Watts began very much as a poetic enthusiast, and spent the rest of his life trying to redeem the wasted energies of his youth by turning his muse, with considerable labour, to the service of practical piety.[26] And what is true of his life's energies is true of his art. He moved away from the enthusiasm of the sublime towards the cultivation of laboured bathos and Parnassian poetic diction.

It is further suggested that the following passage from the 1709 preface to *Horae Lyricae* amounts to a manifesto of preromanticism:

If the heart were first inflamed from heaven, and the Muse were not left alone to form the devotion and pursue a cold scent, but only called in as an assistant to the worship, then the song would end, where the inspiration ceases; the whole composure would be of a piece, all meridian light and meridian fervour.[27]

Watts indeed seems to be suggesting all sorts of exciting aesthetic possibilities. The attack on the muse left alone could be construed as a con-

---

[20] Pinto, *Essays and Studies,* XX (1935), 86.
[21] *Hymns,* II, Preface (1709). Watts, IV, 150.
[22] Alfred Edward Housman, *The Name and Nature of Poetry* (Cambridge: University Press, 1935), p. 31.
[23] Pinto, *Essays and Studies,* XX (1935), 102.
[24] See Reuben A. Brewer, "Lady Winchilsea and the Poetic Tradition of the 17th Century," *Studies in Philology,* XLII (1945), 61-80. Brewer concludes that Lady Winchilsea is neither a Metaphysical nor a preromantic.
[25] Pinto, *Essays and Studies,* XX (1935), 92-93. Cf. T. E. Hulme's belief that Romanticism is spilt religion.
[26] See *The Improvement of the Mind,* Watts, V, 380.
[27] Watts, IV, 323. See Pinto, *Essays and Studies,* XX (1935), 94.

demnation of Parnassian, and the proposed alternative sounds like a 19th century inspirational aesthetic. But it would be unfair to draw too enthusiastic a conclusion from this paragraph. These ideas are couched in the syntax of the conditional, and the aesthetic possibilities they contain represent an ideal at once religious and artistic. Such possibilities would be in perfect consonance with Watts's theory of divine poetry. Watts in fact mentions "Mr Norris's essays in verse" as meeting the requirements of his ideal.[28] And if the ideal stems partially from one strand of the late Metaphysical tradition, it also has distinct overtones of classicism. How, after all, is one to make sure that the song will end when the inspiration ceases, except through the rigour of a formal control, which Romantic poets tended to ignore. Watts may have been criticising poetic diction for too often pursuing a cold scent, but he can hardly be interpreted as advocating an inspirational aesthetic of a "spasmodic" kind as exemplified by, say, James Clarence Mangan's "Dark Rosaleen." [29]

The only other occasion when Watts echoes the tone and sentiments of his allegedly preromantic manifesto is in *The Improvement of the Mind*, where he observes:

In heroic verse, but especially in the grander lyrics, there are sometimes such noble elevations of thought and passion as illuminate all things around us, and convey to the soul the most exalted and magnificent images and sublime sentiments.[30]

If the previous passage, with its call for meridian light and meridian fervour, is an expression of the theory of divine poetry, then this parallel plea for poetry which illuminates all things around us is an explicit expression of the aesthetics of the sublime. Both passages thus primarily reflect prevailing tendencies of Watts's age, and have no need of a hypothetical preromantic aesthetic to account for their tone or content.

A third argument in favour of Watts's preromanticism is drawn from a peculiarly un-18th century quality identified in his poems and equated with that elusively Platonic phenomenon, pure poetry. The quality in question can be detected, it is alleged, in these lines:

> We are a garden walled around,
> Chosen and made peculiar ground;
> A little spot, inclosed by grace,
> Out of the world's wild wilderness.[31]

[28] Watts, IV, 323.
[29] See A. T. Quiller-Couch (ed.), *The Oxford Book of English Verse* (Oxford: Clarendon Press, 1900), p. 772.
[30] Watts, V, 313.
[31] *Hymns*, I, 74. Watts, IV, 172. Quoted in Pinto, *Essays and Studies*, XX (1935), 94.

One may well be able to talk, with these lines in mind, of pure poetry, symbolic use of language, and Romantic potential; but it would be misleading to do so before interpreting the lines in their context. This verse of a hymn is an adaptation from the Song of Solomon: "A garden inclosed is my sister, my spouse, a spring shut up, a fountain sealed." [32] There was a long tradition of such adaptations, which continued well into the 18th century.[33] The credit for the pure poetry must go to the author of the original, not to the latter-day imitators.

In this particular case, Watts is refining and sinking what had been a highly erotic genre, capable of expressing the private and the personal, into a public and congregational idiom. He does this through purity of diction and strength of syntax, qualities not primarily associated with Romanticism. As always, he is doing what Dr Johnson said he did, showing the Dissenters that "zeal and purity might be expressed and enforced by polished diction." [34] In his poetry at large Watts refined on a Metaphysical aesthetic, experimented with the aesthetics of sublimity and, in his own idiom, perfected the aesthetics of classicism.

[32] Song of Solomon, iv, 12.
[33] Cf. Mrs Rowe's version: "A garden well enclosed, a fountain sealed / From all unholy and profane access, / Such is my love to me." *Poems on Several Occasions,* p. 52. This was written in 1735.
[34] Johnson, *Lives of the Poets,* II, 382.

CHAPTER SIXTEEN

THE SUBLIME

Watts's devotion to the aesthetics of the sublime went further than paying lip-service to a theory of divine poetry. It helped to consummate those factors which, in the poetry of More and Norris, were reflecting the modern consciousness and contributing to the disappearance of any living Metaphysical tradition. In Watts's poetry these various factors – a desire for expressionism, an interest in the aesthetics of infinity, a cultivation of Platonic rhapsody, an assertion of introspective egotism and a taste for the prospect poem – come together and are seen to be connected. Many of these factors are aesthetic expressions of aspects of the Enlightenment mind, and it is not surprising that they should be found together in the work of one whose thought so faithfully reflects the nature of the English Enlightenment.

That aesthetic and philosophical factors interlock has already become apparent. The cult of the sublime is defined by its context, and in Watts it is the aesthetic expression of his Free Philosophy. One need look no further than Farquhar to discover a corroborative parallel. Farquhar, in his *Discourse upon Comedy* (1702), makes the distinction between the spurious sublime, whereby Scholasticism sought to control man's highest thoughts, and the true sublime, which dispenses with man-made rules. He writes:

How natural is it for aspiring Schoolmen to attempt matters of the highest reach; the wonderful creation of the world (which nothing but the almighty power that ordered it can describe) is brought into mood and figure by the arrogance of philosophy. But till I can believe that the vertigos of Cartesius, or the atoms of Epicurus can determine the Almighty Fiat, they must give me leave to question the infallibility of their rules in respect of poetry.[1]

Farquhar's analogy between the poet and God the creator, and his slighting reference to "the atoms of Epicurus," are like passing bells announcing the revaluation of poetry made by Blake and Coleridge. But in context,

[1] Farquhar, p. 69.

Farquhar is expressing a view he shares with Watts, namely that poetry, religion and philosophy must be free if they are to flourish in their natural state of sublimity. Farquhar and Watts were uniting the interests of art and thought in a common front to combat the gothic chain and the circles of Metaphysical similitude.

In this perspective the sublime belongs with classicism to the age of the Enlightenment, and is an important manifestation of the cultural revolution which overthrew the spirit and methods of the Renaissance. In the words of Michel Foucault:

Par le jeu de la convenance, de l'émulation, et de la sympathie surtout, la similitude au xvi siècle triomphait de l'espace et du temps: car il appartenait au signe de ramener et de réunir. Avec le classicisme, au contraire, le signe se caractérise par son essentielle dispersion. Le monde circulaire des signes convergents est remplacé par un déploiement à l'infini.[2]

This is the revolution that has been called "The Breaking of the Circle." [3] The enemy of the sublime was the circle of similitude. Compelled by the inexorable laws of the microcosm to play out the sterile game of resemblances, poets seized on the sublime as a possible way out. Ralph Knevet, a minor poet writing in the Metaphysical tradition, was perhaps unwittingly setting himself up as an apostle of the sublime, when he wrote before 1671:

> Man is no Microcosm, and they detract
> From his dimensions, who apply
> This narrow term to his immensity.
> Heaven, Earth and Hell in him are packt.[4]

At the other end of the period of Enlightenment and classicism, Mark Akenside celebrated the indisputable fact that "England spurns her Gothic chain / And equal laws and social science reign." [5] For Watts, the sublime was no mere literary fashion; it was part and parcel of the modern struggle to rid European culture of the chains and circles of an outmoded system in art, thought and society.

Watts's adherence to Free Philosophy goes hand in hand with his cultivation of the sublime in poetic expression. It is significant that his poem "Free Philosophy" contains the most explicit manifesto of this aesthetic. Watts expressly associates the sublime with Protestant individualism as well as with Free Philosophy, and sets it up against the gothic both in

---

[2] Foucault, p. 74.
[3] M. H. Nicolson, *The Breaking of the Circle.*
[4] Ralph Knevet, "The Habitation," in *Rare Poems,* ed. Marshall, p. 137.
[5] Akenside, *Odes,* II, 1. Chalmers, XIV, 110.

learning and in art. The object of attack is identified as "custom," which binds the philosopher and poet; and Watts links the poet and philosopher in a common cause by fighting "custom" with his own "genius":

> My genius storms her throne:
> No more, ye slaves, with awe profound
> Beat the dull track, nor dance the round;
> Loose hands, and quit the enchanted ground,
> Knowledge invites us each alone.
>
> . . . .
>
> A genius which no chain controls
> Roves with delight, or deep, or high:
> Swift I survey the globe around,
> Dive to the centre through the solid ground,
> Or travel o'er the sky.[6]

Just as Enlightenment philosophy would break the gothic chain of the Schools, so the sublime in poetry would break the circle of the Metaphysical tradition.

It is true that More and Norris had made incursions into this circle. Their poetry already reflects the growing weakness of an aesthetic tradition based on a seriously held philosophy of microcosm and correspondences. But these incursions were incomplete because not enforced by an alternative philosophy to replace the gothic chain. Watts was able to break the circle because his aesthetics reflected his philosophy and because both provided a positive alternative to decaying traditions. From the standpoint of his Free Philosophy, he was in a position to dispense with the traditional security of the circle, and to attack the way in which "hand in hand ourselves we bind, / And drag the age along." [7]

The Enlightenment took Watts's manifesto to heart; the 18th century did "loose hands and quit the enchanted ground." So strong was the impulse to do so, that generations later, Joseph Warton, generally considered a pioneer of the neo-gothic, felt himself obliged to conform to the philosophic and aesthetic orthodoxy of Sir Joshua Reynolds. Warton's address to Reynolds is all too revealing:

---

[6] *Horae Lyricae*, II. Watts, IV, 393.
[7] "The Way of the Multitude," *Horae Lyricae*, II. Watts, IV, 394. Cf. "Two Happy Rivals, Devotion and the Muse," *Horae Lyricae*, I, where he writes: "Wild as the lightning, various as the moon, / Roves my Pindaric song. . . . / Such is the Muse: Lo she disdains / The links and chains / Measures and rules of vulgar strains." Watts, IV, 368-369.

> Sudden the sombrous imagery is fled,
> Which late my visionary rapture fed:
> Thy powerful hand has broke the Gothic chain,
> And brought my bosom home to truth again;
> To truth, by no peculiar taste confined,
> Whose universal pattern strikes mankind.[8]

Reynolds was doing the correct 18th century thing; he was continuing the good work of Watts, smashing the gothic chain, and Warton was not sufficiently sure of his preromantic instincts to say nay. The history of 18th century philosophy and aesthetics is the history of how Watts's revolutionary principles of liberation became in their turn a chain of Enlightenment orthodoxy, inhibiting art and thought until Blake rose up and said that Reynolds was wrong.

Although the aesthetics of the sublime were largely instrumental in establishing a poetry liberated from the Metaphysical tradition and capable of expressing the thought of the Enlightenment, they did so, not through any tendency inherent in the sublime as such, but because the tradition of the sublime was extricated from its Metaphysical connections in the medieval cosmos, and used in the service of the Cartesian revolution. The impact of this revolution was two-fold – as it affected man, and as it affected the cosmos. Cartesian dualism divided mind from matter, and man from the cosmos. The function of the sublime after Descartes was thus to celebrate the mind of man and the matter of the universe, and link the two through their only common ground, infinity. Before Descartes on the other hand, the sublime had been simply part of the gothic or Metaphysical set-up, whereby cosmic sublimity, among other things, was available to man's mind through the magical correspondences of the microcosm.

The way in which the circle was broken, and the sublime extricated from the Metaphysical tradition and used to give aesthetic expression to Cartesian dualism, can nowhere more clearly be seen than in successive English versions of the odes of Casimire Sarbiewski.[9] These odes were a Christianised combination of classical and neoplatonic influences, their themes derived partly from the odes of Horace and the Georgics of Virgil, and partly from the pseudo-writings of Hermes Trismegistus. The Hermetic element lent itself naturally to the expression of microcosmic corre-

---

[8] Joseph Warton, "Verses on Sir Joshua Reynolds' Painted Window." Quoted in Fairchild, II, 347.

[9] Casimire Sarbiewski (1595-1640), a Polish Jesuit, published his neo-latin Horatian odes and biblical paraphrases in 1625 and 1628. English versions include those of G. Hils (1646), Henry Vaughan (1651), Cowley, Norris, Watts, and John Hughes (1720).

spondences and Metaphysical conceits. Casimire's first English translator, G. Hils, combined a Jonsonian smoothness with a Metaphysical taste for "wit pure and quaint, with rich conceits." [10] Subsequent versions, and notably the paraphrases made by Norris and Watts, eliminated the quaintness and cultivated the smoothness. But Horace and Virgil only supplied sources for classicism; they did not authorise a taste for the sublime. This had to come out of the Hermetic and therefore the gothic and Metaphysical traditions.

Of those who knew and translated Casimire, Watts did most to isolate the Hermetic tradition of neoplatonic aspiration from its gothic framework and build out of it an aesthetic of the sublime fit for the use of the Enlightenment. There are three parts of the *Hermetica* [11] which stand out as salient sources of the sublime. In the first, Libellus I, the Hermetic writer speaks of thoughts soaring "high aloft" (section 1), of a "boundless view" (section 4), and of breaking "through the bounding circle of orbits" (section 13b), before going on to describe man's flight upwards through the seven zones of heaven (sections 25-26). Such material is easily detachable from its gothic context. Casimire himself set the trend by paraphrasing sections 25-26 in his most important and most translated ode, "E Rebus Humanis Excessus." [12] The strictly Hermetic material – the description of the bodily senses going back "to their own sources, becoming parts of the universe, and entering into fresh combinations to do other work" (section 24) – was eschewed and eliminated as unfit for lyrical sublimity.

The same observations apply to Libellus X. It is not difficult to see in the following extract an ideological basis for the aesthetics of sublimity: "None of the gods of heaven will quit heaven and come down to earth; but man ascends even to heaven, and measures it, and what is more than all beside, he mounts to heaven without quitting the earth." [13] The Hermetic basis for the flight to the sublime – the fact that the "pious soul is daemonic and divine and becomes mind throughout" (section 19a) in a universe which "is a living creature inasmuch as its body is made with soul in it" (section 11) – all this gothic clutter can be discarded, and the extract of sublimity transferred to the pure Cartesian cosmos.

[10] Mathias Casimire Sarbiewski, *Odes,* trans. G. Hils, ed. Maren-Sofie Rostvig ("Augustan Reprint Society," No. 44; Los Angeles: University of California Press, 1953), p. 105. This phrase is taken from Hils' version of Ode 1, Lib. Epod.

[11] Hermes Trismegistus, *Hermetica,* ed. Walter Scott (4 vols.; Oxford: Clarendon Press, 1924).

[12] See Miss Rostvig's preface, Sarbiewski, p. iii.

[13] *Hermetica,* X, 25.

A third example is to be found in Libellus XI (ii). Here there is a passage strongly suggestive of Watts's own concept of the sublime:

The incorporeal cannot be enclosed by anything; but it can itself enclose all things. . . . Think of yourself. Bid your soul travel to any land you choose, and sooner than you can bid it go, it will be there. Bid it fly up to heaven, and it will have no need of wings; nothing can bar its way, neither the fiery heat of the sun, nor the swirl of the planet spheres; cleaving its way through all, it will fly up till it reaches the outermost of all corporeal things. And should you wish to break forth from the universe itself, and gaze on the things outside the Kosmos, even that is permitted to you.[14]

But reading on, we find that the conclusion to this passage represents just that kind of gothic philosophy and mystical divinity which Watts condemned in Malebranche: "You must understand that it is in this way that God contains within himself the Kosmos and himself and all that is; it is as thoughts which God thinks, that all things are contained in him." [15] Norris, to the extent that he embraced this view, was making any aesthetic of the sublime to which he was attracted subservient to a philosophical truth.[16] Watts, on the other hand, threw out the old philosophy root and branch, leaving the aesthetic principle high and dry in a Cartesian cosmos. Thus, when Watts writes in the sublime mode, he writes without any Hermetic infrastructure:

> Heaven is my home, and I must use my wings;
> Sublime above the globe my flight aspires.
>
> . . . .
>
> I have a soul was made for infinite desires.[17]

In saying this, Watts is by no means committed to a belief that "man is made in the image of the Kosmos," [18] or to the view that "space is incorporeal"; [19] he follows the Hermetic tradition only in so far as he wants to "grow wings and soar into the air." [20]

Watts's adaptation of the Hermetic tradition was influential. It made available to a wide public a Christianised neoplatonism, shorn of its cosmic

[14] *Ibid.*, XI (ii), 18-19.
[15] *Ibid.*, 20a.
[16] Coleridge may well have found in Casimire some degree of philosophical truth as well as aesthetic appeal, but though "while still a young man, Coleridge planned a complete translation of Casimire's odes," he never got round to completing "more than the ode 'Ad Lyram.' " Sarbiewski, pp. iii-iv.
[17] "True Wisdom," *Horae Lyricae,* I. Watts, IV, 351.
[18] *Hermetica,* VIII, 5.
[19] *Ibid.*, II, 4a.
[20] *Ibid.*, V, 5. Watts had grown his wings as early as 1694, when in his first extant poem he paid enthusiastic tribute to Casimire. An English translation of Watts's latin original is printed in Gibbons, pp. 16-17.

intricacies, refined out of its Metaphysical framework, and capable of carrying a stereotyped form of lyrical piety, which lingered on in the effusions of the Victorian hymn-writers. Without the lead which Watts gave, it is for example unlikely that Anne Steele (1717-1778), a Baptist lay-preacher, would have imitated in her turn the "E Rebus Humanis Excessus" of the Polish Jesuit poet.[21] Watts however was doing more than imitating a neoclassical model; he was bringing together aesthetic and philosophical factors, until then separate, with the result that the sublime was available to the age of Enlightenment.

In the poem entitled "The Adventurous Muse," Watts transposes the issue of philosophical freedom onto the aesthetic plane:

> Whilst little skiffs along the mortal shores
> With humble toil in order creep,
> Coasting in sight of one another's oars,
> Nor venture through the boundless deep,
> Such low pretending souls are they
> Who dwell enclosed in solid orbs of skull;
> Plodding along their sober way,
> The snail o'ertakes them in their wildest play.[22]

To these plodders Watts opposes his own adventurous muse. As a poet who found corroboration for the freedom of man's mind in the infinity of the cosmos, Watts made several ventures in aesthetic experiment. He has been recognised as perhaps the "inventor of lyrical blank verse." [23] He has been singled out for his success in Sapphics, and praised for his metrical experiments.[24] Above all he has been called one of the "few important writers of non-dramatic blank verse between Milton and Thomson." [25]

In this last sphere his adventurousness did not always go beyond competent imitation. The following passage, for example, would be a parody or a plagiarism were it not so well executed:

> Then the sweet day of sacred rest returns,
> Sweet day of rest, devote to God and heaven,
> And heavenly business, purposes divine,

---

[21] See Fairchild, II, 113.
[22] *Horae Lyricae,* II. Watts, IV, 398.
[23] Pinto, *Essays and Studies,* XX (1935), 103.
[24] Dobrée, pp. 154-157.
[25] Pinto, *Essays and Studies,* XX (1935), 103.

> Angelic work; but not to me returns
> Rest with the day.[26]

Watts's imitation of Milton is so successful that there is not a word out of place to betray his own handiwork; the disciple hides beneath his master's mantle.

But Watts was no purveyor of derivative Miltonics; he is perhaps the first effective moderniser of Milton. His manifesto on this issue deserves attention since it steers a way between the options of slavish imitation and deliberate avoidance of Miltonic influence. Tradition and the individual talent are fused. Watts writes with considerable critical acumen:

In the essays without rhyme, I have not set up Milton for a perfect pattern; though he shall be for ever honoured as our deliverer from the bondage. . . . I could never believe that roughness and obscurity added anything to the true grandeur of a poem: Nor will I ever affect archaisms, exoticisms, and a quaint uncouthness of speech, in order to become perfectly Miltonian. It is my opinion that blank verse may be written with all due elevation of thought in a modern style, without borrowing anything from Chaucer's Tales, or running back so far as the days of Colin the shepherd, and the reign of the Fairy Queen. The oddness of an antic sound gives but a false pleasure to the ear, and abuses the true relish, even when it works delight. . . . So the ill-drawn postures and distortions of shape that we meet with in Chinese pictures, charm a sickly fancy by their very awkwardness; so a distempered appetite will chew coals and sand, and pronounce it gustful.[27]

These are the guide-lines Watts sets himself. In his concern to modernise, while maintaining grandeur and elevation, he follows in the footsteps of Dryden. Like Dryden, he condemns, not wit, but wit without propriety. Like Dryden, he believes that the sublime must be subject to the discipline of classicism, and that the chinoiserie of baroque and neo-gothic fashions must at all costs be eschewed.

Again like Dryden, and this is the heart of the matter, he practises what he preaches, and evolves out of Milton his own modernised blank verse idiom. The following passage illustrates the quality he was capable of attaining:

> O thou dear engine,
> Thou little brass accomptant of my life,
> Would but the mighty wheels of heaven and nature
> Once imitate thy movements, how my hand

[26] "The Wearisome Weeks of Sickness" (1712-13), *Reliquiae Juveniles,* Watts, IV, 528. Cf. *Paradise Lost,* III, 41.
[27] *Horae Lyricae,* Preface. Watts, IV, 326.

Should drive thy dented pinions round their centres
With more than ten-fold flight, and whirl away
These clouded wintry suns, these tedious moons,
These midnights; every star should speed its race,
And the slow bears precipitate their way
Around the frozen pole. Then promised health
That rides with rosy cheeks and blooming grace
On a May sunbeam should attend me here
Before tomorrow sheds its evening dew.[28]

This is Watts's own unique sublimity. Syntax and diction are handled with inspired mastery, moulding the blank verse idiom to create the rise and fall of the emotion. The unwanted suns become totally abject as they are stripped of their impoverished attributes and lost in a stark unqualified midnight. The changes in mood and movement are subtle and seamless, discreetly polarised around the antithetical "slow bears" (signifying, by its cadence, death) and "on a May sunbeam" (signifying, by its cadence, life). In the idiom of lyrical blank verse Watts's adventurous muse finds wings to sustain its flight to the sublime.

Watts of course would not have called Milton "our deliverer from the bondage" on purely technical grounds; and when justice has been done to Watts's originality in the field of metrical experiment, his taste for the sublime cannot be separated from his philosophical and religious interests. In Watts's conception of things there is a direct correspondence between the sublime and Dissent. On one occasion he explicitly contrasts the unconfined aspirations of the Dissenters with the plodding qualities of the Church of England:

Here a solemn form
Of ancient words keeps the devotion warm,
And guides but bounds our wishes: there the mind
Feels its own fire, and kindles unconfined
With bolder hopes.[29]

Watts clearly felt that the established church, surrounded by its laws of conformity, militated not only against the free conscience, but also against the aspiring mind and the flight of genius. It was not enough to plod along in the way of the multitude; given scope, such as Watts felt

[28] "Encouraged to Hope for Health in May. December 1712," *Reliquiae Juveniles*, Watts, IV, 527-528.
[29] "To Her Majesty," *Horae Lyricae*, II. Watts, IV, 383.

was available in the tradition of Dissent, each and every mind was capable of aspiring to sublimity, of stretching its genius. It is thus no coincidence that missionary zeal and a taste for the sublime were qualities cultivated by non-jurors and Dissenters rather than by conformists. Watts pioneered the Christian Pindaric, and both gospel and genius were expanded to infinity during the reign of Queen Anne.[30]

It is not only by aspiring to infinity that Watts refined the Hermetic tradition and polished the Metaphysical elements present in the first English translation of Casimire. He also developed out of Casimire and the *Hermetica* the cult of introspection, making available to the modern consciousness, as More had done before him, the mode of the egotistical sublime. It is true that the flight to infinity, with its overtones of Platonic rhapsody, was also expressive of the egotistical sublime. But introspection, at a moment in the history of thought when the microcosm had been rationalised but not quite eliminated, offered even more exciting possibilities of expressing sublimity.

In "True Riches" Watts writes:

'Tis enough that I can say,
I've possessed myself today:
Then if haply midnight-death
Seize my flesh and stop my breath,
Yet tomorrow I shall be
Heir to the best part of me.[31]

The quaintness of the last two lines is the result of direct borrowing from Hils's Casimire.[32] But Watts is not interested in exploiting the quaintness; he prefers to emphasise the sublimity of introspection:

When I view my spacious soul
And survey myself awhole,
And enjoy myself alone,
I'm a kingdom of my own.

I've a mighty part within
That the world hath never seen.

. . . .

Nothing can describe the soul:

---

[30] Cf. Elkanah Settle's "Pindaric Poem on the Propagation of the Gospel in Foreign Parts" (1711). Settle refers to the "extensive . . . zeal" of England's "apostolic sons," and to "the expanded Gospel, unconfined as air." Quoted in Fairchild, I, 64.
[31] *Horae Lyricae*, II. Watts, IV, 397.
[32] Casimire, VI, 3: "Heir to myself alone." Sarbiewski, p. 49.

'Tis a region half unknown,
That has treasures of its own,
More remote from public view
Than the bowels of Peru;
Broader 'tis and brighter far,
Than the golden Indies are.[33]

The geographical references, with their trace of the microcosm, are borrowed from Hils.[34] Similarly in "Happy Solitude," Watts exploits the ecstasy of introspection:

When I within myself retreat,
I shut the doors against the great;
My busy eyeballs inward roll,
And there with large survey I see
All the wide theatre of me,
And view the various scenes of my retiring soul.[35]

Once again the hint of a microcosmic correspondence is borrowed from Hils.[36]

Unfortunately Watts's dislike of quaintness often leads him into involuntary bathos. This is perhaps inevitable when Watts is too consciously cultivating the sublime. For example, at the end of one of his best Pindaric flights he reduces the whole poem to the absurdity of conscious artifice by writing:

Thus my bold harp profusely played
Pindarical; then on a branchy shade
I hung my harp aloft, myself beneath it laid.
Nature that listened to my strain,
Resumed the theme and acted it again.[37]

Genius is here bound hand and foot to a highly derivative and decadent literary artifice, and the bathos of the final couplet is the result of replacing the quaintness of a microcosmic setting with an over-conscious pathetic fallacy. Watts's attempts at sublimity were thus largely dependant on the religious and philosophical tradition which nourished his

[33] Watts, IV, 397-398.
[34] Casimire, VI, 3: "A great part of my mind lies close, more wide / Than the rich Indies are." Sarbiewski, p. 51.
[35] Horae Lyricae, II. Watts, IV, 414.
[36] Casimire, IV, 12: "I enjoy myself, what need I more? / Of every sense I lock the door; (...) / The theatre of my life I view / My own spectator." Sarbiewski, p. 67.
[37] "Freedom," Horae Lyricae, II. Watts, IV, 396.

aspiration and introspection. They can hardly be said to stand on the basis of an independent aesthetic; but they are made to express and support a view of genius inherent in his divine theory of poetry.[38]

Before proceeding to analyse Watts's use of the sublime in the idiom of the prospect poem, it is worth drawing a line of demarcation between Watts as an exponent of the classical sublime and Young as an exponent of the preromantic sublime. Watts's position has been described in relation to Milton's influence. Young goes beyond Watts in three respects. He uses Casimire to transcend the limits of classicism, he reduces the last relics of the Metaphysical style to serve the mood of the poet rather than to create the tone of the poem, and he reflects the disintegration of the Renaissance and the rise of a Romantic sense of alienation.

In his essay "On Lyric Poetry", Young subtly modifies the critical balance maintained by Dryden and Watts, by suggesting that lyrical poetry in particular must transcend the norms of classicism:

Judgment . . . that masculine power of the mind, in ode, as in all compositions, should bear the supreme sway. . . . The Imagination, like a very beautiful mistress, is indulged in the appearance of domineering. . . . It must be very enterprising; it must, in Shakespeare's style, have hair-breadth 'scapes; and often tread the very brink of error. . . . Such is Casimire's strain among the moderns.[39]

Young pays lip-service to the conventional conceptions of classicism, but his emphasis is on indulgence to the domineering mistress, Imagination. Young's interpretation of Casimire clearly differs from Watts's in this respect.

Different too is Young's use of the microcosm. It no longer discovers truth through its own structure, as it still can do, though faintly, in Watts. It is broken down into a rhetorical apostrophe, geared, in this instance, to the fashionable histrionic indulgence in ruins and melancholy:

> A part how small of the terraqueous globe
> Is tenanted by man! The rest a waste,
> Rocks, deserts, frozen seas, and burning sands:
> Wild haunts of monsters, poisons, stings and death.
> Such is Earth's melancholy map! But, far
> More sad! this Earth is a true map of man.
> So bounded are its haughty lord's delights
> To woe's wide empire.[40]

---

[38] See especially "Two Happy Rivals, Devotion and the Muse," where there is an explicit interpenetration of Genius and Piety. *Ibid.*, IV, 369.

[39] Chalmers, XIII, 403-404.

[40] Young, *Night Thoughts,* I. *Ibid.,* XIII, 422.

In the third place, Young takes lugubrious delight in bewailing the disintegration of the chain of being:

> From Nature's continent, immensely wide,
> Immensely blest, this little isle of life,
> This dark, incarcerated colony,
> Divides us.[41]

The morality of the microcosm pointed by Donne – "No man is an
island" – no longer prevails. Man is alienated from nature; nature (here
the Augustans and the Romantics are at one) is the supreme good; and
the scene is set for that archetypal agony which constitutes the Romantic
Sublime, with man striving to commune with nature. For the Romantics,
the sublime came to be seen as a basic response to man's condition. For
Watts, on the other hand, it was still basically a Hermetic or neoplatonic convention, which coincided with the requirements of his divine
theory of poetry and with the insights of Dissent.

In his views of social sublimity, Watts follows Pomfret in laying down
a via media between the solitude of a "hermit saint" and the business of
the "city crowd." [42] In "The Happy Man" he rejects wealth, pomp,
music, food, drink and lawless love, but accepts a kindred soul, Myrrha,
claiming that "souls are for social bliss designed." [43] In one respect he
outdid Pomfret whose ideal prospect was situated within easy reach of
a town. His own bourgeois prospect included the bustle of industry and
commerce: he enjoyed

> A large round prospect of the spreading plain,
> The wealthy river and his winding train,
> The smoky city, and the busy men.[44]

But Watts's attitude to nature and landscape reveals not only the views
of a middle-class Dissenter, but also the way in which puritanism and
Platonism interlocked as sources for the 18th century prospect poem.

The Platonic sources of the prospect poem have been traced in the
poetry of More and Norris. The prospect became in the 18th century a
means of indulging in otherwise gratuitous natural description; but before the colours were filled in and the lines made more precise, the pros-

---

[41] Young, *Night Thoughts*, IV. *Ibid.*, XIII, 437.
[42] "The Discontented and Unquiet," *Horae Lyricae*, II. Watts, IV, 412. In this
poem, developed out of Casimire (IV, 5), Sylvia is condemned for going from one
extreme to another.
[43] Watts, IV, 409.
[44] "Funeral Poem for Thomas Gunston," *Horae Lyricae*, III. Watts, IV, 442. This
poem was written in the same year as Pomfret's *Choice* (1700).

pect was a means of deriving sublimity from nature. The sublimity arose from the fact that nature was viewed from a distance, and from the belief that, if viewed from an infinite distance, nature could be perceived as infinite. The sublime prospect thus became a means of achieving angelic fruition and bypassing the "weakness of our reason to see far into things at once," or "to take in all . . . with a single view." [45] In the context of the puritan tradition, this meant that the prospect approximated to a prelapsarian vision, and that fallen nature was no longer fallen when viewed from a distance. Thus Watts writes:

> Earth with her scenes of gay delight
> Is but a landscape rudely drawn
> With glaring colours and false light;
> Distance commends it to the sight.[46]

Watts believed, with Thomas Burnet, that the earth's landscape was "rudely drawn" as a result of the Fall. In his *Ruin and Recovery of Mankind* (1740) he relies on Burnet's theories to express his distaste of nature's irregularities.[47]

Both puritanism and Platonism prompted Watts to take an extensive view and achieve a sublimity in which the aesthetic was part and parcel of a religious view incorporating eternity and the resurrection of the dead.[48] In the last resort, Watts placed the prospect in the apocalyptic context laid down by Thomas Burnet, who wrote:

The spheres of men's understandings are as different as prospects upon the earth. Some stand upon a rock, or mountain, and see far round about; others are in an hollow, or in a cave, and have no prospect at all. . . . And yet the fairest prospect in this life is not to be compared to the least we shall have in another. Our clearest day here is misty and hazy: we see not far, and what we do see is in a bad light. But when we have got better bodies in the first resurrection, . . . better senses and a better understanding, a clearer light and an higher station, our horizon will be enlarged every way, both as to the natural world and as to the intellectual.[49]

For Burnet, Watts and the English Enlightenment, sublimity was no mere aesthetic option; it was a means of expressing man's desire for the absolute in the context of the philosophical and religious lights available.

---

[45] *Logic,* Watts, V, 2, 163.
[46] "Earth and Heaven," *Horae Lyricae,* I. Watts, IV, 337.
[47] See Rostvig, II, 185-186 and Watts, VI, 192.
[48] Prospects of this kind were one of Mrs Rowe's specialities. For the extent of her indulgence in celestial landscape gardening, see especially *Friendship in Death in 20 Letters from the Dead to the Living* (London: Henry Lintot, 1743), pp. 7-8, 17.
[49] Thomas Burnet, *The Theory of the Earth* (1684), 3rd ed. 1697, quoted in Rostvig, II, 35.

CHAPTER SEVENTEEN

THE METAPHYSICAL TRADITION

One of the characteristics of the later Metaphysical tradition is the way in which it merges into the sublime. Cowley and Norris are obvious examples.[1] Long before Watts, these two poets had been drawn to the works of Casimire, not for their Metaphysical qualities but for their sublimity.[2] From the poems of Norris one would deduce that the Metaphysical tradition was moribund; and in the poems of Watts, a generation later, one would not expect to find more than pale traces of its demise. Readers of Cowley and Cleveland have perhaps too readily assumed that the Metaphysical tradition died out as a result of its own excesses and decadence. The poetry of Edward Taylor, however, suggests that the tradition could assimilate a strong element of Clevelandism without sinking into the effeminate; and Taylor continued to be nourished by the Metaphysical tradition well into the 18th century.

In the 1680s Taylor could write, "I'm but a flesh and blood bag: Oh! do thou / Sill, plate, ridge, rib, and rafter me with Grace." [3] Almost two hundred years later, Gerard Manley Hopkins had access to this idiom, and wrote, "I am soft sift / In an hourglass . . . / But roped with . . . a vein / Of the gospel." [4] What Taylor and Hopkins have in common is not so much their place at the end of a tradition, Metaphysical or Romantic, as their immunity to the repercussions of the scientific revolution, Cartesian or Darwinian. Since most poets were not immune, the impact of the Cartesian revolution on the later Metaphysical tradition must be shown.

Rosemond Tuve has pointed out that one of the assumptions behind Renaissance rhetoric is "that the universe is . . . full of barely capturable

---

[1] See G. Walton, Chapters 3-5 on Cowley and Chapter 7 on Norris.
[2] See T. A. Birrell, *English Studies,* **XXXVIII** (1956), p. 127.
[3] *Sacramental Meditations,* I, 30 (1688), Taylor, *Poems,* ed. Stanford, p. 49.
[4] *The Wreck of the Deutschland,* I, 4.

significances." [5] M. C. Bradbrook, describing the cosmic background to the poetry of Marvell, has written: "The stars still rained influences, the earth still gave out humours. There was no such thing as inanimate nature, and no possibility of a pathetic fallacy." [6] These assumptions, which informed the nature of Elizabethan and Metaphysical poetry, were denied by the Cartesian revolution. Thus Traherne, in whose work the Metaphysical tradition undergoes a peculiar metamorphosis, noted, neither sadly nor joyfully, that "the material world is dead and feeleth nothing." [7] And in her introduction to the poems of Lady Winchilsea, Myra Reynolds claims that the impact of the Cartesian philosophy can be traced in the work of Lady Winchilsea from 1703. In her early work Lady Winchilsea was nourished by the later Metaphysical tradition. From 1703 an Augustan style goes hand in hand with a Cartesian attitude towards nature and the cosmos. Miss Reynolds identifies the new style in the elegy on Sir William Twysden, in which Lady Winchilsea

says she rejects the customary invocation to flocks and fields and flowers to join her in her grief because to her mind it is false and but a poet's dream that eternal nature is moved by man's sorrow. She is conscious that no human woe can deprive the spring of joy in her fragrant odours and purple violets. It is vain that mourners attempt to force on inanimate things some portion of their grief. Nature, unconcerned for our sorrows, "pursues her settled path, her fixed and steady course." [8]

In an age when the ideological basis of the Romantic agony was being laid, the Metaphysical tradition could not but dwindle; and Watts, brought up in this intellectual milieu, and beginning to write verse at the turn of the century, could not but be affected.

Like his contemporaries, Watts displays an awkwardness of imagery characteristic of the uneasy transition from Metaphysical to Augustan. Like Norris, he introduces mechanical aids into the poetry of vision:

> The cruel shade applied
> A dark long tube, and a false tinctured glass
> Deceitful.
>
> .   .   .   .
>
> Now Urania feels the cheat
> And breaks the hated optic in disdain.

---

[5] Rosemond Tuve, *Elizabethan and Metaphysical Imagery*, p. 105.

[6] M. C. Bradbrook and M. G. Lloyd Thomas, *Andrew Marvell* (Cambridge: University Press, 1940), p. 55.

[7] Thomas Traherne, *Poems, Centuries and Three Thanksgivings*, ed. Anne Ridler (London: Oxford University Press, 1966), p. 255.

[8] Lady Winchilsea, p. cxxxi. See *ibid.*, pp. 61-62 for the passage here paraphrased.

Swift vanishes the sullen forms, and lo,
The scene shines bright with bliss.[9]

Our eyes the radiant saint pursue
Through liquid telescopes of tears.[10]

A. P. Davis quotes the second of these passages to illustrate "a belated Metaphysical tendency." [11] This choice is unfortunate and does Watts scant justice. Such relics do not justify our attaching him to the Metaphysical tradition. Watts however derived more from Norris than the occasional mechanical image; for in Norris he found not only the vein of Cowley and a Metaphysical tradition ready to disintegrate, but also the vein of Herbert.

In 1697 the Dissenters had published a volume of *Select Hymns taken out of Mr Herbert's Temple*, for use in private and family devotions.[12] The adapter in his preface remarked: "How much more fit is Herbert's *Temple* to be set to the lute, than Cowley's *Mistress*." This volume may have been less popular than either John Mason's *Spiritual Songs* (1683) or Watts's *Hymns* (1707), but it does point to a hitherto unexplored influence on the religious lyric of the late 17th and early 18th centuries.[13] This volume must have helped crystallise the influence of Herbert into a tradition. Thus we find John Reynolds (1666-1727), a Presbyterian minister and intimate friend of Watts, writing a poem "To the Memory of George Herbert," in which he declares that he prefers Herbert to Cowley.[14] The relics of an earlier Metaphysical tradition in the poetry of Watts, while by no means evidence of Herbert's direct influence, begin to make sense in the light of this tradition's continuity in the spiritual songs of Dissent. Watts is preserving these relics, not with the aim of refining them into sublimity, but of polishing them into classicism.

[9] "The Bright Vision," *Horae Lyricae,* II. Watts, IV, 418.
[10] "On the Sudden Death of Mrs Mary Peacock," *Horae Lyricae,* III. Watts, IV, 432.
[11] Davis, p. 183.
[12] *Select Hymns taken out of Mr Herbert's Temple,* ed. W. E. Stephenson ("Augustan Reprint Society," No. 98; Los Angeles: University of California Press, 1962).
[13] It may also help to account for the very considerable influence of Herbert on the work of Edward Taylor. In the manner of Herbert's "Jordan I," "Jordan II" and "The Forerunners," Taylor persistently complains that his "rags and jags" never realise his ideal of "a damask web of velvet verse." *Sacramental Meditations,* II, 56, Taylor, *Poems,* ed. Stanford, p. 175. Cf. also I, 13; I, 26; II, 36; II, 82; II, 142.
For one influence of Herbert's that has been explored, see John Sparrow's "George Herbert and John Donne among the Moravians" in Martha Winburn England and John Sparrow, *Hymns Unbidden: Donne, Herbert, Blake, Emily Dickinson and the Hymnographers* (New York Public Library: Astor Lenox and Tilden Foundations, 1966), pp. 1-28.
[14] See Fairchild, , 151.

There is some evidence that Norris directly influenced Watts, even if his predecessor at Bemerton did not. Thus both Norris and Watts quote Horace in defence of the theory of divine poetry.[15] And it is perhaps their common concern for the welfare of religious lyricism which leads them to address angels in their poems. As a philosopher Watts was adamant in his conviction that an extended spirit was a contradiction in terms.[16] But he was not prepared to abandon the Cartesian hypothesis of spiritual beings until someone produced a better hypothesis.[17] And he did not accept Locke's theories on intellectual beings.[18] Hence he was free, as those who accepted Locke on this point were not, to address angels in his poems.

Norris had written in a Metaphysical moment void of sublimity: "Some courteous ghost, tell this great secrecy, / What 'tis you are, and we must be." [19] The third edition of Norris's poems were published in 1699, and in 1701 Watts included the following line in his "Indian Philosopher": "Some courteous angel, tell me where." [20] In 1707 he incorporated in a hymn a similar line: "O for some courteous angel nigh." [21] The adjective obviously appealed to Watts, but it was sufficiently Metaphysical in tone to be changed to "guardian" in the 1709 edition of his *Hymns*.[22] "Guardian angel" was an innocuous and generalised term which could be used without embarrassment even by those who not only disbelieved in angels but also saw no point in making contact with them for poetic purposes.

Most of the instances of an earlier Metaphysical tradition's survival in Watts's poetry follow the pattern of his "courteous angel"; they are brief and isolated, to the extent that one feels they might disappear in revision. They mark *Horae Lyricae* as an early work, written before Watts had had time to put into practice his new theories of syntax and diction. They link Watts with Herbert and Norris, and show that he was not prepared to jettison certain elements of the Metaphysical tradition which allowed religious experience to be expressed with a precision and homeliness incompatible with the loftiness of the sublime.

---

[15] See Escott, p. 39.
[16] *Philosophical Essays,* Watts, V, 502, 513.
[17] *Ibid.,* V, 502, 504.
[18] *Ibid.,* V, 503.
[19] Norris, *Miscellanies* (1687), p. 25.
[20] *Horae Lyricae,* II. Watts, IV, 408.
[21] *Hymns* (1707), II, 28, stanza 5. This first edition variant is quoted in Selma L. Bishop, *Isaac Watts, Hymns and Spiritual Songs 1707-1748. A Study in Early 18th Century Language Changes* (London: Faith Press, 1962), introduction.
[22] Watts, IV, 209.

There is a deliberate diminution of sublimity in the spiritual realism of the phrase, "It was a brave attempt!" [23] The tone is at once wry and ecstatic. Watts valued that kind of spiritual acrobatics practised by Herbert, which could not be carried out weightless in aether and necessitated the presence of at least one foot on the ground. And even if he did, in a second attempt, manage to launch himself into eternity, he could cheat the infinity of the sublime by landing in heaven; "thus I'll leap ashore / Joyful and fearless on the immortal coast." [24]

Watts could also indulge in spiritual anatomy, claiming in the tone of King's "Exequy," "Yet tomorrow I shall be / Heir to the best part of me." [25] From anatomised parts he could create new coherences, claiming in the tone of Donne's "Good Morrow," "I'd live and die with you, / For both our souls are one." [26] It is not simply the thought which is reminiscent of King and Donne; the "yet" and the "for" show that the thought is used in the poems to argue and persuade.

Metaphysical proof based on spiritual anatomy was frowned on as barbarous by the 18th century. As a Cartesian, Watts was incapable of taking the microcosmic world of correspondences seriously, and yet he is not above an occasional rhetorical exploitation of the much in the little. He can use it to enforce an argument:

> We are a little kingdom; but the man
> That chains his rebel will to reason's throne,
> Forms it a large one.[27]

Or he can use it in an elegy as a hyperbole to raise his grief:

> Come, mingle grief with me,
> And drown your little streams in my unbounded sea.
>
> . . . .
>
> Passion, methinks, should rise from all my groans,
> Give sense to rocks, and sympathy to stones.[28]

The 18th century would not condemn such figures, but would use them without Watts's close attention to the microcosmic context.

Nor was Watts completely cut off from the 17th century tradition of religious preciosity. When he wrote the following, he was closer to Crashaw than to Wesley or Cowper:

[23] "Launching into Eternity," *Horae Lyricae,* I. Watts, IV, 364.
[24] "True Courage," *Horae Lyricae,* II. Watts, IV, 393.
[25] "True Riches," *ibid.,* IV, 397.
[26] "Happy Solitude," *ibid.,* IV, 414.
[27] "True Monarchy," *ibid.,* IV, 391.
[28] "Funeral Poem on Thomas Gunston," *Horae Lyricae,* III. Watts, IV, 443.

> I'll carve our passion on the bark,
> And every wounded tree
> Shall drop and bear some mystic mark
> That Jesus died for me.[29]

It is not only the application of profane to sacred which constitutes this verse's preciosity; it is also the symbolic exploitation of nature as a divine hieroglyph. Reference to a "wounded tree" comes oddly from the pen of one whose list of metaphysical impossibilities included "conscious matter." [30] It is important to realise the attraction to preciosity which Watts, writing at the turn of the century, must have felt. He wrestled with this attraction in his *Hymns*, and did not always overcome.[31]

There are four poems in *Horae Lyricae* which belong uncompromisingly to the 17th century, and where the Metaphysical relics are neither brief nor isolated. "Freedom" (1697) must rank as one of the most successful English Pindarics. While the metrical structure is loose and free, the syntax is strong and the language precise and energetic. As such it can be compared to the best Metaphysical and classical poems. While it has the smoothness of Dryden's energy, it has distinct verbal echoes of Donne's *Songs and Sonets*. The following stanza not only provides evidence of an unrejected Metaphysical tradition behind Watts; it also proves that it was possible to draw on this tradition, and renovate it by transposing it into a classical idiom:

> Tempt me no more. My soul can ne'er comport
> With the gay slaveries of a court;
> I've an aversion to those charms,
> And hug dear liberty in both mine arms.
> Go, vassal-souls, go, cringe and wait,
> And dance attendance at Honorio's gate,
> Then run in troops before him to compose his state;
> Move as he moves; and when he loiters, stand;
> You're but the shadows of a man.
> Bend when he speaks; and kiss the ground:

---

[29] "Meditation in a Grove," *Horae Lyricae*, I. Watts, IV, 371.
[30] *Philosophical Essays*, Watts, V, 553.
[31] See for example, *Hymns*, II, 61, stanza 5:
> "How we should scorn these clothes of flesh,
> These fetters and this load;
> And long for evening, to undress,
> That we may rest with God."

Watts, IV, 220. This is a good example of what can happen to preciosity when it is sunk.

> Go, catch the impertinence of sound:
> Adore the follies of the great;
> Wait till he smiles: But lo, the idol frowned
> And drove them to their fate.[32]

The energetic imperatives belong to a pre-Augustan idiom, such as used by Donne in "The Sunne Rising" and "Go and Catch a Falling Star"; but Watts has clearly gone a long way towards polishing this idiom. The verse of Dryden and Pope and the prose of Swift represent a similar achievement writ large.

"Against Tears" (1699) provides another example of the way in which Watts bridges the gap between Donne and Pope. The poem contains several qualities of the Metaphysical tradition, including gratuitous rhetorical speculation, outlandish hyperbole and far-fetched analogy. And yet throughout there is an energetic attempt to sink the patently Metaphysical tone through clarity of syntax and purity of diction. Like "Freedom," this poem unites the strengths of Metaphysical and classical idioms; and it does this in a more obvious way than the more celebrated elegies of Dryden and Pope:

> Madam, persuade me tears are good
> To wash our mortal cares away;
> These eyes shall weep a sudden flood
> And stream into a briny sea.
>
> Or if these orbs are hard and dry
> (These orbs that never use to rain),
> Some star direct me where to buy
> One sovereign drop for all my pain.
>
> Were both the golden Indies mine
> I'd give both Indies for a tear;
> I'd barter all but what's divine:
> Nor shall I think the bargain dear.
>
> But tears alas! are trifling things,
> They rather feed than heal our woe;
> From trickling eyes new sorrow springs,
> As weeds in rainy seasons grow.

[32] *Horae Lyricae*, II. Watts, IV, 396.

Thus weeping urges weeping on;
In vain our miseries hope relief,
For one drop calls another down,
Till we are drowned in seas of grief.

Then let these useless streams be staid;
Wear native courage on your face:
These vulgar things were never made
For souls of a superior race.

If 'tis a rugged path you go,
And thousand foes your steps surround,
Tread the thorns down, charge through the foe:
The hardest fight is highest crowned.[33]

The theme, the structure and the argument belong to the Metaphysical
tradition; but to purify and polish this tradition Watts uses the same
classical craftsmanship with which he shaped and revised his hymns.

A third example can be found in "Few Happy Matches" (1701). The
poem is built up from a series of negative definitions of what are not
happy matches; and far-fetched analogies from vegetable and mineral
nature are used to enforce the definitions. The analogies are half way
between arguments by conceit in the Metaphysical idiom, and moral
illustrations in the Augustan idiom. The didactic diction prevents the
Metaphysical tone from overriding the purpose of the poem, but is itself
strengthened by the range of Metaphysical reference:

Say, mighty love, and teach my song,
To whom my sweetest joys belong,
And who the happy pairs
Whose yielding hearts, and joining hands,
Find blessings twisted with their bands,
To soften all their cares.

Not the wild herd of nymphs and swains
That thoughtless fly into the chains,
As custom leads the way:
If there be bliss without design,
Ivies and oaks may grow and twine,
And be as blest as they.

[33] *Ibid.*, IV, 402.

Not sordid souls of earthly mould
Who drawn by kindred charms of gold
To dull embraces move:
So two rich mountains of Peru
May rush to wealthy marriage too,
And make a world of love.

Not the mad tribe that hell inspires
With wanton flames; those raging fires
The purer bliss destroy:
On Etna's top let furies wed,
And sheets of lightning dress the bed
To improve the burning joy.

Nor the dull pairs whose marble forms
None of the melting passions warms,
Can mingle hearts and hands:
Logs of green wood that quench the coals
Are married just like Stoic souls,
With osiers for their bands.[34]

In a sense, Watts is here illustrating in verse his belief that "conscious matter" is a metaphysical impossibility. But though the definitions and illustrations are negative, they are derived from the 17th century mind to which vegetable love meant something. Watts may be arguing for an Augustan via media in the passions, for a love that is neither too hot nor too cold, and yet it is the two extremes which get all the attention and provoke an expressionism that is both forceful and quaint. Watts may be attacking the 17th century mind, but he is doing so in a 17th century idiom, arguing by means of conceits, and anthropomorphising natural phenomena as seriously, if not as wittily, as Marvell.

The last of Watts's poems to belong uncompromisingly to the 17th century is "To the Memory of Gunston" (1702), a classical example of the puritan funeral elegy. As J. W. Draper has noticed, this poem "unites the 17th century horror of death with a suggestion of the 18th century fondness for the pensive sadness of lingering memories." [35] The 18th century note is authentic — "weighty sorrow nods on every plume" — but it is the strength of the 17th century tradition which strikes the reader:

[34] *Ibid*. These are the first five of nine stanzas.
[35] Draper, p. 250.

> Earthy fogs embrace his head,
> And noisome vapours glide along his face
> Rising perpetual. Muse, forsake the place,
> Flee the raw damps of the unwholesome clay,
> Look to his airy spacious hall, and say,
> How has he changed it for a lonesome cave,
> Confined and crowded in a narrow grave! [36]

It may be that Watts's muse did forsake the place in succeeding years, and according to Draper his later elegies show more restraint and less horror.[37] If by restraint is meant an increase in the volume of the 18th century note, then Draper is right; but the 17th century horror does not disappear. It is merely coated with the rather nauseous varnish of 18th century indulgence.

This is especially apparent in Watts's treatment of the theme of smallpox. In elegies written in 1707 and 1711 he maintains a basic element of preciosity such as is to be found par excellence in Dryden's "Upon the Death of the Lord Hastings" (1650).[38] In the 1707 elegy, the 18th century varnish is laid on thick; through the "fondness for the pensive sadness of lingering memories," the precise symptoms of smallpox barely show:

> I look and mourn and gaze with greedy view
> Of melancholy fondness. Tears bedewing
> That form so late desired, so late beloved,
> How loathsome and unlovely. Base disease
> That leagued with nature's sharpest pains, and spoiled
> So sweet a structure! The impoisoning taint
> O'erspreads the building wrought with skill divine,
> And ruins the rich temple to the dust! [39]

Here the Metaphysical preciosity is obscured by layers of sublimity and sentiment. In the 1711 elegy the physical symptoms of smallpox are given more attention, but their horror is covered by the elegant poetic diction and smooth syntax:

> Unkind disease, to veil that rosy face
> With tumours of a mortal pale,

---

[36] *Horae Lyricae,* III. Watts, IV, 439-440.
[37] Draper, p. 252.
[38] See especially lines 52-64 for the preciosity of Dryden's treatment of smallpox.
[39] "An Elegiac Thought on Mrs Anne Warner who died of the Smallpox" (1707), *Horae Lyricae,* III. Watts, IV, 435.

> While mortal purples with their dismal grace
> And double horror spot the veil.[40]

The syntactical variation given to the word "veil" and the metrical variation given to the word "mortal" control the movement and create the ritual effect of the stanza. The circumlocutory function of the poetic diction blurs the preciosity without eliminating it. There is no doubt that the strength of the Metaphysical tradition lies behind Watts's restraint; and this becomes more evident when one compares Watts on death with Lady Winchilsea and Edward Young.

In a poem entitled "To Death," Lady Winchilsea wrote: "Gently thy fatal sceptre on me lay, / And take to thy cold arms, insensibly, thy prey." [41] In this couplet Lady Winchilsea achieves a rare balance between 17th century preciosity and 18th century indulgence; but there is no doubt that, in these lines at least, she is nearer to Marvell than to Young. The same cannot always be said of Watts. But on the whole his classical restraint operates in the same way as Lady Winchilsea's; that is, it keeps the Metaphysical strength from spilling over into preromanticism. This is perhaps more evident in his hymns than in his elegies. The following verses may stand as samples:

> Stoop down, my thoughts, that use to rise,
> Converse a while with Death.
> Think how a gasping mortal lies,
> And pants away his breath.[42]

> Jesus, to thy dear faithful hand
> My naked soul I trust;
> And my flesh waits for thy command,
> To drop into my dust.[43]

> There the dark Earth and gloomy Shades
> Shall clasp their naked body round,
> And welcome their delicious limbs
> With the cold kisses of the ground.[44]

---

[40] "An Elegy on Sophronia who died of the Smallpox" (1711), *Reliquiae Juveniles*, Watts, IV, 542.

[41] Lady Winchilsea, p. 270.

[42] *Hymns*, II, 28, stanza 1. Watts, IV, 208.

[43] *Ibid.*, stanza 6, IV, 209.

[44] *Hymns* (1707), I, 24, stanza 5. This stanza appeared only in the first edition; it was dropped and, much altered, made part of Psalm 49 in 1719. See Louis F. Benson, "The Early Editions of Watts's Hymns," *Journal of the Presbyterian Historical Society* (Philadelphia), Vol. 1, No. 4 (June 1902), 269. Benson considers this verse to be "perhaps the most objectionable in the whole collection."

While Watts is further from the idiom of Marvell than Lady Winchilsea, he is far nearer it than his contemporary, Young. To the preromantics, as Draper has pointed out, "the funeral elegy supplied what neither the classics nor the Renaissance could give, a diction and metaphor of the emotions, and a whole technique of ecstasy and lamentation." [45] In the idiom of hymn and psalm Watts managed to sink his diction and metaphors and to avoid the indulgence of ecstasy and lamentation. The striking feature about the last stanza quoted above is that it creates an ecstatic note and yet avoids the pitfalls of preciosity and indulgence; it is strong and sweet in the best Metaphysical manner. This was an exceptionally difficult task where death was concerned, and it is to Watts's credit that, even on the verge of the precious and the mawkish, he does not quite succumb. The strength of the Metaphysical tradition, controlled by his classical techniques, sustains him.

In Young on the other hand, one is face to face with "that perfect exemplar of respectable and egregious bereavement, who carried his bleeding heart into the home of every British tradesman." [46] Draper's jibe is not unwarranted. In his incredibly popular "Poem on the Last Day" (1713), Young was capable of, amongst other things, the following:

> Now monuments prove faithful to their trust,
> And render back their long-committed dust.
> Now charnels rattle; scattered limbs, and all
> The various bones, obsequious to the call,
> Self-moved advance; the neck perhaps to meet
> The distant head; the distant legs the feet.
> **Dreadful to view, see through the dusky sky**
> Fragments of bodies in confusion fly,
> To distant regions journeying, there to claim
> Deserted members and complete the frame.[47]

There can be few passages in English verse as downright bad as this. It combines the worst sins of Metaphysical subject-matter with the most inane pomposities of 18th century poetic diction. In Young the faults of preromanticism are writ large. Most of his contemporaries succumbed to this kind of mannerism. Hence the indulgence of the graveyard school of poets; hence the pseudo-Jacobean decadence of William Thompson's five-book poem on "Sickness":

[45] Draper, p. 313.
[46] *Ibid.*, p. 248.
[47] Chalmers, XIII, 371-372.

> The dews of death
> Hung, clammy, on my forehead, like the damps
> Of midnight sepulchres; which
>
> . . . .
>
> Yawn hideous on the moon, and blast the stars
> With pestilential reek.[48]

In the light of the preromantics' treatment of death, Watts's restraint is indeed remarkable.

It is only fair to present here what slight evidence there is in Watts's prose of a mind exploiting the Metaphysical tradition. One would not expect the evidence to be more than slight, for the poems examined above were written when Watts was a young man, and he wrote most, and published all, of his prose long after the first editions of *Horae Lyricae*. His dedication to prose carried with it an implied renunciation of poetry, and such is the utilitarian weight and seriousness of the former that it is almost impossible to discover stylistic slips, let alone modes of thinking, which betray a 17th century mind. Such was his devotion to the plain style in prose, that he felt it necessary to apologise for any sally into figurative speech he may inadvertently have made. Thus in the dedication to his first volume of sermons (1721), he hopes that his "friendly readers will now and then indulge a metaphor, to one who from his earliest years has dealt a little in sacred poesy." [49] Thomas Gibbons, writing in 1780, paid the following compliment to Watts's prose style:

Perspicuity . . . is most eminent in all Dr Watts's works, and perhaps no author ever excelled him in this first glory of composition. . . . He brings down the highest subjects to the level of a common capacity by the perspicuous manner in which he treats them. . . . Where are there any puns or jingles, affected antitheses, fantastic conceits, or disgusting levities? [50]

The clarity of Watts's prose cannot be called in question. His style is set on an even keel. The rare echoes of Metaphysical prose by no means disturb the basic classical balance; but they are there all the same.

In *The Ruin and Recovery of Mankind* (1740), Watts takes up the old 17th century view of the world as a hospital or lazar-house:

And methinks, when I take my justest survey of this lower world, with all the inhabitants of it, I can look upon it no otherwise than as a huge and magnificent structure in ruins, and turned into a prison and a lazar-house or hospital,

---

[48] *Ibid.*, XV, 39.
[49] Watts, I, xxii.
[50] Gibbons, pp. 167, 168, 172.

wherein lie millions of criminals and rebels against their creator, under condemnation to misery and death; who are at the same time sick of a mortal
distemper.[51]

William Drummond of Hawthornden had written in his *Cypress Grove*
(1623): "O! who if before he had a being, he could have knowledge of
the manifold miseries of it, would enter this woeful hospital of the world,
and accept of life upon such hard conditions?" [52] There were surely
some Augustans who would have condemned such writing as in bad
taste. On the strict criterion of perspicuity, Watts is here open to the
charge of purveying at least "fantastic conceits" if not "disgusting
levities."

Nor can one overlook, with particular reference to the language, a
sentence already quoted for its theological implications, and one which
could not be left out of any complete account of the development of
Metaphysical prose:

When I have given my thoughts a loose, and let them rove without confinement, sometimes I seem to have carried reason with me even to the camp of
Socinus; but then St John gives my soul a twitch, and St Paul bears me back
again . . . almost to the tents of John Calvin.[53]

Perspicuity is here heightened by a dose of conceit and levity, though it
is doubtful whether the Augustans of Thomas Gibbons' generation would
have found it to their taste.

On another occasion Watts produced one sentence which, in its use
of syllogistic wit, reminds one strongly of Swift's technique of irony. "I
have heard it hinted," he writes, "that the name of Christ has been
banished out of polite sermons, because it is a monosyllable of so many
consonants, and so harsh a sound." [54] Irony of this calibre depended on
purity of diction and classical precision; but its underlying structure and
satiric bite are products of the 17th century mind, as they are in Swift.
The 18th century gradually dissipated such intellectual rigour and the
accompanying linguistic and satiric violence.

The 18th century also dissipated what was left of the rather more
eccentric rigour of Metaphysical prose, so that after Swift and Watts
quaint wit became indulgent whimsy. A. P. Davis has noted that "Watts's
Metaphysical fancy sometimes led him into quaint surmises." [55] This is
certainly true, but on such rare occasions Watts shows that he is not

[51] Watts, VI, 220.
[52] William Drummond of Hawthornden, *Poetical Works, with "A Cypress Grove,"*
ed. L. E. Kastner (2 vols.; Edinburgh: Blackwood, 1913), II, 80.
[53] *Reliquiae Juveniles,* No 49, Watts, IV, 532.
[54] *The Improvement of the Mind,* Watts, V, 351.
[55] Davis, p. 150.

indulging in gratuitous speculation, but trying to answer questions which were still being asked in the early 18th century. Davis remarks that Watts "was concerned with the state of Methuselah's body in the next world," and quotes his statement that "all the atoms that ever belonged to the animal body of Methuselah in nine hundred and sixty years would make a most bulky and disproportionate figure at the resurrection." [56] What Davis does not say is that Watts qualifies this surmise as "a vain and groundless conceit," and concludes with the relatively useful and sensible answer that "it cannot be the very same body ... that shall be raised." [57] Still, the speculation is there, and belongs to the line of prose inaugurated by Sir Thomas Browne.

A second gem quoted by Davis is equally fanciful, but again taken slightly out of context. Davis does not quote the introductory remark which certainly qualifies what follows. Watts begins: "Some persons have been very solicitous to know how the soul goes out of the body when a good man dies." [58] The gem Davis quotes continues: "They are yet further puzzled to conceive whether a soul departing from any place, for example, from London at noon, would find out its friend who died there the foregoing midnight, since a direct ascent would increase their distance and separation, far as the zenith is from the nadir." [59] Such speculation is not therefore properly Watts's; it is merely referred to as a form of enquiry indulged in by over-inquisitive people. Sir Thomas Browne would have come down on one side or the other in any such enquiry; Watts concludes rather lamely that "these things cannot be fully determined by us." [60] These instances then are residual rather than representative. They do however point to a 17th century mind on which the Metaphysical tradition left some few traces.

There is one aspect of Watts's inheritance of the Metaphysical tradition which calls for special attention. This is his exploitation of eroticism in the religious lyric. Like the religious poets of the 17th century, he relied heavily on transferring the vocabulary and imagery of profane love to the context of divine love. But what the 17th century encouraged, the 18th and 19th centuries condemned.

John Wesley, in a sermon entitled "Knowing Christ after the Flesh," agreed with "a person of deep piety as well as judgment" who had brought Watts's eroticism to his attention. According to Wesley's friend,

[56] *Ibid.* The quote is from *Philosophical Essays,* Watts, V, 583.
[57] *Ibid.*
[58] *Ibid.,* V, 576.
[59] *Ibid.* Quoted in Davis, p. 150.
[60] Watts, V, 576.

"some of the hymns printed in his *Horae Lyricae,* dedicated to Divine
Love, were (as he phrased it) 'too amorous, and fitter to be addressed by
a lover to his fellow-mortal, than by a sinner to the most high God.' " [61]
Wesley extends the attack to Watts's hymns:

Are they not full of expressions which strongly savour of "knowing Christ
after the flesh"? yea, and in a more gross manner, than anything which was
ever before published in the English tongue? What pity is it, that those coarse
expressions should appear in many truly spiritual hymns! [62]

Wesley urges his listeners to "avoid every fondling expression" when
referring to Christ.[63] In his own writing, and with less success in the
hymns of his brother Charles, this avoidance was elevated into a fine art;
and Watts, in revising his own hymns, went a long way towards meeting
Wesley's criteria.

If Wesley spoke for the 18th century, then Southey undoubtedly
speaks for the 19th century. In the preface to his edition of *Horae Lyricae,* published in the year of Queen Victoria's accession, he writes:

Pure as was the mind of Dr Watts – and its purity was equal to the lucid
clearness of his style – he has in many of these pieces, made so bold a use of the
sensible imagery proper to amatory verse, that while the unspiritual reader
is apt to linger, if not finally to rest, in the mere external sense, there is no
small danger, at least in these times, lest the more pious and refined should
experience a feeling bordering on disgust.[64]

It would be difficult to find clearer proof that Victorian culture and 17th
century puritan culture were diametrically opposed. Southey was an Anglican, and the sources of Victorian nonconformity are to be found in the
18th century. Wesley's attack on Watts was but one stage in a rapid pro-
gression from the age of Marvell, with which Watts was not without
contact, to the age of Southey, which claimed contact with Watts.

Wesley in turn was attacked on the same score by those for whom
enthusiasm was an un-18th century activity. Nathaniel Lancaster (1701-
1775), in his *Methodism Triumphant* (1767), attributes a quantity of
fondling expressions to Wesley and his followers.[65] And William Cowper
earns a place as a Victorian avant la lettre for toning down the languish-
ing eroticism of the French pietist, Mme Guion, some of whose poems
he translated in 1782.[66] It is worthwhile examining the nature of Watts's

---

[61] Sermon 117, John Wesley, *Works,* VII, 293.
[62] *Ibid.*
[63] *Ibid.*
[64] Southey's preface to his edition of *Horae Lyricae* (1837), quoted in Birrell,
English Studies, XXXVIII (1956), 130.
[65] See Fairchild, II, 129.
[66] See *ibid.,* II, 183.

alleged eroticism, not only to judge whether subsequent moves towards Victorianism were justified, but also to discover how close Watts was in this respect to the 17th century tradition drawn on so liberally by the Metaphysical poets.

It is significant that what amounts to a manifesto of the 17th century tradition of religious eroticism can be found in the 1697 Dissenters' version of Herbert's *Temple*. In the preface to this volume, not without affinities to the prefaces to Norris's *Miscellanies* and Watts's *Horae Lyricae*, the editor states his aim in terms of the divine theory of poetry; he wishes "to rescue the high flights and lofty strains found in the most celebrated poets, from their sacrilegious applications to carnal love and restore them to the divine love." And he goes on to justify this theory by referring to the tradition of religious eroticism derived from Crashaw:

I do not find it hath been made a matter of scruple to turn the temples built for idols into churches. . . . And who can doubt but the church may take her own, wherever she finds it, whether in an idolatrous Mass-book or profane Love-song? It was a noble resolution of him that said,
>   I'll consecrate my Magdalene to thee –
The eyes, mouth, hair, which had been abused to lust and vanity were used to wash, kiss, wipe the feet of a Saviour.[67]

This is of course not only a defence of religious eroticism, but also a defence of the Dissenters' appropriation of a lyrical tradition previously practised almost exclusively by high-church Anglicans and Roman Catholics. The lateness of the manifesto does something to explain the persistence of religious eroticism in the poetry of the Dissenters well into the 18th century. Mrs Rowe, who modelled much of her verse on Watts, went on writing in this tradition as late as 1735.

Mrs Rowe was a key figure in the development of early 18th century eroticism. Soon after her husband's death in 1715, she composed her *History of Joseph* (published in 1736). Joseph is clearly a sublimation of her dead husband, and the poem is not so much an epic as a romance. Mrs Rowe enjoyed great popularity. As Fairchild has noted, there is "something sentimental, hectic, and even a little sensational about her writings." [68] Her epic-romance is in fact an "extensive adaptation of the Song of Solomon along the lines of 'virgin minds that feel the sacred violence of love.'" [69] Fairchild concludes his description with this wry comment: "Doubtless these spirits love God, but apparently they spend a great deal of their time in loving each other." [70] It is thus surprising to

[67] *Select Hymns,* Preface.
[68] Fairchild, I, 137.
[69] *Ibid.,* I, 138.
[70] *Ibid.,* I, 137.

discover that Mrs Rowe enjoyed the admiration not only of a wide public but also of Watts and Wesley.

Wesley, whose strictures on Watts's erotic tendencies have been noted, was not daunted by the works of Mrs Rowe; he included 24 items by Mrs Rowe in his 1744 anthology of "moral and sacred poems." [71] Watts, in his 1737 preface to Mrs Rowe's posthumous *Devout Exercises,* seems to have been particularly concerned to rescue her from some of the implications of her sensational popularity. He agrees that "the style . . . is raised above that of common meditation," but reminds his readers that "she was no common Christian." [72] He explicitly denies that she ever indulged in mystical ecstasies.[73] His only criticisms are hidden behind the unobtrusive note that "here and there a too venturous flight is a little moderated" [74] – which being interpreted means that he has tampered with her text –, and behind the bland recognition that tastes have changed since their younger days when "it was much the fashion, . . . even among some divines of eminence, to express the fervours of devout love to our Saviour in the style of the Song of Solomon." [75]

The kind of writing which Watts and Wesley must have found distasteful can be seen in Mrs Rowe's "Paraphrase on the Canticles" (1735). Some of the erotic tendencies in this work are inevitable, given the original. Such are the comparisons of lips to "threads of scarlet," and of breasts to "twins of gentle roes." [76] But there is something indulgently hectic and sensational about the following two extracts:

> 'Twas night when on my restless bed I sought,
> But sought in vain the partner of my cares,
> For he was now withdrawn.[77]

> I am sick of love – O let me lean
> My drooping head upon thy downy breast;
> While thy left hand supports me, let thy right
> Kindly enfold me in a chaste embrace.[78]

[71] John Wesley (ed.), *A Collection of Moral and Sacred Poems from the most celebrated English Authors* (3 vols.; Bristol, 1744). Mrs Rowe is way ahead of the other contributors; Watts is second with 13 items, Pope third with 8. See Fairchild, I, 91-92.
[72] Elizabeth Rowe, *Devout Exercises of the Heart,* ed. Isaac Watts (London: C. Cooke, n.d.), Preface, p. 40.
[73] *Ibid.,* p. 41.
[74] *Ibid.,* p. 44.
[75] *Ibid.,* p. 40.
[76] Elizabeth Rowe, *Poems on Several Occasions,* p. 51.
[77] *Ibid.,* p. 48.
[78] *Ibid.,* p. 49.

It is surely the precision of locality and the detail of position, created very largely by the simple words "bed," "left" and "right," which give this writing a hectic solidity beyond the requirements of paraphrase.

Compared to Mrs Rowe's effusions, Watts's *Horae Lyricae* is almost void of eroticism. Watts employs the erotic with a good deal of care, not to say trepidation. Either he couches it in negative syntax, or he betrays a consciousness of transferring it from where it belongs to a metaphorical use. And yet is must be passages like the following which offended Wesley:

> I'm tired with visits, modes and forms,
> And flatteries made to fellow-worms:
> Their conversation cloys;
> Their vain amours, and empty stuff:
> But I can ne'er enjoy enough
> Of thy best company, my Lord, thou life of all my joys.
>
> . . . .
>
> My soul disdains that little snare
> The tangles of Amira's hair:
> Thine arms my God are sweeter bands, nor can my heart remove.[79]

By sobriety of syntax and imagery, Watts keeps his distance, and can hardly be accused of "fondling Christ." Like Milton, Watts introduces his eroticism with an unequivocal negative. Thus:

> Not Danaë's lap could equal treasure boast
> When Jove came down in golden showers.[80]

Still, guilty or not, Watts certainly felt guilty.

In *A Guide to Prayer* (1715) he is considerably more outspoken on this issue than in his 1737 preface to Mrs Rowe's *Devout Exercises*. The insistent amplification of his advice against "fondling Christ" surely betrays excessive sensitivity to his own lapses. He is of course writing an art of prayer, not of poetry; but his critique needs no modification for it to be highly relevant to the religious eroticism of his own early verse, and more particularly of Mrs Rowe's verse. He writes:

---

[79] "Converse with Christ," *Horae Lyricae*, I. Watts, IV, 374-375.

[80] "The Happy Man," *Horae Lyricae*, II. Watts, IV, 409. Cf. Mrs Rowe's *History of Joseph*:

> "Not he that in Sabea's fragrant grove
> (As poets sung) enflamed the queen of love,
> Nor Hylas, nor Narcissus looked so gay."

Poems on Several Occasions, p. 137.

Avoid mean and coarse and too familiar expressions. . . . There is no necessity of being rough and slovenly, in order to be sincere. Sometimes persons have been guilty of great indecencies, and exposed religion to vain scoffs, by a too familiar mention of the name of Christ, and by irreverent freedoms when they speak of God. I cannot approve of the phrases of rolling upon Christ, of swimming upon Christ to dry land, of taking a lease of Christ for all eternity. . . . Persons are sometimes in danger of indecencies in borrowing mean and trivial, or uncleanly similitudes: they rake all the sinks of nastiness to fetch metaphors for their sins, and praying for the coming of Christ, they fold up the heavens like an old cloak, and shovel days out of the way. . . . Some expressions, that might appear decent threescore years ago, would be highly improper, and offensive to the ears of the present age.[81]

There could be no plainer demonstration that the indictment against religious eroticism is part and parcel of the reaction against the Metaphysical tradition. Watts himself was sufficiently conscious of the attraction of this tradition to spend a good deal of his energy trying to purge his youthful poems of their erotic tendencies.

In the second edition of *Horae Lyricae* he paid particular attention to the titles of the "Poems of Divine Love," seeking to root out their sensuous connotations.[82] In the second edition of his *Hymns* most of his revision was devoted to a systematic eradication of elements which could be frowned on as erotic or Metaphysical. Fortunately Watts chose to bracket as optional, rather than erase, verses which constitute his strongest writing. One such verse, bracketed in 1709, runs as follows:

> Jesus! the vision of thy face
> Hath overpowering charms!
> Scarce shall I feel death's cold embrace,
> If Christ be in my arms.[83]

Here again one can assess Watts's achievement by measuring his closeness to, and his attempt to be distant from, a tradition which nourished Metaphysical religious poetry. The Metaphysical qualities of Watts's verse are few and far between, because he was working on his diction and syntax as a classicist, and successfully sinking such qualities. When they do occur however, they reveal the strength of a tradition which sustains the polish of Watts's craftsmanship.

---

[81] Watts, III, 146.
[82] See list of variants in Escott, p. 40.
[83] *Hymns,* I, 19, stanza 5. Watts, IV, 157.

CHAPTER EIGHTEEN

CLASSICISM: THE ART OF SINKING

Watts renovated the religious lyric by purifying its diction and strengthening its syntax. He thus demonstrated that sublimity was no substitute for a redundant Metaphysical tradition. He is a classicist not because, like numerous minor poets, he used the stylistic devices of Dryden and Pope, but because he cultivated what can only be called the art of sinking. His art appropriated lyrical resources until then the monopoly of the Metaphysical poets, and consolidated the stock on which Blake and Wordsworth were to draw.

As an aesthetic theoretician, Watts was principally interested in defining his art of sinking. His only reference to classical literary theory of the kind set out in Pope's *Essay on Criticism* is a passing remark in "A Brief Scheme of Ontology" to the figure of antithesis. As he points out,

all opposites placed near one another give a mutual illustration to each other, and make their distinct characters appear plainer. Hence proceeds the reason of foils among painters and jewellers, orators and poets.[1]

The aesthetics of antithesis, like the Cartesian ideology, demanded plainness and distinctness. Cartesian dualism was instrumental in metamorphosing the correspondences of Metaphysical poetry into the antitheses of classical poetry. It is however important to realise that the material involved was often the same. The far-fetched analogies of the Metaphysicals were exploited as antitheses by the classical poets. It follows that the strength of the classical couplet is derived from the strength of Metaphysical rhetoric, pruned of its gratuitous ornament and copious amplification, and reduced to the bare bones of elementary syntax and diction.

Watts is not concerned with either the couplet in itself or the couplet within the paragraph. When he writes "She loathes her patches, pins and paints," [2] he is reducing satiric alliteration to a level of diction where it

---

[1] *Philosophical Essays,* Watts, V, 665.
[2] "The Discontented and Unquiet," *Horae Lyricae,* II. Watts, IV, 412.

becomes possible to make use of it in the couplet; and when he writes of
those who "sweat to be correctly dull," [3] he is using antithesis as the basis
of satiric bathos, with a compression of syntax which makes the figure
available for exploitation within the couplet. Similarly, when he rides the
high horse of paragraphic rhythm, he uses the syntax of blank verse to
modulate the key in which the antithesis is set:

> Ye frighted nymphs, who on the bridal bed
> Clasped in your arms your lovers cold and dead,
> Come; in the pomp of all your wild despair,
> With flowing eyelids and disordered hair,
> Death in your looks.[4]

The syntax in which "eyelids" and "hair," with their matching epithets,
are set, belongs to the rhythm of the couplet; while "looks," the third item
in the antithesis between love and death, is set in the syntax of blank verse.
For Watts, in other words, the couplet and the paragraph are not absolute
forms with their own mutually exclusive rules, but fluid and interchangea-
ble idioms in which experiments in syntactical variation could be made.

Antithesis also contributes to the way in which Watts sank the 17th
century lyric into its classical form. If the lyric was to survive, it had to
limit the element of personal vision and express philosophical truths which
had a bearing on mankind in general. But to do this was to threaten the
very essence of the lyric, to deny its sweetness and its sense of the marvellous. There was only one way out, and that was the development of the
gnomic lyric, whereby the truth, although obvious and agreed, was expressed in a semi-symbolical, semi-mystical way, so that there was a certain
amount of haze surrounding the precise literal meaning.

The presence of antithetical symbols could be used to create paradox,
and thus express the mystery of truth. Hence Watts writes: "Roses grow
on thorns, and honey wears a sting." [5] He means that there is more to
pleasure than meets the eye. But he is prepared to use the antithesis or
paradox, not merely as a philosophical illustration, but as an argument in
the poem. The essence of the gnomic lyric is that the simile or metaphor is
not an ornament but a proof. In this vein, Watts argues from the antithesis
between rivers and the sea, to prove that life and the divine vision are incompatible, because the flow of life ends in the sea of vision.[6] And from the
antithesis between diamonds worn on the neck and the thorn of humour

---

[3] "The Adventurous Muse," *ibid.*, IV, 399.
[4] "Funeral Poem on Thomas Gunston," *Horae Lyricae*, III. Watts, IV, 443.
[5] "Earth and Heaven," *Horae Lyricae*, I. Watts, IV, 337.
[6] "The Fairest and Only Beloved," *ibid.*, IV, 372.

stuck in the heart, he can prove that the life of a hermit-saint is not necessarily any happier than the life of a courtier, because a humour is more
difficult to get rid of than a necklace.[7] In the gnomic lyric the old water-
tight syllogistic conceit is submerged in a haze of axiomatic probability.
The figures of antithesis and paradox thus represent a survival of Renaissance rhetoric in a sunk and simplified form.

Watts is not above using gnomic imagery in his prose as a method of
argument. Because gnomic imagery is half visual and half conceptual, it
is peculiarly suited to the purposes of persuasion. Because, through the
haze of probability, it expresses axiomatic opposites in a clear and distinct
manner, it could not be condemned as the work of either idle fancy or
imaginative enthusiasm. Even Locke could allow himself to talk of the
blank sheet of a child's mind. Hence Watts can argue gnomically that "it
is not reasonable to put out our candle and sit still in the dark, because we
have not the light of sunbeams." [8] And he can indulge in a sustained metaphor when he is sure of his ground:

The passions never clear the understanding, but raise darkness, clouds and
confusion in the soul: Human nature is like water which has mud at the bottom of it, it may be clear while it is calm and undisturbed, and the ideas, like
pebbles, appear bright at the bottom; but when once it is stirred and moved
by passion, the mud rises uppermost, and spreads confusion and darkness over
all the ideas.[9]

Blake was a great exponent of the art of gnomic imagery; his taste for opposites (like the clod and the pebble), and his use of paradox and antithesis
arose out of the techniques of classicism. Looking back from Blake through
Watts, it is possible to trace gnomic imagery to its Metaphysical sources.
Blake's opposites have their origins in the 17th century consciousness, in
the mind capable of conceiving far-fetched analogies. Classicism saw opposites where the Metaphysical mind saw correspondences. Blake renewed
the far-fetched nature of the truth opposites were capable of expressing.

Take, for example, Watts's analogy between stoic souls and married
logs.[10] This is used as part of an extended antithesis; it exploits the absurdity of comparing a soul to a log, and depends for its point in the poem
on the reader's acceptance that a log and a soul can have nothing to do
with each other. But the exploitation of the absurdity is itself dependent on
a previous generation's acceptance of such analogies as capable of discovering truth via wit. Romanticism in its turn sought to rediscover the

[7] "The Discontented and Unquiet," *Horae Lyricae*, II. Watts, IV, 412.
[8] *The Improvement of the Mind*, Watts, V, 338.
[9] *Ibid.*, V, 330.
[10] *Horae Lyricae*, II. Watts, IV, 402.

sense of the Metaphysical analogy by subjecting the classical opposite to the plastic power of the imagination, which could somehow reunite the log and the soul, if not rationally in the intellect or scientifically in the cosmos, than at least poetically on the page. Wordsworth's leech-gatherer is a striking example of this rediscovery. But it was not a rediscovery which could revert to a 17th century consciousness and ignore the classical experiment. The Romantics set themselves up against 18th century poetic diction, but they flexed their imaginations in the idiom of classical syntax, which Watts and others had created out of the techniques of the Renaissance.

Classicism, if it was followed methodically and consistently, had a severely inhibiting effect on the religious lyric. Such were the pressures of strong syntax and pure diction that the lyrical life as such was being squeezed out of the idiom. Watts went far enough to realise that classicism meant turning the religious lyric into a hymn. The only way of stopping short of the hymn was to use gnomic imagery, with its minimum of visualisation. Classicism shunned the particular vision, sensory or imaginative; and there can be few poets so consistent in their avoidance of the visual than Watts.

In his gnomic imagery there is often only the merest glimmer of the visual. It usually sustains the lyricism, as when he writes of "picking shells and pebbles" from the "narrow shores of flesh and sense," [11] and of those who will not "loose hands" and who "hand in hand" "drag the age along." [12] In the last two verses of one of his elegies, only the alliteration and the gnomic word "dusky" (half visual and half moral) stand out from the classical syntax and diction, and prevent the lyricism from sinking into the cold shape of a hymn:

> Move faster on great nature's wheel,
> Be kind, ye rolling powers,
> Hurl my days headlong down the hill
> With undistinguished hours.
>
> Be dusky, all my rising suns,
> Nor smile upon a slave:
> Darkness and death, make haste at once
> To hide me in the grave.[13]

---

[11] "True Riches," *Horae Lyricae,* II. Watts, IV, 398.
[12] "Free Philosophy" and "The Way of the Multitude," *ibid.,* IV, 393-394.
[13] "The Afflictions of a Friend," *ibid.,* IV, 400.

It is to Watts's credit that he valued lyricism as much as he valued classicism; in his use of gnomic imagery it is possible to trace an important phase of the lyric.

By taking the Metaphysical lyric, sinking its redundancies, and subjecting it to the criteria of classicism, Watts was consolidating the formal stock of the idiom. In allowing the gnomic image, he was admitting that the imagination, in however subterranean a way, could teach:

> Methinks a mould'ring pyramid
> Said all that the old sages said;
> For me these shattered tombs contain
> More morals than the Vatican.[14]

The Metaphysical poet had linked tombs and pyramids to man by the quaint device of the microcosm; the correspondences with which he played in his poems reflected philosophical convictions which he could justify by syllogistic reasoning and preach with the aid of rhetoric. Watts rationalises these correspondences, sets them apart, but does not remove the possibility of influence. It is for this reason, and not because he displays elements of an eternally latent preromanticism, that Watts prefigures Wordsworth so closely. Lyricism would flourish again when poets believed that a mouldering pyramid or a vernal wood could say more than the sages.

Gnomic imagery had to be couched in strong syntax and pure diction if it was to be effective, and Watts's classicism resides most strikingly in his development, in theory and in practice, of the art of sinking. It is difficult to believe that Pope did not have Watts, among others, in mind, when he composed his *Peri Bathous, or The Art of Sinking in Poetry* (1728). In that work, inspired no doubt by Swift and Arbuthnot, Pope singles out for special opprobrium

the *Flying Fishes*: These are writers who now and then rise upon their fins, and fly out of the Profound; but their wings are soon dry, and they drop down to the bottom.[15]

Watts is certainly one of the masters of bathos; but whereas many an 18th century poet fell into bathos naturally and unawares, Watts cultivated it as an art.

Indeed a parallel may be drawn between Watts and that other major practitioner of bathos, Wordsworth.[16] Watts, in proclaiming and prac-

---

[14] "The Hero's School of Morality," *ibid.*, IV, 395.

[15] Alexander Pope, *Works,* ed. W. L. Bowles (10 vols.; London: J. Johnson etc., 1806), VI, 206-207.

[16] This affinity has been noted by Bernard Lord Manning, *The Hymns of Wesley and Watts* (London: Epworth Press, 1942), p. 88: "Watts out-Wordsworth's Words-

tising the art of sinking in poetry, seems to have been aiming at much the same thing as Wordsworth: the purification of diction and the strengthening of syntax through the infusion into poetic tradition of a fresh stream of common language and spoken English. Both poets issued manifestos of their intentions along with their first attempts to put them into practice. Both achieved a measure of success in their early work, and both fell victim to their own theories in the many revisions which followed a comparatively early loss of vision. The parallel is instructive too, for it suggests that classicism and Romanticism are not necessarily opposites, and had the ideal and decadence of bathos in common.

The bathetic ideal led Watts to write: "I have a soul was made to pity kings, / And all their little glittering things." [17] The artificial sublimity of the first line is punctured by the bathos of the second. Noone is interested in whether Watts has a soul made to pity kings, and to proclaim this in a poem is absurd bombast; but the poetic diction is rejuvenated by the childish concept and spoken rhythm of "little glittering things." Bathos introduces into poetry phrases that seem too common, too trite and too obvious. In similar vein elsewhere, Watts gets his bathetic effect through deliberate use of the slipshod, indeterminate word "things":

> The towering heights, and flightful falls,
> The ruined heaps and funerals,
> Of smoking kingdoms and their kings,
> Tell me a thousand mournful things
> In melancholy silence.[18]

Here again the elevated style and conception of the first three lines are made relevant as poetry by the conversational triteness of the last two. Bathos thus allows the poet to indulge in the occasional piece of taut sublimity; it provides an escape valve to prevent the bubble bursting.

There were of course pitfalls, and Watts frequently stumbled. If you are cultivating the art of bathos, you are bound to reach the point where it becomes impossible to guarantee success. If there is no vision to communicate the self-sufficient technique falls flat. Wordsworth had the same trouble, and a lot of bad Victorian poetry displays the kind of decadence that Watts is guilty of in the following:

worth in his love of simple, everyday language; and as Wordsworth at times made the sublime ridiculous by his kindergarten expressions so also did Watts."

[17] "True Wisdom," *Horae Lyricae*, I. Watts, IV, 351.
[18] "The Hero's School of Morality," *Horae Lyricae*, II. Watts, IV, 395.

My heart, how dreadful hard it is!
How heavy here it lies;
Heavy and cold within my breast,
Just like a rock of ice! [19]

The trouble here is that Watts has nothing to sink, and that his bathos is therefore redundant; but the many failures, in which he appears to be floundering in a dead sea of profundity like a flying fish, do not invalidate the guiding principle of the art of sinking.

Watts worked out this principle in the idiom of the hymn. The hymn was an essentially classical and 18th century form, which grew out of the 17th century religious lyric. It is difficult to draw a clear line between the lyric and the hymn, but it is significant that the first recognisable hymn-book was the work of a Roman Catholic. John Austin (1613-1669) issued his *Devotions in the Ancient Way of Offices* in 1668. It incorporated 39 hymns, including a couple by Crashaw. This volume went through four Roman Catholic editions, but in 1687 it was edited by George Hickes and became the hymn-book of the non-jurors.[20] Roman Catholics and non-jurors were followed by the Dissenters.

The hymns of the Dissenters evolved from the same source – the early 17th century high-church devotional lyric. But the colours of stained glass were too rich for the Dissenters, and though the lyrics of Herbert and Quarles were used in private and family devotions, it was some time before hymns replaced psalms in congregational use. The change occurred in the 1690s, partly because John Mason, in his *Spiritual Songs* (1683), provided what James Montgomery was to call "a middle tint between the raw colouring of Quarles and the daylight clearness of Watts." [21] Even then there was still strong opposition to spiritual songs or hymns being used in public worship, and as late as 1697 they were still not permitted to compete with the traditional paraphrases of the psalms.[22] The ground was prepared for some radical innovation, but it was left to Watts to tip the scale.

Watts himself was also prepared for the inauguration of a new lyrical idiom. Here the influence of John Wilkins and the linguistic ideals of the Royal Society were decisive. As H. Escott has very pertinently noted, "the language of the Royal Society was not natural to Watts; he was more at home with the soaring expressions of Casimire and the Metaphysical con-

---

[19] "Hardness of Heart Complained of," *Hymns*, II, 97, stanza 1. Watts, IV, 233.
[20] See Escott, p. 76.
[21] Quoted in *ibid.*, p. 79.
[22] See *Select Hymns*, pp. i-ii.

ceits of the 17th century devotional poets." But, as Escott goes on to say, "the discipline of writing hymns for a definite congregation of lowly folk" led him to perform an

artistic kenosis; Watts had to lay his poetic glories aside, and dress the profound message of the gospel in homespun verse and the language of the people. Only when he turned from the lyric to the hymn did he wholeheartedly adopt the language and ideals of the Royal Society.[23]

This kenosis principle is useful; it accounts for the arduous efforts with which Watts tackled his art of sinking.

On the basis of this art, Watts set about his work, which included lyrics, psalms and hymns. It is slightly misleading to suggest that he turned from the lyric to the hymn; the art of sinking applies to all three genres, and, as far as we know, he began writing lyrics, psalms and hymns together before 1700.[24] Probably the initial challenge arose out of a consideration of the impoverished versions of the psalms then available. The Elizabethan work of Sternhold and Hopkins was still being used, and Watts was anxious to rid public worship of its sclerotic grip. *Horae Lyricae* (1706) and the *Hymns* (1707) constitute a revolutionary vanguard in themselves, but they were seen by Watts at the time as kites flown to prepare the ground for the world-shattering revision of Sternhold and Hopkins which Watts held back until 1719. Thus in the preface to *Horae Lyricae* Watts complains:

They will venture to sing a dull hymn or two at church, in tunes of equal dulness; but still they persuade themselves, and their children, that the beauties of poesy are vain and dangerous. All that arises a degree above Mr Sternhold is too airy for worship, and hardly escapes the sentence of unclean and abominable.[25]

It is clear from this passage how closely interlocked were Watts's aims in lyric, hymn and psalm. To revise Sternhold and Hopkins he had first to introduce the "soaring expressions of Casimire and the Metaphysical conceits of the 17th century devotional poets." Only then could he practise his art of sinking, and prune his muse to meet the linguistic ideals of the Royal Society.

Two milestones in the development of a new lyrical idiom need to be noted. One was singled out for special praise by Watts. It was the appearance in 1679 of John Patrick's *Century of Select Psalms and Portions of*

---

[23] Escott, p. 26. Watts had a youthful fondness for the writings of Wilkins, some of which were on the syllabus at Newington Green Academy. In his *Guide to Prayer* (1715) he drew heavily on Wilkins's *Discourse Concerning the Gift of Prayer* (1653). See Watts, III, 108.

[24] See Davis, pp. 200-201.

[25] *Horae Lyricae,* Preface. Watts, IV, 318.

Psalms, especially those of praise. Patrick was the first to "evangelise the Royal Psalmist." [26] Watts acknowledged his debt to this work when he described Patrick's invaluable innovations:

He hath made use of the present language of Christians in several psalms, and left out many of the judaisms. . . . There are scarce any that have departed farther from the inspired words of scripture than he hath often done, in order to suit his thoughts to the state and worship of Christianity. This I esteem his peculiar excellency.[27]

The possibility of such a liturgical revolution was the inevitable prerequisite to Watts's efforts; without it he was deprived of his audience.

The second milestone coincided with the beginning of Watts's work; this was the appearance in 1697 of *Select Hymns taken out of Mr Herbert's Temple.* In this work the art of sinking, as employed by Watts, was applied with the explicit aim of making the personal lyric available for congregational use. As its modern editor points out,

the adapter avoided poems with an identifiable single speaker, or with two speakers addressing each other in dramatic dialogue. He made the "I" of the *Select Hymns* always a spokesman for an entire group, expressing attitudes all men might find true of themselves. He even avoided poems where too extremely and personally "fanciful" an attitude is taken.[28]

Watts continued this trend in his search for expressions "such as are capable of an extensive sense"; [29] and in revision, any added stanzas were designed to give the hymns "a more general and extensive sense." [30] The danger of course was that in doing this one might lapse into the obvious and trite. On the many occasions when Watts defines his art of sinking, he shows that he is aware of this danger.

Watts's initial manifesto of the art of sinking, "A Short Essay Toward the Improvement of Psalmody," was appended to the first edition of his *Hymns* in 1707.[31] Although he never got round to expanding this essay into the full-length treatise promised, its basic ideas are developed in one form or another in many of his most important subsequent works. In the essay itself, Watts urges the need for singing with understanding and for uniformity of interpretation. As a premise to the effective operation of the

---

[26] Davis, p. 190.
[27] *Psalms,* Preface. Watts, IV, xii.
[28] *Select Hymns,* p. v.
[29] *Hymns,* 1709 Preface. Watts, IV, 149.
[30] *Ibid.,* Advertisement i. Not included in Watts's *Works.* Quoted in Escott, p. 176.
[31] This essay was dropped from subsequent editions of the *Hymns,* pending its expansion into a full-length treatise. The treatise did not materialise, and the original essay was reprinted in the collected works (Watts, IV, 273-291).

art of sinking, he emphasises that the hymn must be lyrical and the vehicle of self-expression:

Songs are generally expressions of our own experiences. There ought to be some turns of expression that make it look at least like our own present meditation, and that may represent it as a history which we ourselves are at that time recollecting.[32]

This point is repeated in his *Guide to Prayer* (1715), where he remarks that "the duty of prayer is very useful to discover to us the frame of our own spirits"; and to support this view he quotes Wilkins, who had written: "While we are clothing the sense of our hearts in fit expressions, and as it were digging the matter of our prayers out of our own feelings and experiences, it must needs keep the heart closer at work." [33] The revolutionary ideal that Watts goes on to set himself in the "Short Essay" is a technical one: "to sink every line to the level of a whole congregation, and yet to keep it above contempt." [34] This is the gist of his manifesto. Although he never loses sight of its relevance to the art of sinking the lyric into the hymn, it is never a mere technical device. Its reiteration in all sorts of places demonstrates that it is the central aesthetic expression of Watts's thinking on a variety of topics.

Since Watts's "Short Essay" was never expanded into a treatise, it is worth noting how he applied its central idea to a variety of tasks which he undertook after 1707. In the preface to the second edition of his *Hymns,* he makes the point that bathos is not a simple art but an arduous one:

The metaphors are generally sunk to the level of vulgar capacities. I have aimed at ease of numbers and smoothness of sound, and endeavoured to make the sense plain and obvious. If the verse appears so gentle and flowing as to incur the censure of feebleness, I may honestly affirm, that sometimes it cost me labour to make it so: Some of the beauties of poesy are neglected, and some wilfully defaced: I have thrown out the lines that were too sonorous, and have given an allay to the verse, lest a more exalted turn of thought and language should darken or disturb the devotion of the weaker souls.[35]

In *The Improvement of the Mind* (1741) Watts returned to this argument. Translating Horace, he wrote:

> Smooth be your style, and plain and natural,
> To strike the sons of Wapping or Whitehall.
> While others think this easy to attain,

[32] Watts, IV, 277.
[33] Watts, III, 125.
[34] Watts, IV, 291.
[35] Watts, IV, 149.

> Let them but try, and with their utmost pain
> They'll sweat and strive to imitate in vain.[36]

Classicism for Watts was a hard task-master; it demanded from him an artistic kenosis.

In 1715 Watts preached the art of sinking in his *Guide to Prayer* and practised it in his *Divine Songs Attempted in Easy Language for the Use of Children*. In the former he urged: "Let your language be grave and decent, which is a medium between magnificence and meanness. Let it be plain but not coarse. Let it be clean, but not at all lofty and glittering." [37] To illustrate his point he gave numerous examples of those expressions – neological, pleonastic or obsolete – which should be sunk.[38] In the preface to the latter he explained his aims: "As I have endeavoured to sink the language to the level of a child's understanding, and yet to keep it if possible above contempt; so I have designed to profit all, if possible, and offend none." [39] The measure of his success can be gauged from the following sample:

> Lord I ascribe it to thy Grace
> And not to chance as others do
> That I was born of Christian race
> And not a heathen or a Jew.[40]

Verses such as these must have made their mark on generations of 18th century and Victorian children; they are easy to parody but almost impossible to imitate. Blake, whose *Songs of Innocence and Experience* appeared as a counterblast against such sentiments, is perhaps the only poet able to sink his vision in diction and syntax as pure and strong as Watts's. Watts certainly raised the cultivation of bathos to a fine art; the effect, in terms of communication of solid piety to successive generations, must have been irresistible.

In 1722 Watts applied his art of sinking to his favourite theological problem. In the preface to *The Christian Doctrine of the Trinity*, he declared:

I have attempted to do all this in such plain and easy language, that every private Christian ... may understand. ... Upon this account I have been watchful against admitting those latin and greek words and terms of art,

---

[36] Watts, V, 233.
[37] Watts, III, 145.
[38] Watts, III, 144.
[39] Watts, IV, 296.
[40] Watts, IV, 299. Cf. "Let dogs delight to bark and bite" (*ibid.*, IV, 303) and "'Tis the voice of the sluggard" (*ibid.*, IV, 309).

which have too often tended to flatter the vanity of men, and make them learned in mere words and syllables, and which have often proved an incumbrance and burden to their faith, rather than a support of it.[41]

The art of sinking, in other words, served to define the context in which he set out to write controversial prose as well as pious verse.

Perhaps the clearest example of Watts's art of sinking is to be found in his *Catechisms composed for Children and Youth, according to their Different Ages* (1730). The Westminster Assembly's catechism was so verbose and complicated that Watts felt it incumbent upon him to produce several briefer versions of it, each to meet the needs and capacities of a particular age-group. In the preface to "The Assembly's Shorter Catechism," designed for children between 12 and 14, he sought to justify his scheme: "Some persons perhaps may think I have explained too many words. . . . But I have been informed of one child who was asked, What the chief end of man was, and he answered, His head; another being asked the same question, answered death." [42] In the dedication to his explanatory "Discourse on the Way of Instruction by Catechism," Watts renewed his claim to be practising a painstaking and arduous art: "The world will hardly believe what pains have been taken in composing these catechisms, . . . that no word, phrase or sentiment might be admitted which could not be brought in some measure within the reach of a child's understanding." [43] The single-minded persistence with which Watts pursued his declared mission as vulgariser-extraordinary to the early 18th century deserves to be acknowledged. It is no doubt because he did not confine his art of sinking to the context of technical devices, that his technical achievement in the lyrics, psalms and hymns is so considerable.

As might be expected, Watts's most sustained reference to the art of sinking, outside his 1707 "Short Essay," occurs in the 1719 preface to his *Psalms*. To this work, all his previous experiments in verse were, to his way of thinking, tentative preludes. In the preface, he crystallises definitively his previous reflections on the art of sinking. There are the customary strictures on the sublime and the bathetic:

In some of the more elevated psalms I have given a little indulgence to my genius; and if it should appear that I have aimed at the sublime, yet I have generally kept within the reach of an unlearned reader. I never thought the art of sublime writing consisted in flying out of sight. . . . In many of these composures I have just permitted my verse to rise above a flat and indolent

---

[41] Watts, VI, 417.
[42] Watts, III, 252-253.
[43] Watts, III, 203.

style; yet I hope it is everywhere supported above the just contempt of the critics: Though I am sensible that I have often subdued it below their esteem; because I would neither indulge any bold metaphors, nor admit of hard words, nor tempt an ignorant worshipper to sing without his understanding.[44]

This passage reflects the extent of Watts's artistic kenosis. He concludes, as he had begun in 1707, in the spirit of a manifesto, drawing together the threads of his argument with fitting eloquence:

A meaner pen may imitate at a distance, but a complete translation, or a just paraphrase, demands a rich treasury of diction, and exalted fancy, a quick taste of devout passion, together with judgment strict and severe to retrench every luxuriant line, and to maintain a religious sovereignty over the whole work. . . . And whensoever there shall appear any paraphrase of the book of psalms, that retains more of the savour of David's piety, discovers more of the style and spirit of the gospel, with a superior dignity of verse, and yet the lines as easy and flowing and the sense and language as level to the lowest capacity, I shall congratulate the world, and consent to say, Let this attempt of mine be buried in silence.[45]

This declaration constitutes Watts's own apology for his classicism. It reflects the core of his aesthetic theory. Its validity can be tested against Watts's lyrics, psalms and hymns. It is perhaps most demonstrably valid in the revolutionary idiom of his hymns, between the first and second editions of which Watts worked hard at revision by the art of sinking.

At the end of 1708, Watts wrote to his friend Samuel Say, asking him to "point me those lines . . . which are offensive to the weak and pious, and shocking or disgustful to the polite, or obscure to the vulgar capacity, or, in short, whatever you think should be mended, and if you please with your amendment; but I entreat it especially for the Hymns in a fortnight's time." [46] In the spring of 1709, when the second edition had come out, he tells Say how he went about the process of revision:

The method I took was, to collect all the remarks together, that several friends had made by word or letter, and got a friend or two together, and spent a whole day in perusing and considering the remarks; I agreed to their judgments I think in all things; in the whole, there are near half a hundred lines altered, I hope always for the better.[47]

In addition to the revisions he made, Watts also made provision for certain of the stanzas to be optional. Those marked with a crotchet

---

[44] Watts, IV, xx.

[45] Watts, IV, xxi.

[46] Letter to Samuel Say, 23 December 1708. Quoted in Thomas Milner, *The Life, Times, and Correspondence of the Rev. Isaac Watts D.D.* (London: Simpkin and Marshall, 1834), p. 229.

[47] Letter to Samuel Say, 12 March 1709. Milner, p. 229.

may be left out in singing without disturbing the sense. Those parts are also included in such crotchets which contain words too poetical for meaner understandings, or too particular for whole congregations to sing.[48]

The way in which Watts practised his art of sinking can be seen by examining the variants between the first and second editions of his *Hymns,* as they are listed in Selma Bishop's variorum edition.[49] Watts's principles of revision, as they are worked out in a series of instances, can be seen to express the preoccupations and techniques of classicism.

From the following select list of variants, the art of sinking can be seen at work:

(i) Be husht into a pious calm (1707)
Be silent at his sovereign will (1709) [50]

The self-centred private emotion is transposed into the public voice. The poetic onomatopoeia of "husht" is sunk into the prose abstraction of "silent," the spatial spread of "into" replaced by the purely copulative "at," and the psychological state of "pious calm" abolished to make room for the theological imperative of "sovereign will." This is a good example of the way in which Watts sought to neglect the beauties of poesy.

(ii) every dainty (1707)
rich provision (1709) [51]

The visual and the particular give way to the abstract and the general. The violence of a conceit which the Metaphysical poets exploited in their stride is toned down into what amounts to poetic diction, sufficiently vague not to be offensive to the weak and pious.

(iii) In a vast Ocean of rich Grace
The milky rivers join
Salvation in abundance flows
Like floods of generous wine. (1707)

Rivers of Love and Mercy here
In a rich Ocean join
Salvation in abundance flows
Like floods of milk and wine. (1709) [52]

[48] *Hymns,* 1709 Preface, Advertisement iii. Not included in Watts's *Works.* Quoted in Escott, p. 176.
[49] Selma Bishop, *Isaac Watts, Hymns and Spiritual Songs 1707-1748.*
[50] *Hymns,* I, 5, stanza 4. Watts, IV, 153.
[51] *Hymns,* I, 7, stanza 3. *Ibid.* Cf. *Hymns,* III, 15, stanza 6, where "dainties" is replaced by "blessings." Watts, IV, 263.
[52] *Hymns,* I, 7, stanza 5. Watts, IV, 153.

The gnomic quality of "milky rivers" is the cause of the obscurity and symbolism of the first version. These poetic excesses are removed by a simple change of syntax. "Rivers" stay as the subject, but are explained by the addition of "Love and Mercy"; and "milky" clarifies itself by becoming a noun and joining "wine." Watts gets rid of an image and its confusion; by strengthening the syntax and purifying the diction, he rationalises the messy conceit into a clear concept.

(iv)   Wrought by the fingers of his son (1707)
       Wrought by the labours of his son (1709) [53]

The physical and particular, with an element of superstitious magic about it, becomes the moral and abstract.

(v)   Our guilt shall vanish all away
       In sacred crimson waves
       Our sins shall sink beneath the sea
       To everlasting graves. (1707)

       Our guilt shall vanish all away
       Though black as hell before
       Our sins shall sink beneath the sea
       And shall be found no more. (1709) [54]

Watts revises to remove the visual. The second line is strengthened by the substitution of an antithesis for a description, but the fourth line is weakened because Watts feels the need to deface a fine gnomic image and substitute a piece of otiose bathos. This fourth line is so utterly emptied of its poetry that it falls below the intended level of bathos into the flatness of metre-fodder. The verse is thus a good example of the strength and weakness inherent in Watts's art of sinking.

(vi)   Defilements (1707)
       Pollution (1709) [55]

The plural, with its emphasis on a series of physical acts, is replaced by a more abstract singular, with its emphasis on a moral state or condition.

(vii)   The Sanctifying Spirit framed
       The needlework of grace
       But Jesus spent his life to work
       The Robe of Righteousness. (1707)

[53] *Hymns,* I, 7, stanza 7. *Ibid.*
[54] *Hymns,* I, 9, stanza 5. Watts, IV, 154.
[55] *Hymns,* I, 9, stanza 6. *Ibid.*
[56] *Hymns,* I, 20, stanza 5. Watts, IV, 158.

> The Spirit wrought my faith and love
> And hope and every grace
> But Jesus spent his life to work
> The Robe of Righteousness. (1709) [56]

The precious Metaphysical conceit of the kind which stud the verse of Edward Taylor is eliminated; [57] but the "Robe of Righteousness" is retained, probably because it has the static quality of an emblem, whereas "needlework of grace" is an active conceit. Unfortunately revision on this criterion has truncated the point of the verse, which is now held together only by the weakened antithesis of "wrought" and "worked," and relies far too heavily on the pure syntax of the copulative "but."

(viii) No more shall hunger pinch their souls (1707)
        No more shall hunger pain their souls (1709) [58]

The physical and figurative is toned down to the moral and literal. This revision is carried out on the grounds that a pinched soul, like an extended spirit, is a metaphysical impossibility.

(ix) Redeemer from the sky (1707)
       Redeemer from on high (1709) [59]

       Thence he arose and climbed the sky (1707)
       Thence he arose ascending high (1709) [60]

       And travel to the skies (1707)
       Upwards our souls shall rise (1709) [61]

"Sky" is one of the words Watts systematically eliminates in revision; it is usually conveniently replacable by "high." The point of the change seems to be not merely a flight from the visual, but also an attempt to modernise theology in the light of Newtonian physics which had abolished the sky.

(x) That was a vast amazing power (1707)
      That was a most amazing power (1709) [62]

This is a simple case of moving from the sublime to the ridiculous via the art of sinking; there is little to choose between the sublimity and the bathos, both equally mediocre if instructive.

---

[57] Cf. in particular Taylor's "Adorn me, Lord with holy huswifry." *Sacramental Meditations,* I, 42 (1691) in *Poems,* ed. Stanford, p. 69.
[58] *Hymns,* I, 40, stanza 4. Watts, IV, 162.
[59] *Hymns,* I, 70, stanza 1. Watts, IV, 171.
[60] *Hymns,* II, 3, stanza 5. Watts, IV, 200.
[61] *Hymns,* II, 25, stanza 6. Watts, IV, 208.
[62] *Hymns,* II, 8, stanza 2. Watts, IV, 202.

(xi)   To the dear crimson of thy veins (1707)
        To the dear fountain of thy blood (1709) [63]

The preciosity of the particular is polished into the commonplace of theo-logical poetic diction.

(xii)   And taste the sweetness of those lips (1707)
        And hear the language of those lips (1709) [64]

For Watts the poet, lips were made for kissing; as a preacher, he would think of them as made for speaking. Watts is forestalling the criticisms of those who accused him of fondling Christ.

(xiii) With ecstasy of fear (1707)
        With most tormenting fear (1709) [65]

The poetic paradox, couched in an oxymoron, is sunk to the level of prosaic common sense.

(xiv)   Then welcome earth and worms
        Ye must refine this flesh (1707)

        Corruption, Earth and Worms
        Shall but refine this flesh (1709) [66]

The 17th century treatment of death as both horrible and attractive is turned into a comfortable pietistic morality. The "welcome," with its tone of serious wit, is jettisoned, and the playful preciosity is changed into com-monplace piety through the syntactical modulation of "then" into "but."

(xv)   Nor shall our Graces sink to death
        Till our redeemer dies (1707)

        Nor shall our Graces sink to death
        For Jesus never dies (1709) [67]

Watts eradicates the figure of hyperbole in the second line, judging it too poetic for the weaker brethren, who will be happier with the unadorned literal truth.

(xvi)   His dying crimson like a robe
        Spreads o'er his body on the tree

---

[63] *Hymns,* II, 90, stanza 4. Watts, IV, 230.
[64] *Hymns,* II, 102, stanza 4. Watts, IV, 235.
[65] *Hymns,* II, 107, stanza 3. Watts, IV, 236.
[66] *Hymns,* II, 110, stanza 2. Watts, IV, 237.
[67] *Hymns,* III, 5, stanza 5. Watts, IV, 259.

> Then am I dead to all the globe
> And all the globe is dead to me. (1707)

This becomes an optional stanza in 1709.[68] The fourth verse of the famous hymn, "When I survey the wondrous cross," it is in fact never sung. It has the personal note of the lyric, expressed in poignant bathos akin to that of Wordsworth's Lucy poems, and is therefore highly unsuited to congregational use. Watts usually manages to sink such expressionism into poetic diction; here however the bathos intensifies rather than flattens the lyricism.

It is thus in the idiom of the hymn that Watts expresses his classical energies most effectively. His success and failure in this idiom are a fair measure of the strength and weakness of classical lyricism. In poetic terms the hymn is a highly restricted idiom with such severe limitations that it is difficult to subject it to critical scrutiny. But whatever became of the hymn in the hands of Wesley and his successors, in the hands of Watts it does illustrate the techniques and ideals of a classical aesthetic. In the work of Watts as a whole, the hymn represents a summit of poetic achievement. Evolved out of his manipulation of the prevailing Metaphysical and sublime traditions, it closely reflects the way in which his thought developed out of the Renaissance into the Enlightenment.

[68] *Hymns,* III, 7, stanza 4. Watts, IV, 259-260.

CONCLUSION

Watts represents one terminal point in the waning of the Renaissance. With his roots in the 17th century, he reflects what in part he created, thought identifiably part of the English Enlightenment and verse identifiably part of English classicism. The achievement was considerable; but it was also short-lived. Neither classicism nor the Enlightenment were capable of replacing the Renaissance as the central and normative tradition in English culture. The lyric had been metamorphosed into the hymn, thanks largely to Watts's own work; and Enlightenment thought, hidebound to the tame sterilities of the deistic controversy, reflects in large perspective the image of Watts chewing the indigestible Trinitarian cud. Neither classicism nor the Enlightenment, as traditions, do more than stagnate once they have been given a modestly definitive expression in Pope's *Essay on Man*.

Our conclusion must be that classicism and the Enlightenment merely cleared the ground and prepared the way for the new Romantic culture which was capable of replacing the Renaissance. We have seen intimations of such an outcome in the work of More, Norris and Watts. In these writers the ultimate rise of Romanticism appears as a necessary concomitant to the waning of the Renaissance. They all grappled with the problems raised by the cultural revolution; they resisted the process as well as contributing to it in varying degrees, and for all their limitations and lack of hindsight they helped "to keep alive the heart in the head." [1]

Watts's resting-place was a temporary one. He had done his work, but even as he wrote at the end of the 1730s the forces of evangelicalism and preromanticism were gathering strength. The movements of religious enthusiasm and poetic imagination were for a long time contained within the epistemological system of the Enlightenment and the Augustan social structure. With the advent of the French Revolution, the poems of Blake and the death of Wesley, the qualitative leap forward was possible and a culture worthy to succeed the Renaissance was in the making.

---

[1] S. T. Coleridge, *Biographia Literaria*, ed. Arthur Symons (London: J. M. Dent, 1906), p. 76 (Chapter 9).

SELECT BIBLIOGRAPHY

1. TEXTS OF PRINCIPAL AUTHORS STUDIED

More, Henry. *A Collection of Several Philosophical Writings*. 2nd ed. enlarged. London: W. Morden, 1662.
—. *The Theological Works*. London: J. Downing, 1708.
—. *Complete Poems*. Edited by A. B. Grosart. "Chertsey Worthies Library." Edinburgh: privately printed, 1878.
—. *Philosophical Writings*. Edited by Flora Isabel Mackinnon. New York: Oxford University Press, 1925.
—. *Philosophical Poems*. Edited by Geoffrey Bullough. Manchester: University Press, 1931.
Nicolson, Marjorie Hope (ed.). *The Conway Letters: The Correspondence of Anne, Viscountess Conway, Henry More, and their friends, 1642-1684*. London: Oxford University Press; New York: Yale University Press, 1930.
Norris, John. *A Collection of Miscellanies*. 3rd ed. London: S. Manship, 1699.
—. *An Essay towards the Theory of the Ideal or Intelligible World*. 2 vols. London: S. Manship, 1701-1704.
Watts, Isaac. *Works*. Edited by D. Jennings and P. Doddridge. 6 vols. London, 1753.

2. SECONDARY TEXTS RELATING TO THE PRINCIPAL AUTHORS

Birrell, T. A. "Sarbiewski, Watts and the Later Metaphysical Tradition," *English Studies*, XXXVIII (1956), 125-132.
Bishop, Selma L. *Isaac Watts, Hymns and Spiritual Songs 1707-1748. A Study in Early 18th Century Language Changes*. London: Faith Press, 1962.
Davis, Arthur Paul. *Isaac Watts, his Life and Works*. New York: Dryden Press, 1943.
Escott, Harry. *Isaac Watts Hymnographer*. London: Independent Press, 1962.
Lichtenstein, Aharon. *Henry More: The Rational Theology of a Cambridge Platonist*. Cambridge, Mass.: Harvard University Press, 1962.
Mackinnon, Flora Isabel. *The Philosophy of John Norris*. "Philosophical Monographs," Vol. 1, No. 2. New York: The Psychological Review, 1910.

Pinto, Vivian de Sola. "Isaac Watts and the Adventurous Muse," *Essays and Studies,* XX (1935), 86-107.

—. "Isaac Watts and William Blake," *Review of English Studies,* XX (1944), 214-223.

Powicke, Frederick J. *A Dissertation on John Norris of Bemerton.* London: George Philip, (1894).

Walton, Geoffrey. *Metaphysical to Augustan: Studies in Tone and Sensibility in the 17th Century.* London: Bowes and Bowes, 1955.

Ward, Richard. *The Life of the Learned and Pious Dr More.* London: J. Downing, 1710.

3. OTHER PRIMARY TEXTS

Addison, Joseph. *Works.* Edited by Henry G. Bohn. 6 vols. London: Bohn's British Classics, 1856.

Bayle, Pierre. *Oeuvres Diverses.* 4 vols. La Haye: P. Husson, 1727-1731.

Berkeley, George. *Alciphron.* Edited by T. E. Jessop. London: Thomas Nelson, 1950.

Bolingbroke, Henry St. John, Viscount. *Works.* Edited by David Mallet. 5 vols. London, 1754.

Chalmers, Alexander (ed.). *The Works of the English Poets from Chaucer to Cowper.* 21 vols. London: J. Johnson, 1810.

Coleridge, Samuel Taylor. *On the 17th Century.* Edited by Roberta Florence Brinkley. Durham, North Carolina: Duke University Press, 1955.

Cudworth, Ralph. *The True Intellectual System of the Universe.* Edited and translated by John Harrison. 3 vols. London: T. Tegg, 1845.

Durfey, Thomas (pseudonym: Gabriel John). *An Essay towards the Theory of the Intelligible World Intuitively Considered. The Archetypally Second Edition.* London, 1707.

Farquhar, George. *Works.* 2nd ed. London: Bernard Lintott, 1711.

Fénelon (Francois de Salignac de la Mothe). *De l'existence et des attributs de Dieu.* Paris: Didot, 1853.

Locke, John. *Works.* 9 vols. 12th ed. London: Rivington, 1824.

Parker, Samuel. *A Free and Impartial Censure of the Platonic Philosophy.* 2nd ed. Oxford, 1667.

Patrick, Simon. *A Brief Account of the New Sect of Latitude Men, together with Some Reflections on the New Philosophy, in answer to a letter from his friend at Oxford.* Edited by T. A. Birrell. "Augustan Reprint Society," No. 100. Los Angeles: University of California Press, 1963.

Sarbiewski, Mathias Casimire. *Odes.* Translated by G. Hils. Edited by Maren-Sofie Rostvig. "Augustan Reprint Society," No. 44. Los Angeles: University of California Press, 1953.

Select Hymns Taken out of Mr Herbert's Temple. Edited by W. E. Stephenson. "Augustan Reprint Society," No. 98. Los Angeles: University of California Press, 1962.

Smith, John. *Select Discourses.* Edited by Henry Griffin Williams. 4th ed. Cambridge: University Press, 1859.

Swift, Jonathan. *Works.* Edited by Herbert Davis. 14 vols. Oxford: Blackwell, 1939-1962.

Taylor, Edward. *Poems.* Edited by Donald E. Stanford. 2nd ed. abridged. New Haven and London: Yale University Press, 1963.

Wesley, John. *Works.* 14 vols. Grand Rapids, Michigan: Zondervan, 1958-1959.

Wilkins, John. *An Essay towards a Real Character and a Philosophical Language.* London: S. Gellibrand and J. Martin, 1668.

Winchilsea, Anne Finch, Countess of. *Poems.* Edited by Myra Reynolds. Chicago: University Press, 1903.

4. OTHER SECONDARY TEXTS

Barth, Karl. *From Rousseau to Ritschl.* London: Student Christian Movement Press, 1959.

Bate, Walter Jackson. *From Classic to Romantic: Premises of Taste in 18th Century England.* New York: Harper, 1961.

Bethell, Samuel Leslie. *The Cultural Revolution of the 17th Century.* London: Dennis Dobson, 1951.

Brett, Raymond Laurence. *Reason and Imagination.* "University of Hull Publications." London: Oxford University Press, 1960.

Bullough, Geoffrey. *Mirror of Minds: Changing Psychological Beliefs in English Poetry.* London: Athlone Press, 1962.

Burtt, Edwin Arthur. *The Metaphysical Foundations of Modern Science.* London: Kegan Paul, Trench, 1925.

Carré, Meyrick. *Phases of Thought in England.* Oxford: Clarendon Press, 1949.

Cassirer, Ernst. *The Philosophy of the Enlightenment.* Boston: Beacon Press, 1951.

—. *The Platonic Renaissance in England.* Edinburgh: Thomas Nelson, 1953.

Colie, Rosalie L. *Light and Enlightenment: A Study of the Cambridge Platonists and the Dutch Arminians.* Cambridge: University Press, 1957.

Cragg, Gerald Robertson. *From Puritanism to the Age of Reason: A Study of Changes in Religious Thought within the Church of England 1660-1700.* Cambridge: University Press, 1950.

Davie, Donald. *Purity of Diction in English Verse.* London: Chatto and Windus, 1952.

—. *Articulate Energy: An Enquiry into the Syntax of English Poetry.* London: Routledge and Kegan Paul, 1955.

De Pauley, William Cecil. *The Candle of the Lord: Studies in the Cambridge Platonists.* London: Society for the Propagation of Christian Knowledge, 1937.

Dobrée, Bonamy. *English Literature in the Early 18th Century 1700-1740.* Oxford: Clarendon Press, 1959.

Draper, John William. *The Funeral Elegy and the Rise of English Romanticism.* New York: University Press, 1929.

England, Martha Winburn, and Sparrow, John. *Hymns Unbidden: Donne,*

Herbert, Blake, Emily Dickinson and the Hymnographers. New York Public Library: Astor Lenox and Tilden Foundations, 1966.

Fairchild, Hoxie Neale. *Religious Trends in English Poetry.* 5 vols. New York: Columbia University Press, 1939-1962.

Foucault, Michel. *Les mots et les choses.* Paris: Gallimard, 1966.

Fussell, Paul. *The Rhetorical World of Augustan Humanism: Ethics and Imagery from Swift to Burke.* Oxford: Clarendon Press, 1965.

Gay, Peter. *The Enlightenment: An Interpretation. The Rise of Modern Paganism.* London: Weidenfeld and Nicolson, 1966.

Hanzo, Thomas A. *Latitude and Restoration Criticism.* "Anglistica," No. 12. Copenhagen: Rosenkilde and Bagger, 1961.

Harrison, John Smith. *Platonism in English Poetry of the 16th and 17th Centuries.* New York: Columbia University Press, 1903.

Hazard, Paul. *La crise de la conscience Européenne 1680-1715.* Paris: Boivin, 1935.

Henderson, P. A. Wright. *The Life and Times of John Wilkins.* Edinburgh: William Blackwood, 1910.

James, David Gwilym. *The Life of Reason: Hobbes, Locke, Bolingbroke.* London: Longmans Green, 1963.

Jones, Richard Foster, and Others. *The 17th Century: Studies in the History of English Thought and Literature from Bacon to Pope.* Stanford: University Press, 1951.

Jones, William Powell. *The Rhetoric of Science: A Study of Scientific Ideas and Imagery in 18th Century English Poetry.* London: Routledge and Kegan Paul, 1966.

Labrousse, Elisabeth. *Pierre Bayle.* 2 vols. The Hague: Nijhoff, 1963-1964.

Locke, Louis G. *Tillotson, A Study in 17th Century Literature.* "Anglistica," No. 4. Copenhagen: Rosenkilde and Bagger, 1954.

Lovejoy, Arthur Oncken. *Essays in the History of Ideas.* Baltimore: John Hopkins Press, 1948.

—. *The Great Chain of Being: A Study in the History of an Idea.* New York: Harper Torchbooks, 1960.

McGiffert, Arthur Cushman. *Protestant Thought Before Kant.* London: Duckworth, 1911.

McLachlan, Herbert. *English Education under the Test Acts: Being the History of the Nonconformist Academies 1660-1820.* Manchester: University Press, 1931.

—. *The Religious Opinions of Milton, Locke and Newton.* Manchester: University Press, 1941.

McLachlan, Herbert John. *Socinianism in 17th Century England.* London: Oxford University Press, 1951.

MacLean, Kenneth. *John Locke and English Literature of the 18th Century.* New Haven: Yale University Press, 1936.

Martz, Louis Lohr. *The Poetry of Meditation: A Study in English Religious Literature of the 17th Century.* Rev. ed. New Haven: Yale University Press, 1962.

Mazzeo, Joseph Anthony, and Others. *Reason and the Imagination: Studies in the History of Ideas 1600-1800.* New York: Columbia University Press, 1962.

Miller, Perry. *The New England Mind: The 17th Century.* Cambridge, Mass.: Harvard University Press, 1939.

Muirhead, John H. *The Platonic Tradition in Anglo-Saxon Philosophy: Studies in the History of Idealism in England and America.* London: Allen and Unwin, 1931.

Nicolson, Marjorie Hope. "The Early Stage of Cartesianism in England," *Studies in Philology,* XXVI (1929), 356-374.

—. *Newton Demands the Muse: Newton's Opticks and the 18th Century Poets.* Princeton: University Press, 1946.

—. *The Breaking of the Circle: Studies in the Effect of the "New Science" upon 17th Century Poetry.* Rev. ed. New York: Columbia University Press, 1960.

Ong, Walter J. "Ramus and the Transit to the Modern Mind," *The Modern Schoolman,* XXXII (May 1955), 301-311.

—. *Ramus: Method and the Decay of Dialogue; From the Art of Discourse to the Art of Reason.* Cambridge, Mass.: Harvard University Press, 1958.

Parker, Irene. *Dissenting Academies in England.* Cambridge: University Press, 1914.

Powicke, Frederick J. *The Cambridge Platonists: A Study.* London: J. M. Dent, 1926.

Reynolds, Myra. *The Learned Lady in England 1650-1760.* Boston and New York: Houghton Mifflin, 1920.

Rodway, Allan. *The Romantic Conflict.* London: Chatto and Windus, 1963.

Rostvig, Maren-Sofie. *The Happy Man: Studies in the Metamorphoses of a Classical Ideal.* 2 vols. "Oslo Studies in English," Nos. 2 and 7. Oslo: Akademisk Forlag; Oxford: Blackwell, 1954-1958.

Stephen, Leslie. *History of English Thought in the 18th Century.* 2 vols. London: Rupert Hart-Davis, 1962.

Stromberg, Roland Nelson. *Religious Liberalism in 18th Century England.* London: Oxford University Press, 1954.

Tulloch, John. *Rational Theology and Christian Philosophy in England in the 17th Century.* 2 vols. Edinburgh: Blackwood, 1874.

Tuve, Rosemond. "Imagery and Logic. Ramus and Metaphysical Poetics," *Journal of the History of Ideas,* III (October 1942), 383-384.

—. *Elizabethan and Metaphysical Imagery.* Chicago: University Press, 1961.

Vereker, Charles. *18th Century Optimism: A Study of the Interrelations of Moral and Social Theory in English and French Thought between 1689 and 1789.* Liverpool: University Press, 1967.

Watson, Richard A. *The Downfall of Cartesianism 1673-1712: A Study of Epistemological Issues in Late 17th Century Cartesianism.* "International Archives of the History of Ideas," No. 2. The Hague: Nijhoff, 1966.

Willey, Basil. *The 17th Century Background.* London: Penguin Books, 1962.

—. *The 18th Century Background.* London: Penguin Books, 1962.

—. *The English Moralists.* London: Methuen, 1965.

INDEX

Addison, Joseph, "The spacious firmament on high," 52, 58-9; and the Enlightenment, 79-80, 115, 143, 149-51; and religion, 186-7

Akenside, Mark, 200

Ancients and Moderns, 80, 99, 159, 169

Angels, 128-9, 216

Anglicanism, 29, 177, 207, 228; and Aristotelianism, 13-14; and the New Philosophy, 30; and More, 39-40; and Quakers, 42; and the Dissenting Academies, 153; and the Enlightenment, 186; and eroticism, 229

Anne, Queen, 143, 147, 208

Aquinas, Thomas, 81, 84, 86

Arbuthnot, John, 237

Arianism, 165, 179, 183; John Wesley on, 178

Aristotelianism, and Ramism, 3, 10; of Anglicans and Presbyterians, 13-14; Coleridge on, 21; and Norris, 80-1, 96; in the universities, 165

Aristotle, 21, 49, 68, 167; and Descartes, 13-14, 96; and Bacon, 79; Norris on, 81, 83, 85; and Plato, 164-5

Arminianism, Dutch, 5, 164; and Platonism, 13; and John Wesley, 119; and Presbyterianism, 182

Arminius, Jacobus, 169

Arnold, Matthew, "Dover Beach," 138-9

Association of ideas, 53-4, 173

Astell, Mary, 93-4; on Plastic Nature, 103

Athanasian Creed, 150, 182, 193

Atheism, 12, 39, 43, 131, 165; and Cudworth, 24, 46, 103-4; More's *Antidote Against Atheism*, 26-7; Casaubon on, 30; Bayle on, 36

Athenian Society, 94-6

Augustans, XII, XV, 25, 51, 55, 63, 131, 139, 143, 220-1, 226, 251; pre-Augustan, 45, 54, 61, 67, 219; Burke, 86; concept of Nature, 99, 211; Lady Winchilsea, 125, 214; Berkeley, 173

Augustine, St., and Norris, 77, 84-5; Fénelon on, 85; and Platonic theology, 112; Bolingbroke on, 185

Austin, John, 239

Bacon, Francis, on Paracelsus, 17; and Descartes, 20, 167-8; v. Aristotle, 79, 167; Bolingbroke on, 145

Baconian, 18, 80, 194; empiricism, 13, 105; reason, 37-8; style, 67; critique of Renaissance, 145, 168; words and things, 167-8, 185

Baptists, 153-4, 176, 183, 205

Barth, Karl, 149; on Wolff, 161; on the Enlightenment, 164

Bathos, in Norris, 131; in Watts, 194, 196, 209, 234, 239, 243-4, 247-8, 250; Pope on, 237; in Wordsworth, 237-8, 250

Bayle, Pierre, 24, 35, 164; on Poiret, 19; on More, 25-6; on Cudworth, 36

Benson, L. F., 223

Bentham, Jeremy, 156

Berkeley, George, 76, 101, 115, 147, 159; on logic, 160; on Shaftesbury, 170-1; and utilitarianism, 173; on Spinoza, 180-1; Bolingbroke on, 185; and irony, 193-4

Bethell, S.L., XII

Birrell, T.A., 228; on latitudinarianism, 29; on Watts, 144; on Casimire, 213

Bishop, S.L., 216, 246

Blair, Robert, *The Grave*, 129, 138

Blake, William, XII, XV, 53, 62, 75, 133,